THE RENEWAL OF CHURCH

The Panel Reports

W. B. Blakemore, *General Editor*

The Panel of Scholars Reports

VOLUME I

The Reformation of Tradition

R. E. OSBORN, Editor

VOLUME II

The Reconstruction of Theology

R. G. WILBURN, Editor

VOLUME III

The Revival of the Churches

W. B. BLAKEMORE, Editor

Volume III

THE REVIVAL OF THE CHURCHES

THE
Revival of the Churches

Edited by

Wm. Barnett Blakemore

The Renewal of Church
The Panel Reports
W. B. Blakemore, Editor

III

The Bethany Press
St. Louis, Missouri
1963

 Library of Congress Catalog Card Number 63-16091

Distributed by Thomas C. Lothian, Melbourne, Australia, and Auckland, New Zealand and by The G. R. Welch Company, Toronto, Canada

Manufactured in the United States of America

Typography and design by David Homeier

Panel of Scholars Membership

July 1956 to March 1962

CHAIRMEN

Howard E. Short: June 1956 to September 1958
W. B. Blakemore: October 1958 to March 1962

MEMBERS

William R. Baird: November 1959 to March 1962
Professor of New Testament
The College of the Bible
Lexington, Kentucky

Paul Hunter Beckelhymer: January 1957 to March 1962
Minister of Hiram Christian Church
Hiram, Ohio

W. B. Blakemore: July 1956 to March 1962
Dean of Disciples Divinity House and
Associate Dean of Rockefeller Memorial Chapel
University of Chicago
Chicago, Illinois

James A. Clague: August 1956 to March 1962
Associate Professor of Systematic Theology
Christian Theological Seminary
Indianapolis, Indiana

Stephen J. England: July 1956 to March 1962
Dean of The Graduate Seminary
Phillips University
Enid, Oklahoma

Frank N. Gardner: July 1956 to March 1962
Professor of Christian Thought
Drake University
Des Moines, Iowa

Virgil V. Hinds: October 1956 to March 1962
Associate Professor of Religion
Lynchburg College
Lynchburg, Virginia

J. Phillip Hyatt: July 1956 to March 1962
Professor of Old Testament of the Divinity School and Chairman of the Department of Religion of the Graduate School
Vanderbilt University
Nashville, Tennessee

Clarence E. Lemmon: July 1956 to March 1962
Minister of First Christian Church
Columbia, Missouri

D. Ray Lindley: July 1956 to March 1962
President of Texas Christian University
Fort Worth, Texas

Ronald E. Osborn: July 1956 to March 1962
Dean and Professor of Church History
Christian Theological Seminary
Indianapolis, Indiana

Eugene H. Peters: December 1959 to March 1962
Associate Professor of Theology
The Graduate Seminary
Phillips University
Enid, Oklahoma

Glenn C. Routt: July 1956 to March 1962
Associate Professor of Theology
Brite College of the Bible
Texas Christian University
Fort Worth, Texas

Howard E. Short: June 1956 to September 1958
Professor of Church History
The College of the Bible
Lexington, Kentucky (until September 1958)
Editor of *The Christian*

DWIGHT E. STEVENSON: June 1956 to October 1959
Professor of Homiletics
The College of the Bible
Lexington, Kentucky

WILLIAM G. WEST: July 1956 to March 1962
Minister of First Christian Church
Chattanooga, Tennessee

RALPH G. WILBURN: July 1956 to March 1962
Dean and Professor of Historical Theology
The College of the Bible
Lexington, Kentucky

THE EDITORIAL AND PUBLICATION COMMITTEE

W. B. Blakemore, Chairman, General Editor and Editor of Volume III

R. E. Osborn, Editor of Volume I

R. G. Wilburn, Editor of Volume II

W. M. Wickizer for the sponsoring agencies

Contents

CONCLUSION

INTRODUCTION

1

Where Thought and Action Meet

W. B. Blakemore

AS the work of the Panel of Scholars reached its climax, there emerged two general insights which dominated the last half of its work. The first insight renewed our understanding of the centrality of Jesus Christ to all that is Christian. The second insight clarified our understanding of the parallel roles of thought and practice in the life of the churches. Each of these insights introduced factors which have shaped the papers in this volume.

I

It may seem a tautology to assert the centrality of Jesus Christ to everything that is Christian, yet the Panel of Scholars would admit that at the outset they did not understand this principle, and in their ignorance they mirrored the mentality of their brotherhood and of most of Christendom. There is always a great variety of concerns which must engage the churches, and any of these may become a preoccupation if not indeed an idol which supplants the Lord Jesus Christ. Evangelistic preaching preoccupied a revivalist age, prophetic utterance and action the social-gospel age, and scriptural words the fundamentalist era. The center of immediate attention has been taken successively by theology, liturgy, and religious education. One segment of the church comes to be dominated with concern about practical technicalities, while another segment is equally overborne concerning theological methodologies. Each may misunderstand the other, and both may lose sight of the foundation center of Christian existence. But if serious questioning begins, either from the practical or the theoretical side, that questioning leads at last to the center. The Panel of Scholars began its questioning with both practical and theoretical problems in mind. Volume I of these reports carries papers on preaching, church organization, and the sociological factors in Disciples' history as well as papers on revelation, faith, salvation, and the Holy Spirit. It was in the midst of these papers that the Panel became aware of the fact that Disciples of Christ have a tradition. The members of the Panel found themselves speaking about "our tradition," and were surprised to hear the phrase on their lips because until recently Disciples of Christ have firmly asserted that they are not traditionalists. But the term "tradition" means "a teaching handed down from generation to generation," and the Panel was becoming aware of the fact that there is a teaching which our forefathers and fathers before us have handed down and have passed on to us. There is a continuity from generation to generation, and this continuity is what gives us a continuing history. We have not taught one thing in one age and something else in another age, which would have meant that we are not a people with a continuing history, which in turn would have meant that we are no people at all.

The Panel's work made plain a tradition which is the perennial focus of Disciple thought and life, and that tradition is Jesus Christ. The decisive papers in this regard were those by D. E. Stevenson, W. G. West, P. H. Beckelhymer, and F. N. Gardner which rightfully stand as the first four chapters of Part I of Volume I which is entitled *The Reformation of Tradition*. That title reflects the insight upon which the Panel had come, namely, that we do have a tradition that we hand on from age to age, and that we must constantly reform our teaching in order to keep it relevant to every new age and to release it from formulations which may have had relevance in an earlier age but have become obsolete.

There were two dominant results of the discovery that Christ is our tradition, that he is the center of our teaching. One result was negative, the other positive. The negative result was the recognition that whatever the historic significance for Disciples of "restorationism," it is not our tradition. Ideas of reform, of restoration, of union, and of merger have had their place, but we are fundamentally a Christian movement, and not a restoration movement, nor a merger movement, and it is precisely because we are a Christian movement that we are concerned about Christian unity. But it is Jesus Christ who has been passed on from age to age and whom we received in the teachings of our parents. It was inevitable that Volume I would contain a "critique of the Restoration Principle" (by R. G. Wilburn), and that Volume II would be a *Reconstruction of Theology* on a Christological base. Jesus Christ and our understanding of him is the center and basis of every chapter of that volume which seeks the renewal of church through a more adequate grasp on the meaning of Christ.

The positive result of the discovery that Christ is our tradition was a renewed impetus in our ecumenical involvement. It was precisely in the period that the Panel of Scholars was rediscovering the meanings of the centrality of Christ that parallel discoveries were characterizing many communions and the ecumenical movement as a whole. Early in the 1950's the Faith and Order Commission of the World Council of Churches discovered that its historic procedure of comparative studies of each other's thought and practice was leading the churches nowhere. Gradually, through the 1950's the center of attention became the Christ who is the One Lord of the church. In him, the churches found their bond of unity. Ecumenical discussion shifted from the differing practices of the churches to the One Lord of the Church. Christians of every sign and creed began the exploration together of the meaning of his lordship. Members of the Panel have various relationships to the ecumenical movement, and it was with great excitement that they recognized their discussions in those relationships drawing ever more closely to their discussions in the Panel. At no point was this excitement greater than in the revival of biblical theology, a movement characteristic of Protestantism as a whole.

Disciples of Christ have always been a biblical people, but their first form of attachment to the Bible was in terms of specifics and patterns. At this point there is a curious contradiction in the beginnings of the movement, a contradiction to be found in Alexander Campbell himself. On the one hand, he pled for the restoration of the ancient order of things regarding worship and ecclesiastical structure. He had a strong tendency to find a specific "Thus saith the Lord," for every item suggested. Apostolic precedent or Jesus' own utterance was necessary. On the other hand, there were times when he said that whereas God had dealt with the Jews in terms of specific prescriptions, with the Christians he was able to take an approach more adult. He provided principles in terms of which the Christian was to work out the appropriate practice for any particular situation. In either instance, Campbell's approach was rationalist and legalist. On the one hand he was advocating the kind of biblical literalism that leads to fundamentalism. On the other hand he was suggesting the Bible as a source of principles from which practice might be deduced—a sort of latter-day Thomism.

The newer biblical theology, widely shared throughout Protestantism, rejects both the idea of literal biblical example and of biblical principle to be deductively reduced to practice. Current biblical theology speaks rather in terms of "biblical concepts or ideas." It searches and finds in the Bible what can best be called guiding and nurturing concepts. When grasped and understood, these do not provide the Christian with precise principles reapplicable in his own day, but they cultivate and enlighten his mind so that as he deals with contemporary problems he does so as a man whose mind is equipped with insights from the Bible and whose spirit has been nurtured by the Bible.

Among Disciples of Christ there is a lively new interest in biblical materials. Chapters in Volume II of this series explore the place of both Old and New Testaments in the church today. The newer understandings of biblical material enable us to escape both literalism and rationalism, and to return to the Bible with a zest and sparkle and delight as it nourishes our spirits. It is no longer the book of the law binding the spirit, but the book of grace feeding the spirit.

Almost miraculous is the fact that became clear in 1962 as the Panel was closing its work. Throughout the 1950's Roman Catholic scholars had been following the same path, rediscovering that the center of their tradition is Christ the Lord and that through biblical studies men become open to the renewal by the Holy Spirit. The conversations surrounding the Second Vatican Council have made clear, as Edgar H. S. Chandler, executive vice-president of the Church Federation of Greater Chicago, remarked recently, "The meeting place of the Roman and Protestant minds will be in Christology, for Christ is the common ground of the faith of both the Roman and the Protestant." Throughout Christendom the discovery is going forward that beneath the variety of the traditions of the churches the tradition that is their common bond is Christ the Lord.

Yet even as the centrality of Christ was rediscovered, it was obvious that a warning must be sounded. This warning applies to several denominations, but to Disciples of Christ especially because of their weekly observance of the Lord's Supper. Disciple liturgical practice insures the remembrance of Jesus in every Sunday service. But it creates the possibility of making Jesus of Nazareth the object of worship instead of the focus through which faith passes on its way to the knowledge of God. We must always be reminded that we must see through and beyond Jesus to the Christ in whom God revealed himself and by whom he reconciles the world to himself. We must not stop with Jesus*ism* or with Christ*ism*. To do so is to fall into the error of a "unitarianism of the Son" which obscures the Father who sent the Son, and in its way is just as erroneous as a "unitarianism of the Father" which denies the divinity of Christ. Disciples of Christ may have to recognize that an inordinate attention to Jesus Christ may lead to a neglect of consideration of the Father (and hence to weak theology) and of the Holy Spirit (and hence to lack of inspiration). But after the warning is sounded, the assertion may be even more confidently made that Christology must be the center and pivot of theology, just as Jesus Christ must be the pivot of Christian understanding of existence in all its parts.

II

The second general insight which came to the Panel is that in the life of the churches thought and practice have parallel roles. All too frequently in the past, thought and practice have become separated from each other, and have indulged in extreme and reactionary claims against each other. There have been periods of excessive theologism when it has been claimed that theology comes first and guides practice. In counter-action the claim has been made that it is in what we do that truth is to be discovered. Belief and action have become divorced into confessional*ism* and pragmat*ism*. But a proper theology is neither a rationalization after the fact nor the *a priori* justification of action. Religious ideas and religious practice alike are "earthly vessels" through which faith is expressed, and they always must have relevance to particular times and places if they are to be effective. That in turn means that both religious ideas and religious practices escape obsolescence only by an eternal and dynamic renewal in the light of new occasions. That in which our faith rests never changes, and in this foundational sense the faith in us does not change. But both the ideological and practical responses by which we relate faith to *our* life in *our* circumstances must undergo change. Oddly enough there have been times when men would allow that one or the other might change, but not both. There have been times when men have allowed considerable variety in practice so long as the creed was held unchanging. There have been other times when men have tolerated all sorts of ideas but cried heresy when some item of the cult or ethical code was changed. Now, however, the instrumental and therefore dynamic character of both organizational and verbal forms is recognized.

Men have recognized that organizational structures are only instruments they have employed to achieve the goals inspired by faith. They have only in recent decades, and only in certain areas of the church (notably in North America) fully recognized the instrumental character of thought. Western man has had a very high opinion of the mind, an esteem which reached its height in the Renaissance. Subsequently, that esteem has altered in two ways. First, men have come to recognize that the mind is bound by the moral limitations of the men in whom minds reside. But, even more radically, they have begun to see that ideas, concepts, terms, definitions, formulas, generalizations, abstractions, and all our intellectual apparatus are but the pots and pans, knives and forks, spoons and platters whereby knowledge is fashioned for our mental nourishment. Indeed, if the facts remain indigestible by one mode of preparation we get at them by another. What geometry will not solve, logarithms may; what does not yield to algebra may be penetrated by trigonometry.

Now we could take a very playful attitude toward these matters of the mind if we were not suddenly aware that just as we are responsible and accountable for our own actions, so we are just as much responsible and accountable for our ideas. It was a shocking travesty when the weaker forms of liberalism fell into the error of declaring that it does not matter what one thinks. That was a tragic misinterpretation of the high liberal claim that since a man is responsible for the thoughts by which he expresses his faith he must be free to think them out. Religious liberty is not only freedom of worship; it is equally freedom of doctrine, for there cannot be freedom of conscience without freedom of thought. Theological and liturgical liberty belong together. Faith and piety must alike be anchored in the unchanging gift of God's Son, but doctrine and practice reach out like the parallel sides of a great cantilever spanning the gulf between earth and heaven. As long as they move forward together, doctrine and practice support each other. When one is suppressed, the other cannot sustain itself. When they no longer are parallel, the whole structure twists and wrenches into collapse.

This third volume may be likened to the struts that connect the two sides of the cantilever, doctrine and practice, as the church moves forward into the future. The volume is not, on the one hand, a manual of practical activities. Nor is it, on the other hand, a repetition of the topics of Volume II. It is a volume of practical theology, a volume which discusses the ways in which we must rebuild our understanding of such practical activities as church order and worship, the ministry, and church-related institutions if there is to be a revival of the life of the churches. The authors do not present these papers as final answers. They do present them as examples of the level of thought which must be tackled if revival is to flourish. And they would insist that the conjunction between doctrine and practice which these papers exemplify is the climax and culmination of their years of work as a Panel of Scholars.

It was soon after the Panel was organized that a new word began to be heard in the assemblies of Disciples of Christ. It was the word "Restructure." The Panel had been brought into existence to help the agencies of the church understand their objectives more clearly. No sooner had the Panel begun its work of rethinking doctrine than churchmen began to talk in terms of restructuring.

The processes of restructure did not wait upon the completion of the work of redefining. The two processes began to flow side by side, and influenced each other immediately, as members of the Panel on the one hand and practical churchmen on the other found themselves in discussion.

The sponsoring agencies were always represented at the meetings of the Panel of Scholars; W. M. Wickizer served most frequently as that representative. He soon became *de facto* if not *de jure* a member of the Panel of Scholars; after a while the rest of us felt it was only fair that he submit a paper for the same kind of critical appraisal the rest of us received. Dr. Wickizer chose to participate in his capacity as a professional religious educator, a happy circumstance since no other member of the Panel was professionally qualified in that area. Dr. Wickizer's paper which uses the terminology of the liberal approach to religion demonstrates the power of that terminology to absorb the implications of the most recent understandings of human nature and of Christian theology. Also included, primarily for its historical interest, is a short paper on "Ideas for Brotherhood Restructure" presented by Dr. Wickizer in 1958 before the Council of Agencies. It represents an early instance of the interaction between theory and practice that the Panel helped to achieve.

When it came to selecting a Panel member to deal with church-related higher education, the Panel was in a quandary. Most, but not all, of the Panel members were school men: seminary deans, department heads, university administrators, professors. Any of us might have written on the topic. The one category our membership lacked was a college president, so for a paper on higher education we reached beyond the Panel. Dr. Orville W. Wake, President of Lynchburg College, Lynchburg, Virginia, was asked if this volume might include a paper most of the Panel heard and discussed at the 1961 meeting of the Board of Higher Education. In that meeting Dr. Wake's paper was given the same kind of critical treatment it would have received in a Panel meeting. He gave his consent, and his informative and valuable paper is here included.

The present volume makes no attempt to be exhaustive. Particularly it omits any discussion of mission to overseas non-Christians. This area has been the concern of a special study group sponsored jointly by The United Christian Missionary Society and the Council on Christian Unity. What would be said by the Panel of Scholars is what all communions today recognize: Church is mission, and only in the renewed advance of the Christian mission can the church find its true being.

With the publication of this volume, the Panel of Scholars finishes its phase of a task which the churches perennially confront: the renewal of thought and of practice. That work goes forward however in many ways among Disciples of Christ. It continues in several organizations established specifically for theological discussion. But it continues much more importantly in the discussions of the Commission on Brotherhood Restructure, and also in the dozens of other "practical" commissions, agencies, boards, and societies of the brotherhood because their thoughts have taken on a new and remarkable theological dimension. Meetings of stewardship committees, benevolence boards, and evangelistic teams no longer proceed without inquiry into the Christian meaning of economics, and charity, and witness. It is obvious that in recent years the practical issues of the Christian Churches are being decided in the light of new depths of understanding regarding the fundamental nature of the church, of the gospel, of Jesus Christ who is Head of the Church, social Lord and personal Savior, and of that God and Father whose love we know through the cross of his Son. The Panel of Scholars made a contribution toward that deepening and strengthening of understanding in the counsels of our brotherhood. To the degree that we have been useful, we are grateful to those who brought us into existence as a Panel, and above all to him who reigns, whose Holy Spirit we ever sought as our guide.

July 22, 1963. W. B. BLAKEMORE

PART ONE

THE CHURCH OF CHRIST ON EARTH

2

Concepts of the New Testament Church

Which Contribute to Disciple Thought About the Church

DWIGHT E. STEVENSON

ONE hundred and fifty years of biblical scholarship have passed since Alexander Campbell enunciated his views on "The Ancient Order" of the New Testament church. How do Campbell's views hold up under the weight of this history? Even more significant: since Disciples of Christ derived their view of church organization largely from Campbell, how well do Disciples of Christ measure up to the present understanding of church organization made available by biblical scholarship? How far have we been right? How far afield are we? What future directions should we take?

This paper falls into three main divisions: (1) Church Organization as Alexander Campbell Saw It, (2) Church Organization in the New Testament as Biblical Scholars Now See It, and (3) Assumptions Reconsidered.

I Church Organization As Alexander Campbell Saw It

BRITISH INDEPENDENTS INFLUENCE CAMPBELL

There is little doubt that Alexander Campbell's approach to church organization began within the fellowship of the Scottish Independents. While he was at the University of Glasgow during the school year of 1808-09, he came under the influence of

Greville Ewing in whose company he spent many long evenings. This influence finally resulted in his severing ties with the Seceder Presbyterians. When he arrived in America in the summer of 1809, he was an Independent.

I shall not attempt to weave the strands of influence into a single fabric, but there were several of these. For example, John Glas about 1727 left his ministry in the Church of Scotland and in time organized a dozen or so independent congregations which emphasized the autonomy of the local church, a weekly communion, the plurality of elders, and lay leadership of worship.[1] The Haldane Brothers were active at the time of Campbell's attendance at Glasgow, although Greville Ewing was drifting away from them because he could not follow them into their insistence upon baptism by immersion. Nevertheless, it was the Haldane influence that Ewing mediated to Campbell, with some modifications. It had been the purpose of the Haldanes to restore the exact pattern of the primitive church in structure, ministry, ordinances, and worship. This included foot washing, the holy kiss, and closed communion.[2] William Ballantine, one of Haldane's evangelists, had written a "Treatise on the Elder's Office" in which he had argued for a plurality of elders in every church and had insisted upon the practice of mutual exhortation by all the lay members as the best means of obtaining elders. This mutual exhortation was regarded not as a mere privilege, but as a duty of all the members. This, as Richardson reported, caused great disorder in the public worship of the Independents and all but destroyed the pastoral office.[3] Ewing seems to have followed Ballantine in a slightly modified way; he introduced, "besides the Lord's Day meeting . . . a weekly church meeting, which was for social worship and mutual exhortation."[4] Ewing had already adopted the practice of weekly communion.

Thus we see that all or nearly all of the essential elements of Campbell's early stand on church order were supplied by the Independents. Richardson characterizes Alexander's stand in 1824 as the adoption of the "weekly breaking of the loaf," the fellowship, the simple order of public worship, and the independence of each church under the care of bishops and elders. This order was in effect at Wellsburg, Brush Run, and Pittsburgh.[5]

There is a good deal of evidence that Campbell was little attracted to the Haldanican emphasis upon mutual exhortation. He favored it, but he felt that it should be safeguarded by placing it under the strict supervision of qualified elders. The following incident is instructive:

> About this period Mr. Scott was one day accompanying Mr. Campbell on his way from Pittsburg home, and they attended together the meeting of the church at Cross Roads, in which the order of the Pittsburg Church had been to a considerable extent adopted. A number of the members having read various Scriptures and spoken at length, Mr. Scott was finally called upon to say something. With this invitation he at once complied, by boldly taking the ground that it was unscriptural to have so many teachers, that the liberty conceded was carried to license, and that each member should be confined, according to the Scripture analogy of the human body, to the particular function for which he was best fitted. At the close of his remarks he inquired with emphasis, in the broad Scotch he sometimes used, "What, my brethren! is the Church to be a' mouth?"[6]

Richardson tells us that Campbell "fully concurred in the justness of Mr. Scott's admonitions." He went on to say:

> He entirely approved mutual exhortation and instruction, but thought it best that a general permission to speak should be confined to private or social meetings of the church, and that at the Lord's day meetings, when the public were expected to attend, only those should be set forward who were best able, from their knowledge of the Bible and their natural gifts, to speak acceptably and profitably to the assembly.[7]

This led him to place increased emphasis upon the authority of the elders or bishops and to insist also that they be paid.[8]

Campbell Looks Beyond the Congregation

The above encounter with the excesses of lay religion is instructive. Campbell had been driven by the excesses of clericalism into the arms of the Independents, but the excesses of the Independents began to repel him. This is the way in which Campbell really arrived at his final positions on church organizations—by reacting to practical difficulties which emerged in the growing movement which he headed. This was true not only within congregations, but among congregations. As long as he operated within the structure of the Baptist Associations, he did not need to concern himself, however, with the scriptural pattern beyond the local congregation. The problem of intercongregational relations had not really emerged. But when the Mahoning Baptist Association, having been captured for the Reformers by Walter Scott, voted itself out of existence in the summer of 1830, Campbell was startled. He rose to his feet and said, "Brethren, what are you going to do? Are you never going to meet again?" These words fell upon the assembly "like a clap of thunder, and caused a speedy change of feelings." Campbell then proposed that they meet annually for preaching, fellowship, and reports of progress on a purely voluntary basis. From this time forward he began to argue with increasing fervor for some plan of church organization that would save the movement from rank congregational anarchy. It was his firm belief that the plan for this organization could be found in the New Testament. But practical needs and problems were at the basis of this search: (1) Evangelists had to be sent out and supported; this was beyond the province or the power of any local church. (2) The training of the ministry could not be done by one church. (3) Without some concert the separate congregations could not protect themselves against roving impostors and charlatans who ordained themselves to the ministry and used "the gift of gab" to exploit the people. (4) The growth and size of the successful movement made state and national assemblies desirable and practically forced some kind of decision about organization. (5) There were disputes and difficulties calling for some machinery of church discipline.

By 1841 Campbell was saying, ". . . our organization and discipline are greatly defective, and essentially inadequate to the present condition and wants of society."[9] "Christ's institution is a kingdom," he said, "not a mob, not a fierce lawless democracy. . . ."[10] There were those who argued that we needed nothing beyond the Bible and the local congregation. This position Campbell vehemently rejected:

> A book is not sufficient to govern the church. No book ever governed any community—not even the Book of the Law, or the Book of the Gospel, else Moses would have resigned when he wrote the Law, and would never have laid his hand upon Joshua; else Jesus would never have sent out Apostles, Prophets, Evangelists, Pastors, and Teachers if the New Testament had been a King and Sovereign executive of his will. After the New Testament had been written out, Paul would not have commanded Timothy and Titus to reprove, to rebuke, or to commit to faithful and competent persons the office of instructing and building up the church."[11]

It was Campbell's view that the church was a comprehensive term embracing nothing less than the whole church. While it was appropriate to speak of the church of a city, district, state, or nation, none of these designations could be exclusive; *the* church was nothing less than the whole church. It was this basic fact of all-embracing community that had to be considered in any plan of church organization. From such a background Campbell argued:

> Now that there are individual, domestic, and social duties needs no demonstration. And that the family and the particular congregation have each their special and appropriate duties, obligation, and jurisdiction, is equally evident; but that there is a community beyond the family, beyond the particular congregation, is equally evident and undeniable; and that it is competent only to that community to select and appoint its own public functionaries, as much as it is to the congregation in any given place, is a proposition which I am prepared to demonstrate. . . .[12]

Campbell was always confident that he could find all that was needed in the New Testament itself. He was willing to appeal neither to the postbiblical tradition of the church nor wholly to expediency:

> Christianity, introduced by the Lord in person, by Apostles, Evangelists, and Prophets, was, as has been often demonstrated, placed under the supervision and administration of elders or bishops. These bishops, though raised up and ordained by certain churches, possessed in some way a supervision over cities and districts of country beyond a single congregation. Bishops were ordained in every city so soon as congregations were formed, and these bishops by consultation, either by the way of occasional or periodical meetings, or by internuncios, messengers, or epistles, consulted, advised, and directed the whole communities of Christians in reference to all matters of public interest in the kingdom.[13]

Endeavoring to enunciate what the New Testament teaches and shows us about church cooperation, Campbell arrived at seven principles of concerted action:

> 1. It inculcates the necessity of co-operation, and specifies instances.
>
> 2. It inculcates the necessity of two distinct classes of officers in every particular community. [Elders and deacons.]
>
> 3. It indicates the necessity of a third class of public functionaries, and gives examples of diverse ministries. [Evangelists.]
>
> 4. It exemplifies the utility and the need for special deliberations, and of conventions on peculiar emergencies.
>
> 5. It allows not persons to send themselves or to ordain themselves to office; but every where intimates the necessity of choice, selection, mission, and ordination.
>
> 6. It inculcates a general superintendency of districts and cities by those who preside over the churches in those districts; that is, it makes it the duty of the Christian ministry, by whatever name it may be called, to take care of the common interests of the kingdom in those places and districts in which it is located and resident.
>
> 7. It claims for every functionary the concurrence of those portions of the community in which he labors, and holds him responsible to those who send, appoint, or ordain him to office.[14]

To do all this Campbell had only three classes of church officers, for "the proper officers of the kingdom are three—Elders or Bishops, Evangelists or Missionaries, Deacons or Ministers."[15] It is clear that many terms are synonymous. For example, the terms elder, bishop, teacher, and pastor are different titles for the same office. He held that the "apostles and prophets have finished their labors, and now live only in print."[16]

Before proceeding to Campbell's full scheme of congregational and intercongregational organization, let us pause to consider two deviations from congregational independency: the church of a city and tribunals for church discipline.

The church in a given city might have several congregations, but it was only one church so organized that the separate congregations lived in concert:

> . . . there was not a city in the Apostolic age that had a plurality of churches, so far as the New Testament indicates. Their government was Episcopal, Presbyterian and Congregational, all three—bishops and elders, are but two names for the same office.[17]

In problems calling for discipline and the settling of disputes Campbell called tribunals into being: "The most common, natural, and indeed scriptural way, is to call for help from some neighboring communities—to invite the eldership of one or more churches, either chosen by the parties or appointed by the church to which they belong . . ."[18]

Asked for scriptural warrant for these tribunals, Campbell pointed to the Council of Jerusalem in Acts 15, and also insisted that the warrant "is found in the constitution of the church itself. The church is one body, composed of many communities, . . . they are subject to the call of one another, and are bound to submit to one another in all cases demanding their action or co-operation."[19]

DETAILS OF A SYSTEM

To get a quick view of Campbell's whole plan of church organization we may refer to Chapter 24 in *The Christian System* or to a somewhat more imaginative passage in the *Millennial Harbinger* of 1843. We shall defer to the latter.

> Suppose, then, for example, an Evangelist or two were sent into the island of Guernsey to publish the gospel and to plant the Christian standard there. They preach the gospel successfully, and, in a few weeks, one hundred converts are made. They continue with them for a year or two, until they are able to take care of themselves. A temporary administration of Elders and Deacons, by and with the consent of the congregation, is appointed by the Evangelists. They then leave the church A; and proceeding to another station, gather a second community, which is called B; . . . and so on till they have thus got into existence the churches A, B, C, D, E, and F.[20]

In five or six years, having revisited the congregations and having spent some time with each community, the evangelists *ordain* bishops and deacons in every church. At this time, although the whole church of Guernsey consists of six congregations, they have no machinery of cooperation (except insofar as it is supplied by the itinerating evangelists). Moreover, certain difficulties have begun to arise: (1) Persons excommunicated from one community are received without question into another. (2) Messengers from one congregation are refused hospitality by another. (3) Individual congregations think of many projects that need to be carried out but they lack resources to undertake them independently. To meet these emerging problems and needs, "all the Elders and Deacons of all the churches meet at Church A, the oldest and most exemplary in the island."[21] This council of church officers sets to work formulating eight propositions, as follows:

> 1. That all Christian communities on earth, however numerous, constituted but one church of Christ.
> 2. That the communities of any one State were the church of that State, as though it were the whole world, and that being placed under the same providential arrangements as to language and political relations, they were to act with a reference to that State just as though it was the whole world, or as the whole church of Christ ought to act towards the whole world.

3. That the church being compared to a *body,* and to *one* body, was an organized community, having two great classes of duties to perform—one class of duties were to be performed to itself and one to the world.

4. That there were in each of these general classes of duties two classes as respected another grand view of the one body—they were public and private duties.

5. That the private duties concerned each particular community, and were to be performed by that community to itself independent. . . .

6. That as private and special consultation meetings were necessary to the complete and perfect discharge of private duties, so public and special meetings were equally . . . necessary. . . .

7. That as private duties respected the economical, moral, and religious bearings of individual members of a single community towards each other . . .; so the public duties of all the churches in their associate character, *as one body,* respected the economical, moral, and religious bearings of all the communities towards each other and the world, with a special reference to their own character, honor, usefulness, and happiness, as one body.

8. That as moral and religious duties are the result of direct and positive enactments, so all economical and prudential duties, not directly and positively enjoined because circumstantial, and contingent on the unstable and mutable forms of political society and human revolutions, are in their nature and design *conventional,* and must be enacted by the authority of a whole community; and then, like the by-laws of all other corporations, when agreed to, are to be conscientiously respected and obeyed by all the good and orderly constituents or members of that community.[22]

The first meeting of the Council is adjourned to be followed some days later by a second with the same persons present together with "certain other brethren of high reputation amongst them" who were appointed by their respective congregations. All of these agreed to six things:

1. That they should act as one body, regarding all the existing congregations of the island, they should recognize certain strictly congregational rights.

Amongst these they enumerated the election and appointment of their congregational officers. That each church should have its own eldership and diaconate, and at least one *President Elder,* whose whole time shall be sacred to the calls and supervision of the church; for which services he shall be supported by the brethren so far as his needs require, and their abilities allow.

2. That every individual community shall respect the private acts and rights of every other community, and not at all interfere with them.

3. That in all cases where public officers, such as messengers of any general character, and especially Evangelists, who are to be regarded as officers of the whole body, *a concurrence of a plurality of churches by their officers,* be regarded as necessary, if not to empower them to discharge official duties in a single congregation, at least necessary to give them general acceptance, and to constitute them public and responsible agents of the whole body.

4. That when any community shall have any case of great difficulty beyond its ability satisfactorily to dispose of, reference may be had to other communities for a council or committee to assist in such case; whose decision shall be final—an end of all farther litigation or debate on the premises.

5. That whenever any great question of finance, or the means of successfully prosecuting any great public object, or any other event of great public interest shall require it, a special general meeting of messengers from all the congregations shall be called by the person who presided at the last general meeting; and that the eldership and diaconates of all the congregations, or so many of them as can attend, shall always be at least a portion of the messengers who attend on such occasions.

6. Finally, that all the public duties of the Christian church shall be attended to as though it were, what it is in fact, *one body,* under the head—the Messiah; and, therefore, arrangements and provisions shall be always made in general meetings for the most faithful, prompt, and satisfactory discharge of these duties.[23]

The above principles were not sufficient, of course, to settle the question of how the six churches of Guernsey would relate themselves to the churches on another island, or how the churches of several islands taken together would express their unity. In other words, it leaves unsolved the relations of districts to states and states to the whole brotherhood. This was the problem which emerged in connection with the first national convention. In the call that went out for the convention of 1849 which finally met at Cincinnati, Campbell gave it as his opinion that the meeting should be a delegated body "of messengers of churches, selected and constituted such by the church—one from every church if possible, or if impossible, one from a district, or some definite number of churches."

Campbell's wishes for a delegate convention were wholly unrealized during his lifetime. By 1869 at Louisville, Kentucky, a new plan was adopted. It was a very rigid plan of pyramided representation from the local churches, through the county and state up to the national convention. When the first assembly of this new General Convention was held a year later, there were 74 delegates from 14 states; but there were also 600 visitors, and these were invited to participate, turning what had promised to be a representative gathering into a mass meeting. Another attempt to get a representative national convention in 1913 failed in much the same way; there were 1,000 delegates, but 1,741 nondelegates; the mass swamped the delegate principle.

Campbell makes it clear in other places that there is an element of expediency which has to be taken into account, though he insists that the general principles of cooperative organization are scripturally given. Here, for example, he writes:

> No written formula could possibly be given for all time, because the conditions of society are ever changing. Hence the necessity of prudential and effective counsel and co-operation changing with times and circumstances. No new doctrine, no formula of doctrine, is wanting. The Christian Scriptures are adequate, in their doctrne and spirit, to every new condition and emergency of the cause. . . . But there is need for *executive counsel* and sound discretion, in order to success. Hence new emergencies, even in the short period of the apostolic age, called for deliberative meetings of the church by her messengers.[24]

There is further light on questions which may be of an expedient nature in a passage from the *Christian System:*

> . . . whether the churches in a given district shall, by letter, mes-

sengers, or stated meetings, once or twice per annum, or oftener, communicate with one another; whether they shall send one, two, or twenty persons, or all go and communicate face to face, or send a letter; and whether they shall annually print, write or publish their statistics, &c. &c. &c., are the mere circumstantials of the Christian institution.[25]

Campbell also makes it clear that he does not want conventions or conferences legislating on matters of belief. Of the councils which he sees meeting in the New Testament church he says:

> Their conferences, consultations and decisions, were neither doctrinal, preceptive, nor speculative, but wholly practical and executive. They were, indeed, neither legislative nor judicial, but simply executive and advisory councils. The churches severally had their own judicial tribunals in all cases of discipline. They were competent to the case; or, if not, to solicit such advice and direction as would ultimately settle the matter.[26]

Campbell's Presuppositions

Before we pass to an examination of what modern light we may have on the organization of the New Testament church, let us pause to state a few of Campbell's basic assumptions underlying the foregoing discussion. Some of these he expressed; others he did not regard as presuppositions at all, but as matters of simple truth:

1. Congregational independency is only a relative term; the church embraces all local congregations everywhere in the world. This unity of the whole church must have institutional expression.
2. The New Testament recognizes this; moreover, it gives us in express command or approved precedent all that we need to guide the modern church in matters of organization.
3. In the New Testament church, organization is everywhere the same, every congregation being developed on the same pattern, and the unity of the whole church being expressed in the same way throughout all its districts.

4. The offices of the New Testament church were definite in name, number, and functions.

5. The New Testament pattern for church organization was essentially static, and was meant to remain so for all subsequent time.

How do these presuppositions fare in the light of modern biblical knowledge?

II Church Organization In The New Testament

EMERGENCE AT JERUSALEM

Thousands of disciples at Jerusalem met in family groupings at numerous private homes to celebrate their own distinctive fellowship. (Acts 2:47; 5:11) But these fellowships were not separate churches. All of them together constituted the church in Jerusalem. Members were conscious of a unity that embraced all the brethren.

1. *Apostles.* The most important persons in the Jerusalem church at first were the apostles. They were twelve in number: eleven of the original Twelve, plus a disciple to replace Judas. The authority of this group was probably spiritual rather than official. Other disciples took notice of them because they had been with Jesus. They were at the heart of the fellowship. (Acts 4:33; 5:12)

Through the apostles the work of Jesus was continued, particularly in preaching, teaching, and healing. They were the incarnate influence of Jesus, extending itself. Because of this spiritual role they came also to have a supervisory capacity. (Acts 6:1-2; 7:14; 11:1, 22) They supervised such temporal matters as the distribution of charity and the table fellowships. As time passed and the church grew in numbers, this task began to divert energy from preaching and teaching, but at the beginning the apostles carried it without helpers. More important they supervised the spread of the church beyond Jerusalem, often going themselves to visit new fellowships and to evangelize in new territories. Thus, Peter and John were sent to investigate and confirm the work of Philip in Samaria, and Barnabas was the official emissary of the apostles to survey the situation at Antioch. This activity of supervision and evangelizing throughout a growing Christendom drew the apostles out of Jerusalem and finally dispersed them throughout the Roman world.

2. *The Seven.* Supervising a church so large, the apostles were seen doing a poor job as business managers of it charities. (Acts 6:1-6) Their answer to the resulting complaints was to call a meeting of the church and ask for an election of seven men who would assume this duty, thus releasing them to educate and evangelize. The church having elected The Seven, the apostles then set them to their task. These men were not deacons, nor were they officers of local congregations. We do not find their office duplicated in any other situation. At least two of these men, Philip and Stephen, became active evangelists to special groups, thus going beyond their elected roles.

3. *Elders.* The elders in the Jerusalem church slip up on us without warning. Seemingly they were not there at the beginning, else the apostles would have called upon them to help with the "daily distribution." But by the time of the Jerusalem conference the elders had appeared and were ranked with the apostles as the spiritual leaders of the church. (Acts 11:30; 15:2, 4, 6, 22; 16:4) They met as a group with the apostles and concerned themselves with the affairs of the whole church; their jurisdiction was not confined to local fellowships.

Israel had had its elders for centuries. In the time of Christ, these Jewish elders ruled the communities and supervised the synagogues. The growth of bodies of elders in the churches must have been a natural, unplanned borrowing from Jewish practice.

4. *James, the brother of Jesus.* This younger brother of Jesus came to occupy a position of authority in Jerusalem superior even to that of the Twelve. (Acts 12:17; 15:13; 21:17-18; Galatians 1:19; 2:9, 12) This prominence may have resulted to some degree from the absence of the apostles from Jerusalem,

but a more important cause was probably James' kinship to Jesus. Support for this view is gained from the fact that after the stoning of James, A.D. 62, Simeon, another kinsman, became the head of the Jerusalem church. Had this practice continued, the Christian church might have been ruled by a hereditary caliphate, as Islam was later to be ruled. This Christian caliphate perished with the second in line for several reasons, the strongest of which was the scattering of the Jerusalem church in the Jewish wars and the destruction of the holy city, A.D. 70. James was the most authoritative single person to emerge in the church during its first twenty-five years.

There is much that we do not know about the Jerusalem church, but what we do know indicates that organization emerged in response to practical needs and problems and that it changed with time.

ANTIOCH

The church at Antioch, which became the capital of the gentile mission, did not follow the pattern of Jerusalem.

1. *Prophets and teachers.* This church was led by prophets and teachers. Five of them are named. (Acts 13:1) Neither elders nor apostles are mentioned, for, although Barnabas and Saul are listed among the five, they are not invested with the title of apostle.

This coincides with what we learn of Syrian churches later on. As late as the *Didache,* published about A.D. 140, there were Syrian churches ruled exclusively by "prophets and teachers." It is a pattern peculiar to this region, to be found neither in the church at Jerusalem nor in the infant churches of the gentile mission.

Now we suddenly learn that there were prophets also in the church at Jerusalem. (Acts 11:28; 15:32) Agabus and Silas were among them. No doubt there were others; but at Jerusalem the apostles and elders held pre-eminence over them, whereas at Antioch men of their sort were in the leadership.

Prophets were preachers possessing extraordinary gifts. Their prototype is found in the prophets of the Old Testament.

Teachers were apparently a little more prosaic. Upon them fell the task of instructing new converts, in all probability.

Why did organization develop along this line at Antioch? We can only surmise. The church there was not founded by apostles but by lay believers scattered from Jerusalem. All of them proclaimed the gospel, but some of them must have done it with marked talent and with unusual power; these would have become the prophets of the community, as those with superior talents for instruction would have become its teachers. In time, what had grown up naturally was confirmed and perpetuated as the form of government best suited to the life of the church in this place.

2. *Apostles.* Although Barnabas and Paul were listed only as "prophets and teachers" before their commission to the Gentiles, afterwards they are referred to as "apostles." (Acts 13:4; 14:4) This means that the church of one city, regarding itself as the channel through which the Holy Spirit operated, created apostles. The original Twelve had nothing to do with this. Paul, it is true, later insisted that his commission was from no man, but from God himself (Gal. 1:1). He dated his own apostolic call from his conversion, but the church may have dated it from the commission at Antioch.

Led by prophets and teachers and sending forth its own apostles, the church at Antioch reflected its missionary origin and its role as the mother of missions.

In the Churches Established by Paul

What did Paul do about organization in the churches which he established? (Acts 14:21-23) Newly established churches needed authorized leaders. In the case of these mission churches there were no apostles in residence and no prophets and teachers who had come from older churches to settle in their midst. Lacking these naturally authoritative men, they had to elevate the most venerable from their own ranks to positions of leadership. What they did was necessary; it was an outgrowth of their situation, and it was simple. The mission churches were led by elders. The office of deacon had not yet come into being.

Why did they call these leaders "elders"? Because Paul, who had more to do than any other with their appointment, thought of the church as the New Israel, inclined naturally to provide a government for the churches similar to that of the synagogues, which were ruled by elders. In fact, Christian churches were Christian synagogues, exhibiting many similarities to their Jewish forerunners.

What did these elders do? If we may generalize from the duties of the Ephesian elders nearly ten years later than this, they were pastors. (Acts 20:17, 28) Significantly, they were in the plural. Single pastors came later.

A half dozen years past the middle of the first century, Paul wrote to the Corinthians in an effort to bring unity into a strife-ridden congregation. Three chapters of that letter (1 Corinthians 12-14) go to the heart of our questions about organization. The church, said Paul, is a living community serving as the body of Christ. The life and authority of Christianity lies in the whole community. (1 Cor. 12:12, 22-25, 27) Every member of this community of faith is a responsible member, holding duties which he can never delegate, because he alone has the talent to make his own unique contribution. (1 Cor. 12:4, 28; 14:26-33)

The church of which Paul wrote was not rigidly crystallized. As he himself said, it had variety. The important thing was that the church had many different kinds of work to be done and that different people possessed different talents. It was an open society, so open, in fact, that it was subject to disorder. Paul's list of God's appointments in the church are not offices; they are ministries or services to be rendered. If there were any officers, they were indicated by the word *administrators* which came seventh in a list of eight.

Later in his missionary career Paul may have moved toward a more formal position. (Phil. 1:1; Romans 16:1; Acts 20:17, 28) He begins his Philippian letter by singling out bishops (*episkopoi* used here as synonymous with elders, *presbyteroi*), and deacons. These officials had apparently become important to him in carrying on the work of the church. In the letter of introduction appended to Romans (but probably intended for Ephesus), we even find him mentioning a deaconess. Again in the latter part of Acts we find Paul using *elders* and *bishops* interchangeably as he lays a heavy responsibility upon these men to guard the flock when he himself had left them forever.

Summarizing church life under Paul, we may say that there is a trend from a church life in which pre-eminence was based upon some spiritual gift to church life in which pre-eminence was based upon holding an office. That is, organization as such became progressively important to Paul as the situation began to pass beyond his powers of personal oversight. Nevertheless, the monarchical bishopric had not yet appeared; bishops and elders were synonymous terms and both were in the plural, with authority apparently restricted to local churches. These bishops or elders were assisted in each local situation by deacons and deaconesses.

Organizational Outcomes

In the New Testament after Paul we glimpse a church in transition. It may help us to evaluate the transition if we look at what emerged in the early Church Fathers. This was the authority of the monarchical bishop.

In its simplest form this meant the rule of one bishop over one church in one city. But other stages soon followed. A second stage, only slightly more advanced in time, was the rule of the bishop at a provincial capital over all the bishops and churches of his province. A third state was reached when the bishop of the capital of the Empire came to rule over all the bishops in provincial capitals, and through them over all the bishops of the

Empire. Such authority grew up naturally. Having lost its spiritual center at Jerusalem, the church in time turned to a new one at Rome. Church history informs us beyond doubt that this was the route that the ecclesiastical structure took in the first three centuries.

In some quarters at least, the church had come to recognize the monarchical bishop by A.D. 110 or 115. This we know from the letters of Ignatius, Bishop of Antioch, written on the way to Roman martyrdom under Trajan. In order to be clear about the evidence in Ignatius, we shall quote from a number of these letters. To Polycarp, bishop of Smyrna, he wrote:

> I am giving myself for those who are obedient to the bishop, the elders, the deacons, and may I have my portion with them, in God. Toil together, struggle together, race together, suffer together, rest together, rise together, as God's managers, assistants, and servants. (Polycarp 6:1)

The organizational picture of a single church is very clear: In the above list of officers in a local church there are a body of deacons, another body of elders, and over them all one bishop. The bishop is really a ruler, as the following quotation from the same letter shows: "If you love good disciples, it is no credit to you; rather induce the more troublesome to subjection by your gentleness. . . . Men who seem plausible but teach a strange doctrine must not appall you. Stand firm like an anvil that is hammered." (Polycarp 2:1; 3:1)

To Ephesus, whose bishop was Onesimus, Ignatius wrote:

> Hence it is proper for you to run your race in harmony with the mind of the bishop, just as you are doing. For your deserving body of elders, worthy of God, is attuned to the bishop as the strings of the harp (Ephesians 4:1). So it is clear that we must look upon the bishop as the Lord himself. So Onesimus himself praises highly your good discipline in God, for you all live in the light of the truth, and no sect has any lodging among you . . . (Ephesus 6:1-2).

That the bishop had considerable power we may not doubt. In his letter to Smyrna, Ignatius says:

It is not permissible to baptize or hold a religious meal without the bishop, but whatever he approves is also pleasing to God, so that everything you do may be secure and valid (8:2). It is well to recognize God and the bishop. Whoever honors the bishop is honored by God. Whoever does anything without the bishop's knowledge is serving the devil (9:1).

One other strand of early evidence from the Apostolic Fathers comes through Clement, who was bishop of Rome from A.D. 88 to 97. About A.D. 95 he wrote a letter in the name of the church at Rome to the church at Corinth. The purpose of the letter was to discipline a quarrel within the church, not unlike those with which Paul had dealt forty years earlier. Evidently Clement felt that he could speak to Corinth with some authority, and he proceeded to do so:

The church of God that is staying in Rome to the church of God that is staying in Corinth. . . . Because of the sudden and repeated misfortunes and calamities that have befallen us (persecution), we think we have been discussed among you and to the foul and impious uprising . . . which a few headstrong and willful men have kindled to such a frenzy that your good name, respected and renowned and universally beloved, has come to be greatly reviled (1:1).

It is disgraceful, dear friends, utterly disgraceful, and unworthy of Christian conduct to have it said that because of one or two people the old, established church of the Corinthians is in revolt against its elders. (47:6)

The significance of Clement's letter lies in the implicit authority of the bishop of Rome who felt duty-bound to undertake to discipline a church as far distant as Corinth. But, the latter is also eloquent by its silence; it does not mention a bishop of Corinth as distinct from the elders.

Ignatius and Clement do show us, however, that by the end of the first century or very soon in the second, *bishop* and *elder* were no longer synonymous terms. A plurality of elders made up a body in a church, but the bishop was one man at the head.

This bishop had binding authority over doctrine and worship. This bishop might be over a local church, or over a province, and even, perhaps over a much larger territory.

AFTER PAUL

What, then, happened in the transitional period, from A.D. 65 to 100? There were elders and deacons in most churches; and evidently there were also deaconesses, though they are not specifically called such. (1 Tim. 3:1, 8, 11; 5:9-11) "The women" and "a widow" seem to be official designations; these terms may perhaps be taken to refer to deaconesses.

Elders exercise considerable authority. (Heb. 13:17; 1 Tim. 5:17; 1 Pet. 5:2, 5) At the same time this authority was new enough that the churches had to be admonished to submit to it. These men had at least two clearly recognized functions in addition to administration: they were also preachers and teachers. Apparently they had taken over the functions of earlier prophets and teachers. (1 Tim. 5:18-19) Moreover, they were paid a salary, and they enjoyed certain immunities from censure because of their office.

The pastoral Epistles do not help us to decide whether the monarchical bishopric had emerged by this period. Titus 1:5-9 can be interpreted either way. Titus was to appoint bishops in several local churches. Does this mean that he appointed one bishop in each of a number of churches? It could mean that. Moreover, what of Titus himself? Was he not exercising the authority of a provincial bishop, ruling over several churches in many cities?

When we pass to the Johannine Epistles, we are on much more definite ground. Now it appears beyond doubt that the bishop is one man who rules over one church, in one instance; and in another instance, he is the head of a church in a provincial capital who also exercises authority over other churches in his province. (3 John 9-10)

Diotrephes was a one-man ruler of the church addressed in

this letter. He held absolute power over worship, hospitality, and church membership. He exercised the right of excommunication. But he would not submit to the authority of the Elder who wrote from a sister church in a neighboring city. This looks very much like an established monarchical bishopric of one city in the days of the emerging provincial bishopric, before prerogatives had been firmly established.

The author of First and Second John, who is unnamed, simply calls himself "the Elder." If he had been an apostle he would surely have asserted his apostolic authority, especially when it was being contested. He does not call himself "an elder" but "the Elder." All of this points to his being the bishop in the capital of the province—and tradition says that the Elder was at Ephesus—writing to a church in another city under his supervision. First he had tried to approach this city through its leader, the bishop Diotrephes, but Diotrephes had rejected his authority; so he had gone over the head of the bishop to appeal directly to the church itself. What is more, he did not intend to let the matter rest with letters. (2 John 12-13) He planned to visit the neighboring church in person. One cannot suppose that he would fail to deal with Diotrephes. The issue at stake was one of authority and it had to be settled. We do not know how it was settled in this case, but we do know how this sort of thing came out in the long run.

It was a long organizational journey which the church of the New Testament had taken: all the way from an informal family fellowship to a formidable ecclesiastical structure shaped on the provincial government of the Roman Empire. But this development was natural and it was necessary.

It was necessary for three reasons: (1) The passing of the Apostles. It takes an institution to transmit a faith from one generation to another; the church developed an institution so that its faith would pass into the future. (2) The disciplining of heresy was an even more powerful factor disposing the church toward definite organization structure. For heresy threatened the unity and peace of the church as well as the continuance of the faith. To put it bluntly, except for the emergence of a strong authority to meet them, early heresies could have killed the church. (3) A third reason for definite structure was the opposition of a highly organized, authoritative state. To fight Rome, the church had to counter authority with authority, organization with organization. Nothing was more natural than that the church should come to duplicate the governmental structure of the Roman Empire.

To recapitulate, we may say that the word "organization" is much too static and formal to fit the early church. Whatever else the church was, it was not an organization; it acquired organization as a tool. But it was first a fellowship and a movement. Both fellowship and movement were growing affairs.

The church began almost without any machinery and gradually evolved a structure of offices as it needed them, suiting that structure to the complex individual situation. Emergence, variety, and vitality characterized the organization of this explosive movement in which the church began; for organization was secondary, a tool hammered out on the anvil of necessity.

III Assumptions Reconsidered

In the light of the above survey, what can be said about Alexander Campbell's presuppositions? Of the five which we attempted to articulate, only the first stands. The remaining four are wholly untenable in light of biblical scholarship. Campbell once said that the church of the New Testament was congregational, presbyterian, and episcopal—all three. It was unfortunate that the absence of the principle of development did not enable him to see deeper into this truth. And it is unfortunate, too, that he insisted upon making the details of church organization a matter of divine revelation, as necessary to Christianity as basic faith and worship.

Failing to see the early church in dynamic rather than in static, legalistic terms, Campbell also failed to see that the death of the

Apostles was bound to force a tighter organization than was needed during their lifetime. Though he felt that the Apostles continued with the church through the written authority of the New Testament, they could not possibly answer the emerging organizational needs of the movement. In the same way—and it is not blasphemy to say this—Campbell failed to assess the importance of his own role in the movement of Disciples of Christ. For all practical purposes he was what the citizens of Bethany and Wellsburg always called him, "Bishop Campbell." We might even say, "Archbishop Campbell" without straying too far from the facts. Campbell himself would have bridled at the suggestion, but he behaved and spoke as though he did hold such authority. J. B. Jeter, one of Campbell's enemies, was reliably objective when he said that Disciples "are held together by the magic of a name, and by a leader whose authority they have indignantly denied, and implicitly followed."[27]

Even Campbell's authority hardly kept the movement united during his lifetime. He came to want a tighter state and national organization than he achieved. But after his death the lack of organizational cohesion proved anarchistic. In this, too, Jeter was prophetic. After making the statement about the magic of Campbell's name, quoted just above, he went on to predict that following Campbell's death the divisive tendencies in the movement would assert themselves and Disciple unity would be shattered. As long as Campbell was alive a strong central government was not needed; when he was dead, it became impossible.

The answer to all of this, as well as our future direction was given by Isaac Errett in 1870, when he wrote, "We have been, for forty or fifty years, carrying on a revolutionary movement, in some respects more *de*structive than *con*structive. . . . This state of things cannot continue. We must come under system. . . . Congregationalism must enlarge its sphere of activity and develop into systematic cooperation for all the grand purposes that enter into the aggressive work of the church."

If Campbell had not been hampered by his own legalistic assumptions about the dependence of church organization upon the letter of the New Testament and about the static character of that organization, he may well have led Disciples into an ordered brotherhood life. His failure lay in the realm of basic presuppositions. Now we can see that the fundamental principle of church organization, even in the New Testament, is expediency. The church as redemptive community is given to mankind by the spirit of God, but this living church directed by the Spirit in ever new, emerging situations must fashion its own organization and it must keep on revising that organization to meet the needs of the growing program of the church and the changing character of the secular order.

NOTES

1. W. E. Garrison, *An American Religious Movement* (St. Louis: Bethany Press, 1945), pp. 20-21.
2. W. E. Garrison and A. T. DeGroot, *The Disciples of Christ, a History* (St. Louis: Bethany Press, 1948), pp. 52-53.
3. Robert Richardson, *The Memoirs of Alexander Campbell,* I, 180. (J. B. Lippincott, 1871).
4. *Ibid.,* 179.
5. *Ibid.,* II, 125.
6. *Ibid.,* II, 126-127.
7. *Ibid.*
8. *Ibid.*
9. *Millennial Harbinger,* 1841, 533.
10. *Ibid.,* 1841, 534.
11. *Ibid.,* 1841, 533-534.
12. *Ibid.,* 1841, 534-535.
13. *Ibid.,* 1842, 60.
14. *Ibid.,* 1842, 62-63.
15. *Ibid.,* 1843, 261.
16. *Ibid.,* 1853, 481.
17. *Ibid.,* 1853, 123.
18. *Ibid.,* 1840, 434.
19. *Ibid.*
20. *Ibid.,* 1843, 83.
21. *Ibid.*
22. *Ibid.,* 1843, 84-85.
23. *Ibid.,* 1843, 85-86.
24. *Ibid.,* 1853, 489.
25. Alexander Campbell, *The Christian System* (John Burns, St. Louis, N. D.), pp. 74-75.
26. *Millennial Harbinger,* 1853, 489.
27. Foreword to *Campbellism Exposed* by A. P. Williams.

3

The Issue of Polity for Disciples Today

W. B. Blakemore

CHURCH polity is now a serious issue for Disciples of Christ though many of them do not realize how serious an issue it is. Most Disciples of Christ probably believe that insofar as polity is an issue the problem lies at the level of maintaining some kind of integrity between our practice and the congregational polity which we have traditionally and currently asserted to be the polity we approve. What few enough realize is that the issue has arisen at the more fundamental level of the very idea of "congregational polity."

Does the term "congregational polity" any longer represent a viable and a valid conception?

As we work our way through to a more adequately Christian conception of church polity, can the term "congregational polity" serve to designate that more adequate conception?

The thesis of this paper is that the answer to both the above questions is "No." This does not mean, however, that we will therefore turn to either presbyterial or episcopal polity which, to many, seem to be the only alternatives to congregational polity. Rather our thesis will demonstrate that what is needed is a conception that transcends all three of these historic doctrines of church polity, and points toward another kind of understanding which may serve a more ecumenical purpose. The bankruptcy of the notion of congregational polity will be an item in the early parts of this article. The later sections of the paper will introduce a theory of association which, we believe, must be taken into account in reconstruction of polity.

During the decade of the 1950's Disciples of Christ carried a Long Range Program to undeniable success, especially in terms of institutional development. But the 1950's were a decade which also saw, just as undeniably, a collapse of the conception of congregational polity. In the first place, the idea of congregational polity was proven ecumenically inadequate. This was evident as early as 1950, though numerous "congregationalists" including Disciples of Christ closed their minds fast shut against that evidence which became clear in connection with the emergence of the United Church of Christ. Second, the conception of congregational polity was found denominationally inadequate as Disciples, during the '50s, came upon problems of "brotherhood" structure for which congregational polity provided no answers, nor even any guidance toward an answer. These two inadequacies will be further amplified, but first the term "congregational polity" must be clarified.

In the course of this paper five conceptions of congregational polity will be presented. This section of the paper will deal with three only. These three are popularly and widely held. The fourth view is one which is emergent among congregationalists at the present time, though it is in many respects a revival of an earlier historic definition. The name of Dr. Douglas Horton is closely associated with this conception today. The fifth conception is really a clarifying restatement of the fourth. The restatement implies that in the long run the fourth overcomes the inadequacies of the first three conceptions but cannot logically be called "congregational polity." These five conceptions of congregational polity are usually, in any single individual mind, mixed and unclarified—a situation which, in part, accounts for some of our contemporary confusions regarding polity.

The first idea of congregational polity is that which asserts the term "church" is properly applied only to local congregations and since this is the only proper usage of the word "church," local congregations should enter into no other kind of association. This point of view does not merely assert, "nothing other than local congregations may be called church." It asserts, "since nothing other than local congregations may be called church, no kinds of religious association other than congregations may be brought into existence." This is the kind of radical localism which is the theory behind the anti-Sunday school movement, the antimissionary organization movement, and other antimeans movements that have been most frequent among the anti-organ Church of Christ and, as a theory at least, among the "Independents." It is, so to speak, the idea that becomes dominant when the words in Thomas Campbell's second Proposition, "The Church of Christ upon earth must necessarily exist in particular and distinct societies, locally separate from one another," are lifted out of context and given more regard than the assertion of constitutional, essential and intentional unity expressed in Proposition One.

The first idea of congregational polity is a radical congregationalism. Its overstatement of the case originally eased the separation of Disciple congregations from "the sects," especially on the Western Reserve. It is the theory by virtue of which Walter Scott carried the day of dissolving the Mahoning Association. For many Disciples this radical way of stating the case became normative even though it was not the theory by which Disciples and Christians, in the same months that the Mahoning Association was dissolved, were moving toward the Union of 1832 and preparing for the emergence of numerous regional and state associations for evangelism. The history of Disciples in the early 1830's is evidence that even at our origins more than one conception of "congregational polity" was in the minds of the forefathers—sometimes they acted in accordance with one and sometimes in accordance with another of these conceptions.

The second conception of "congregational polity" admits associations of Christians other than local congregations as "means" of carrying on various desirable religious works. These functional associations are in no sense considered "church," and they were organized originally as private corporations rather than as ecclesiastical corporations, i.e., as associations of persons, not as associations of congregations. For many decades Diciples of Christ were quite content with this kind of arrangement and an amazing proportion of the present structure of the brotherhood was brought into existence under the aegis of this conception. Even so recent an entity as the Disciples of Christ Historical Society emerged as a private corporation which only subsequently has sought some kind of "official" relationship.

It is fair to state that through the greater part of the history of Disciples of Christ this second conception has been the one which has accompanied the development of their cooperative life. At the present time, however, there is a strong tendency to adopt the third conception as a re-explanation of and guide for that cooperative life.

The third conception of congregational polity has had a slow emergence. In its mature form this third theory admits the inevitability of supralocal organization and asserts that while this level of organization in none of its parts may be called "church," it should all be under the control of the local congregation. While this notion of government of the overhead structure by the local congregations is relatively new amongst Disciples of Christ, there were instances of it very early in the history of the movement. The Missionary Society of the Christian Churches of North Carolina has always in one sense been an association of local congregations. But for the vast majority of Disciples of Christ the shift from the second to the third idea is a very recent matter and not yet by any means completed. The fact that this shift is going on means that much of the organizational debate in the denomination is in terms of "associations of persons" versus "associations of churches." So long as the debate is at this level Diciples of Christ only intensify an organizational impasse, though it is correct also to say that what changes are taking place—state unification, the drive toward delegate conventions, the increase of representative boards as over against self-perpetuating boards, the subtle nuances in the change from "International Convention of Disciples of Christ" to "International Convention of Christian Churches," etc.—are supported theoretically by the notion that while supralocal organization in none of its parts may be denominated church, it should all be under control of the local congregations.

The most widely spread and popular idea of congregational polity amongst Disciples of Christ today is this third conception which calls for the government of everything else in the brotherhood by the local congregations. Furthermore, it was the popular and most widespread doctrine of congregational polity amongst the Congregational–Christians a decade ago when they sought to form the United Church of Christ. It was because Cadman Memorial Church in Brooklyn knew that this was by far the most widely held doctrine of congregational polity among the Congregational–Christian Churches that it confidently took court action to block the merger because in terms of that doctrine the merger could not logically take place. Ultimately the merger succeeded, not because it was demonstrated that the majority held a different point of view but because the majority point of view was demonstrated to be illogical and irrelevant, a tissue of ambiguous terms arranged into propositions which have no reality in history or present fact. This charge of bankruptcy is not hyperbole. It is a literal statement because the third idea of congregational polity collapses in the face of logic and reality, exhibiting neither inner coherence nor correspondence with reality when closely examined.

The demonstration of the incoherence of the third version of congregational polity is made in a pair of slim but important documents published in 1954 which few enough Disciples of

Christ have read. The procedures which produced these two documents began in 1950 when the General Council of the Congregational–Christian Churches appointed a Committee to Study Free Church Polity and Unity. The committee was appointed because the denomination was already in the law courts. The Cadman Memorial Church had instituted a suit against the General Council to prevent the merger that would result in the United Church of Christ. On January 26, 1950, Justice Meyer Steinbrink of the New York Supreme Court handed down a decision upholding the plea of Cadman Memorial Church. One of the ideas in Justice Steinbrink's decision was that congregational polity "is that system of church organization which recognizes the independence and autonomy of the local church in all matters temporal or spiritual, and the association of churches through voluntary independent organizations devised for fellowship and cooperation is without ecclesiastical authority." Justice Steinbrink made it perfectly plain that his decision was based on what he believed was the standard Congregational-Christian interpretation of congregational polity. It was perfectly obvious that if Judge Steinbrink's decision were to be sustained, no congregationalist bodies would ever be able to unite with any other because all of them favored that idea of congregational polity. *The Christian Century,* particularly in its issue for February 8, 1950 (Vol. 67, No. 6), remarked the decision and warned that since the end of the road had come for traditional congregational polity all congregational-type bodies should reconsider their ideas of their structural and organizational functioning. It was against such a background that the General Council appointed its committee to study free church polity in relation to Christian unity.

Before the *Report* of that committee was in, the New York State Court of Appeals in 1953 ruled that the civil courts were without jurisdiction in the Cadman case. The General Council was therefore free to effect its merger with the United Church of Christ. The reaction has been something like a vast sigh of relief as left-wing Protestantism has thought "perhaps we can be ecumenical without rethinking our polity after all." But the shock of the Steinbrink decision cannot be forgotten and some rethinking has been going on, though nothing like the radical and heart-searching inquiry which *The Christian Century* recognized a decade ago as essential.

It was not until 1954 that the Committee on Free Church Polity and Unity rendered its Report to the General Council (hereafter the *Report* will be referred to simply as the *Report*).[1] At the same time the legal Counsel of the General Council submitted a *Letter* concerning the *Report* (the *Letter* hereafter will be referred to as the *Letter*).[2]

Despite what had happened four years earlier, the rigidities of the human mind and its entrapments in habit are such that the Committee handed in a *Report* which, so far as congregational polity is concerned, in no way reflected the significance of Judge Steinbrink's decision. Indeed, we saw the strange spectacle of the body that wanted to form the United Church of Christ reiterating the very doctrine on the basis of which Judge Steinbrink had ruled against the merger. In other words, at the practical level these good people voted for the merger and voted also for a doctrine which would not allow it. (It should be remembered that the legal reversal was not in terms of a repudiation of Judge Steinbrink's argument but an assertion of no jurisdiction.)

Fortunately, the General Council of the Congregational-Christian Churches seems to have recognized that the ordinary ways of stating congregational polity needed to be corrected, and received the *Letter* from Counsel which aids in that clarification. It is in the *Letter* that the traditional version of congregational polity is demolished. That version which we have heretofore stated as the assertion that all supralocal organization while not in any sense Church is to be controlled by the local congregations is widely held by Congregationalists and Disciples of Christ. Perhaps the way in which the doctrine is most often stated is that the agencies are the creatures of the churches which govern the agencies through representatives. Certain passages from the *Letter* which give a critique of this idea bear repetition even at some length.

> If, as the *Report* says, the "wider bodies are the agents of the churches, then these bodies are governed by 5,600 principals, each of which, admittedly is free to select its own Christian theology, determine its own practices and hold its own views of its relation to the wider bodies. If the *Report* is correct, then to which of these principals is the "wider body" "responsible"? If not all of the 5,600 agree, then which conflicting view should it accept? If *1* or 100 disagree, should the "wider bodies" be "accountable" to those "Principals" or to the 5,599 or 5,500 which approve? Attention is drawn to a special situation. In the case of *Cadman v. Kenyon,* the New York Congregational-Christian Conference sought to file a brief in the Court of Appeals as a friend of the court for the purpose of presenting its views. Eighty-three per cent of its members and 79.93% of the 332 churches in the Conference had voted in favor of the Plan in The Basis of Union. Nevertheless, counsel for the Cadman Church argued that the Conference was a representative body of the churches in New York State, was "supposed to be operated for the benefit of all of them" and since, counsel alleged, five of the "large and prominent churches" in Brooklyn were of a contrary position, the Conference should not be permitted to file the brief. Here was an attempt by an individual church to create enforced "responsibility" to its views to the exclusion of the view of the other churches concerned. (The attempt failed since the Court permitted the filing of the brief.) This of course is but one example of the application of these premises to our denominational life; yet it evidences the confusion and frustration which would prevail in the organs of our fellowship. (p. 8)

Then follows this statement:

> It can therefore be seen that there is no limit to the use which could be made of the premises in this *Report.* The consequences are not confined to denominational unions and the ecumenical movement, but will invade every fact of denominational life. If accepted, the functioning of the Associations, Conferences, the General Council and the Boards would become impossible. (pp. 8 & 9)

The full force of this sentence should be felt. It asserts, as did the *Christian Century* article mentioned earlier, that the doctrine of congregational polity typically held by Congregational-Christians and other congregationalists such as Disciples and probably by Baptists, is such that if it were to be taken seriously, nothing in the nature of an associated life between the congregations could occur. Of course the doctrine is not to be taken seriously because an associated life within these denominations is currently taking place; yet the accepted theory simply does not explicate how that can be. At this point it is obivous that the doctrine does not correspond to practice, but there can be no talk of bringing practice back into line with doctrine because there never could be established a practice to which this doctrine could correspond. The doctrine is patently impracticable. Furthermore, as we shall see, despite the fact that congregationalists suppose that the doctrine truly reflects a past historical condition, even this shall be shown not to have been the case. The doctrine never did, has not now, and it never can correspond to any reality. In these senses the doctrine is impracticable, and the root of the impracticality lies in its incoherence which will now be pointed out.

The Counsel's *Letter* examines several terms which are commonly used in the jargon of congregationalist bodies when they are talking about ecclesiastical structure. These terms, says the *Letter,* are full of ambiguity and have no guiding significance without a new firmness of definition.

The paragraphs in which the Letter examines the word "agency," "representative bodies," "responsible to the churches," by which they were "created," are very important for Disciples of Christ.

With respect to the need for greater definition, "The word 'agency'," says the *Report,* "is an outstanding example." The *Letter* continues:

> It is historically a word of common use within the denomination, having no particular legal significance to it. However, in the argument for the Cadman Church in *Cadman v. Kenyon,* there was an emphatic effort to give it the technical meaning of "agent" in the legal sense of principal and agent. Since the historic meaning

of the word was thus questioned, it becomes important to know in which sense it is used in the *Report*. The word can justify its currency hereafter only if it is recognized by all as being used in its ordinary sense of a "means" or a "channel." An agency in this ordinary sense can be and usually is an independent body established for the purpose of performing certain functions and services and to which people can resort to accomplish certain purposes. The Red Cross, and similar charitable agencies, are familiar examples of bodies which are not "agents" of the public but are agencies through which the public can act. A critical examination of the documents of the denomination indicates that "agency" has always been used in this general sense and should be so read and defined in the *Report*. (p. 9).

The *Letter* next deals with the notion of the "creation" of the wider bodies by the churches.

The Report speaks at several places of the "creation" of wider bodies by the churches. To accomplish this it would have been necessary for the churches to have sent instructed delegates to the meetings at which the wider bodies were formed. Such evidence as we have indicates that they were not formed by any such delegates bearing the authority of the churches, but rather by individuals, seeking to create organizations of which the churches might avail themselves. Many of the Associations, for example, were "voluntary clubs of ministers" to which the churches eventually attached themselves. (p. 9)

When we honestly recall Disciple history, we have to recognize that at the outset many, if indeed not all, of our agencies were even opposed by vigorous and vocal groups—and even by majorities. Fortunately, votes upon the matter were not possible, otherwise majority opinion at the time would have prevented the origination of virtually every one of our present agencies.

Philosophically more fundamental are the paragraphs which deal with the ideas of "representative bodies," and "responsible to the churches."

The Report speaks of the Associations, Conferences and General Council as "representative bodies." The word "representative" has several possible meanings. If it is intended to mean a representative form of membership where the members come under instructions from their churches. it presupposes that the churches have already passed upon the matters to be submitted to the wider body. If it is used in the Report to mean that they are "representative bodies" in the sense that they draw from large areas and from different shades of opinion and thus produce a distillation of a collective wisdom, then the use is factually correct.

The Report speaks to the Associations, Conferences, and General Council as being "responsible" to the churches. The word "responsible" may have been used figuratively to convey the fact that they seek to know the views of the members of the churches and to act in harmony with prevailing opinion. However, if it was used to connote legal responsibility enforceable by law, the Report is in error. (pp. 9 and 10)

These paragraphs are enough to indicate the idea of agencies as representative bodies responsible to the congregations by which they were created is an incoherent notion. The confusion is particularly evident in another sentence or two from the *Letter*. At one point the *Report* asserts that the associations are clearly and directly responsible agents of the congregation. The *Letter* then says

Those who hold this theory that the wider bodies are the agents of the churches fail to recognize that the churches then become responsible and are bound by the action of their agents within the scope of their authority. No individual church has ever taken the position that it is responsible for or bound by the actions of the General Council or other wider bodies. (p. 14)

Certainly Disciple churches have always insisted that the action of the wider bodies are not binding upon the congregations but are only "advisory." They have even vigorously asserted that they are not responsible to the agencies, and therefore they cannot look upon the agencies as their agents.

So much for the fact that the third interpretation of congregational polity is neither coherent nor has correspondence to reality, and so much for the fact that in and of itself it has no relevance for ecumenical activity. In what has already been said the inadequacies with respect to the inner aspects of denominational life have become obvious. Amongst Disciples of Christ this inadequacy is apparent in a present impasse regarding the relative spheres of national and state societies. This problem is mentioned, though not clarified, in those sections from Dr. Harold E. Fey's *Christian Century* report in its issue for September 23, 1959 (p. 1077, Vol. 76, No. 38), of the election of Loren Lair, state secretary of Iowa Disciples, as president of the International Convention of Christian Churches:

> In recent years the power of the denominational boards located in Indianapolis has grown; some wariness has developed in the churches of the collectivity known as "Indianapolis." One group of men who are considered—erroneously in my opinion—to be in a position to challenge "Indianapolis" consists of the secretaries of state societies.

Wariness of "Indianapolis" is nothing new amongst Disciples. That kind of wariness at the national level dates back to 1849 when our first national agency was organized. There is also just as much wariness in any state regarding its state organization—and these are burgeoning—and in the metropolitan regions regarding the associations there. Wherever this wariness has been extreme, it has led to "independency." But the vast majority of Disciples have accepted the need of organization beyond the local congregation and the problem is no longer that of trying to control a single power center, namely "Indianapolis," but of discovering the principles whereby an appropriate distribution of powers and responsibilities between local, regional, state, and national organizations can be recognized and respected. One inadequacy of congregational polity is that it has nothing to say with respect to the distribution of powers and responsibilities between a state and a national organization. Disciples of Christ have reached a situation organizationally in which their traditional polity is no longer relevant. Something else will have to be found.

We shall now turn our attention to the emergence of a fourth interpretation of congregational polity. It has emerged chiefly amongst the Congregational-Christians and is the ideological weapon by which they have rationalized in terms of the third interpretation of congregational polity. It is to be noted that the rationalization has taken place by means of the term "congregational" and in a sense this is most curious. But the nature of human thought and emotions is such that a new procedure may be tolerated if some way can be found to justify calling it by the old name. When that is done, people feel that they can still think about things—whereas if a new name were introduced, or one strange to the group, it would cause intellectual confusion. Actually it is an illusion to believe that in all instances true thinking can continue when the old terms are declared applicable to the new situation, but at least this usage of the older term allows organizational change to take place.

Among congregationalists of all stripes, during the present century, the term "congregational autonomy" has come into use. It has often appeared in a variation: "local autonomy," or "the autonomy of the local church." The provenance of this latter term is obscure. It was certainly not in wide use amongst congregationalists prior to 1910 and it is hardly discoverable prior to 1900. But by 1940 it was everywhere asserted as the key item of congregational polity. Amongst Congregationalists, Baptists, and Disciples alike, around 1940 everything that was done had to make a deep bow in the direction of the term "local autonomy." This is a very different thing from saying that everything had to adjust to the principle of local autonomy. The term was and is a shibboleth. As we enter the '60's it is fair to state that the term "autonomy of the local congregation" does not have the kind of dominance which it enjoyed twenty years ago. But to this term, congregationalist polity had to accommodate itself as the Congregationalist-Christians moved toward merger. This task of accommodation was performed primarily by Dr. Douglas Horton in a book entitled *Congregationalism.*[3] The book would be worth little if it were simply an exercise in semantic gymnastics. It is also an excellent little study in the history of congregational practice regarding supralocal church organizations. What Horton demonstrated is that in the early period of Congregationalism, it was recognized that associations wider in scope than the local congregation had spheres of their own responsibility, autonomy, and power. But Horton could not have carried his point simply by asserting on historical ground the autonomy of councils and associations. The phrase "autonomy of general councils" could find no precedent in congregationalist terminology, despite the fact that it could be found in congregationalist practice. So Douglas Horton went all the way around and propounded an argument to the effect that associations, councils, etc., must really be understood as falling under the category of "congregations." Therefore, the argument runs, "We believe in congregational autonomy. Associations and councils are congregations. Therefore they rightfully have autonomy, and it can be demonstrated that historically they have had it." So much for the circumloculations that have proved necessary in the twentieth century!

The important and kernel matter in Douglas Horton's book is the recognition that in early Congregationalism it was recognized that associations, councils, and other bodies wider in scope than local congregations have their rightful areas of responsibility and power just as congregations have their rightful areas of responsibility and power. It is important to remember that there were at least two stages in the emergence of Congregationalism during the seventeenth century:

A. A claim for the rights of local congregations in the midst of a larger church in which other rights exist at other levels, and in particular a claim that those other levels must not transgress the rights of local congregations.

B. So great a preoccupation with the rights of local congregations that the rights of any other kinds of bodies were either forgotten about or even openly denied—an attitude which indeed led eventually to the denial of the validity of the existence of any other bodies and finally reached the point of absurdity of denying the very existence of any other kinds of bodies.

There is no need to recount the historical circumstances which led to the increasing radicalism of "B" above. It emerged historically somewhat later than "A." In the earlier part of this paper, however, what is "B" above corresponds to what we have called the "first" interpretation of congregationalist polity. To present-day congregationalists—certainly for Disciples, this latter view (i.e., B, "first") usually sounds more simple and therefore seems to have a historical priority. This feeling of its historical priority is heightened for Disciples because it was the dominant view when they emerged around 1820—and it was the view of the church which, by their reading it back into the New Testament, seemed to have also primitive scriptural priority. However, the development from this "first" point of view through what we have earlier called the "second" and "third" points of view to a "fourth" point of view, is in many respects a recapturing in our own day of "A" above which is historically the first stage of emergence of Congregationalism. This does not imply that we are on our way back to that from which Congregationalism emerged. It does mean that in the realm of ecclesiastical polity we are all in need of new understandings. In parlance that is popular in our own day the assertion is often made that we need a theology of the church. This is no doubt true, but that simple statement ought to be expanded to say that we need to understand theologically what denominations are, what councils and federations are, and how ecclesiastical organization and polity are to be understood. Such assertions mean that biblical, historical, and doctrinal concerns will have to be taken into account—and indeed that is exactly what has been going on during a half century of vigorous Faith and Order discussions in the ecumenical movements. However, we seem to be at some kind of impasse so far as the ordinary theological ways of thinking about church organization are concerned. There has not as yet appeared any body of thought or group of ideas which resolves the debates between episcopal, presbyterial, and congregational points of view.

It is the thesis of this paper that the source of the confusion does not lie at the theological level alone but lies in part at a more abstract level involving certain general notions regarding organization, notions which have largely gone unexamined and therefore have tyrannized our thought regarding polity. These presuppositions need to be brought to light in order that their grip upon our minds can be relinquished and that our thoughts may control them rather than be controlled by them. Two such presuppositions in particular to be examined here are: (a) the notion of "fundamental unit," and (b) the notion of a "single locus of power."

Underlying most contemporary congregationalist ideology in the twentieth century is the notion that in Christianity it is the congregation which is the "fundamental unit." This means that from the congregationalist point of view one presupposes that all thinking about religious organizations begins by accepting the local congregation as fundamental. The local congregations are the foundation on which everything else stands, so to speak.

It should be remarked in passing that this kind of emphasis upon the local congregation is a twentieth-century characteristic. In the nineteenth century there would have been much more of a tendency to assert that the Christian individual is the fundamental unit and that the church comes into existence by the gathering together of individual Christians in the name of Christ. From this nineteenth-century point of view the local congregation takes on its Christian character because of the Christian character of those who gather together and the Lord who is in their midst. In the twentieth century even congregationalists assert that a Christian individual is not the fundamental unit because he is not a Christian except in relation to the church (which for congregationalists means a local congregation) and membership in it. From this point of view there cannot be such a thing as an isolated Christian and a church cannot be formed by bringing individual Christians together. Individuals who are part of a congregation have Christian character which they derive from the Church, but the church does not get its character from them. This twentieth-century idea of the local congregation as the "fundamental unit" is a mild form of collectivism in the sense that something collective is considered more fundamental than the individuals in the collective.

The difference between contemporary congregationalist polity and most other polities is no longer with respect to whether the individual or a collective is the fundamental unit. The difference is with respect to which collective is considered the fundamental unit. Congregationalist polity makes the local congregation that unit. The Roman Catholic church, of course, declares that the fundamental unit is the whole totality of the church; local parishes have no churchly quality in and of themselves but only as they derive it through the vicar of Christ. National or established churches tend to declare that the collectivity which is the fundamental unit is to be found at the national level. Disciples of Christ should realize that Thomas Campbell did not look upon the local congregation as the fundamental unit in the way in which most later Disciples of Christ have. For Thomas Campbell it is the whole Church of Christ on earth, comprising all those in every place who do profess Christian faith and obedience, which is essentially and intentionally and constitutionally one. For him this one church necessarily exists in local assemblies, but it is not made up of those local assemblies. It is made up of the whole body of professing Christians.

Closely associated with the notion of fundamental unit is the assumption of a single locus of power. It is simply presupposed that rights, powers, and responsibilities derive from somewhere and that there is a singularity of location with respect to this somewhere. Because of this presupposition, the political debate, and therefore the debate with respect to ecclesiastical polity, has for the greatest part of history been a repetitious and doleful argument regarding whether power and authority originate at the top and proceed down, or whether they originate at the bottom and proceed upward. In episcopacy of all sorts the dominant notion is that powers originate in God, descend to the vicar of Christ or the bishops (episcopacy), then down through priest and deacon to the people who only exercise such powers as have been delegated to them from above. The congregationalist point of view claims to be more democratic. Power and authority originate in God who has delegated them to the "people." The "people" delegate them up through congregations and associations; the ministry at local and general executive levels is thought of as having only such powers as have been granted by the people. Whatever is the fundamental unit tends also to be thought of as the single source from which all powers within the church derive.

There is an alternative to the two erroneous doctrines of "top down and bottom up" and "single locus of power." The alternative lies in the recognition that an act of association, at whatever level, for the purpose of fulfilling a function or functions creates new power and new ability, new responsibility and therefore new authority. This is true whether the association comes from the emergence of a wider body including members of more local bodies or whether it comes about by the emergence within a larger body of a smaller unit. An example of the emergence of a wider body is missionary societies. Examples of the emergence of a smaller unit within a larger body are the Campbell Institute, or the Panel of Scholars or the Commission on Restructure, or for that matter any local congregation.

The emergence of a local congregation as an instance of the emergence of a smaller unit out of a larger one requires some explanation. The statement is valid only if in some sense the whole Church of Christ is prior to any particular congregation. But there is another sense in which we must assert that the Church of Christ which on earth is essentially, intentionally, and constitutionally one does not exist except in local congregations. It might therefore be very easy to say that the local congregations are prior to the whole Church of Christ. It is at this point that the illogicality of the notion of a "fundamental unit" becomes obvious. In the history of the Christian church larger and smaller units emerge, have a life span, change character, and sometimes go out of existence. It is probably incorrect to say that these units emerge within each other or out of each other though in some way they certainly emerge in relation to each other.

I have felt that this little explanatory paragraph above is necessary in order to prevent me from being misunderstood when I say that the emergence of a local congregation is an example of the emergence of a smaller unit within a larger body. This does not mean that the larger body—which I am certainly not identifying as the International Convention, or The Methodist Church in the U.S.A., or the Roman Catholic Church, or any other specific body—has any priority with respect to authority or rights which it may or may not delegate to the new emergent congregation. But while no *specific organization* is prior to the local congregation which emerges, we must assert that what is prior is that very *concrete* entity: *the Church of Christ on earth* which is essentially, intentionally, and constitutionally one and is *composed of all those in every place who do profess their faith in Jesus Christ and obedience to him* in all things according to the scripture and who do manifest the same by their conduct in life. In this sense this same *concrete* entity is prior not only to every specific local congregation, it is prior also to every specific association of persons whereby our agencies have been formed, it is prior to every state convention and to the International Convention. In other words, all of these various units do not derive from each other but only from the Church of Christ in the Campbellite sense though all of these entities are certainly ecclesiastically related to each other. What the specific form of that relationship should be is part of the task to be undertaken by a Commission on Restructure of the Brotherhood. That task has a theoretical portion which we hope this chapter may assist, but certainly the task must be informed also by rich involvements in the specific and practical activities of the brotherhood.

Let us return to some exploration of the idea that it is in the act of association for the fulfillment of a function that new powers, abilities, responsibilities, and authority are created. This is to me a very lively and precious concept.

The precious quality of this understanding lies in what it tells us about creation and creativity. It points to the fact that an act of association or cooperation is actually productive of new power that did not exist prior to the act of cooperation. It points toward the possibility of getting things done that cannot be done apart from cooperation. If one local congregation alone cannot carry on a particular missionary program but can carry on a service of worship, two congregations standing side by side but not in cooperation cannot carry on that missionary program though they will succeed in providing worship for twice as many persons. Three local congregations standing side by side but not in cooperation cannot yet carry on that missionary program but will succeed in providing worship for three times as many persons. The missionary program will be carried on only as an association adequate to it emerges. One might say that grains of sand could be piled upon each other forever without getting to a missionary program though the addition of each grain of sand does multiply the things that belong to single grains of sand. The number of local congregations could be increased *ad infinitum* and in so doing those activities which belong to local congregations would be increased without ever beginning to accomplish those things which any one local congregation by itself cannot acomplish. In other words when association takes place there does occur something that is more than the sum of the parts. New power and new abilities actually come into existence. An analogy is provided in the new cosmological theory that new matter is constantly being created in intergalactic space; there is also some way in which new power and abilities can be created in intercongregational space. The difficulty with the analogy is that it is not obvious that the relationship between the galaxies is what produces the new matter, whereas it is obviously an act of association between persons or groups which does produce new abilities and power.

Our churches have not been bereft of a sense that an act of association creates new power. I do not have the reference immediately at hand but in some history of Disciples in Illinois there is an account of an effort about 1870 to form or to increase state missionary work. The argument against the action was that it would provide power which would be subject to abuse. In what was obviously an impassioned reply, a proponent for the scheme cried out, "Are we always to be so afraid of abuse of power that we fail to lay hold upon it." What we need to understand is that certain levels of association are capable of fulfilling certain functions and those particular associations must in some way be recognized with respect to both responsibility and authority regarding their appropriate abilities and functions. As congregationalists have long since pointed out, an overhead body simply has no ability to conduct those functions which only a local congregation can carry out. Certainly the provision of worship through which to serve God every Lord's day is an ability peculiarly relevant to local congregations, and congregationalist bodies have always insisted upon safeguarding the local congregation from transgression of its ability and rights related to worship. Similarly there are functions that can be carried on by state organizations, and other functions which can be carried on by national organizations, and insofar as the abilities lie with any particular organization it does have something that might be called "autonomy." I do not believe that in order to confirm this fact we ought to say associations wider than local congregations are also to be understood as "congregations" and therefore should exercise "congregational autonomy." What we must recognize is that the term "autonomy" may point to the rightful prerogatives and areas of function of a particular level of organization, but the term autonomy does not give that level of organization control over any other level. And ultimately the term "autonomy" itself is inadequate because it fails to indicate either the fact or character of the rightful associations within the life of the church.

The important insight that the term "autonomy" may protect is that the powers of any particular level of association originate with it and do not derive from elsewhere. In this respect there was in the *Report* (paragraph 51) an assertion that: The General Council possesses all of the powers specifically given to it by the churches." In rejoinder the *Letter* points out: "At no time in its history or in the history of its predecessor (the National Council) have powers been given to it by the churches as such. Its powers originate with it and have been recognized by the churches through their continued support" (p. 14).

In the light of this understanding we must notice the true character of "delegates" or "representatives." Their true character is first that they constitute the body to which they are delegated or on which they serve. They are that body and therefore they carry the primary responsibility for making sure that the proper functions of that particular body are fulfilled. They also bear the responsibility for making sure that the fulfillment of those functions is not wrongfully impeded by actions taken by other bodies.

The delegates or representatives that constitute any particular body may have been placed in office by any one of a number of different procedures. Sometimes persons are appointed from above to a particular position as when a chairman of a committee appoints subcommittee members, or persons may be elected from below. They may hold membership "ex-officio." Or they may be constituent members of an organization by personal choice—as when a church member voluntarily joins a Sunday church school class. In any complicated organization a variety of these processes will be operative. Appointment from above is very frequently used within democratic organizations. It is also often used in very autocratic organizations. It is not the fact that it is an appointment from above which makes it either democratic or autocratic. In the case of a chairman appointing a subcommittee we think that the procedure is democratic. In the case of kings appointing bishops we think that it is autocratic. All of these ideas probably miss the main point. That point is whether or not the person appointed acts as a free and very responsible agent with respect to the appointment and without subservience to the appointer. Inside a supposedly democratic organization, if an appointed person is very subservient and is really only carrying out the hidden agenda of the chairman who appointed him, this is full-fledge autocracy. The most famous instance in history of real responsibility to an appointed position is the instance of Thomas Becket. When King Henry II of England appointed Thomas Becket to be Archbishop of Canterbury, Henry thought that he was putting "the King's man" into the primacy of England. Becket had a different understanding. While he had been an officer of state he had understood himself as the King's man. It was the King who had appointed him Archbishop, but the appointment from Becket's point of view meant that now Becket was the Church's man. He acted upon his belief and lost his life because of it. England, the mother of democracy, rightfully made him her chief saint and martyr. In the history of the control of tyrants and the development of democracy his role is equal to if not more important than that of the barons who wrested the Magna Carta from King John, and England rightfully made Canterbury and not Runnymede the place of pilgrimage.

Whether an association is constituted by election from below or by appointment from above or by delegation from some other kind of bodies, the important point is that those who form the association have their primary responsibility to that association and not to those from whence they have come. As Disciples of Christ move toward delegate conventions, which they seem to be doing, we will find ourselves ultimately in very great difficulty unless we realize that the chief function of a delegate is to carry on the work of the convention and not to "represent the churches." We will be in difficulty unless we recognize the fact that one of the rights of a delegate from a congregation to a convention will be to represent the rights and claims and authority of the convention over the congregation from which that delegate has come. Disciples of Christ should recognize as they move toward a delegate convention—if they really want to move toward a delegate convention—that its significance will lie in the appropriate control of that convention over the congregations. There is hardly any point in moving toward delegate conventions if these are still to be only "advisory to the churches." It is only when we have made some discovery of the rightful kinds of *mutual* relationships and responsibilities that we can truly propose a polity. We must come to recognize that when we vote as a majority, we do not vote in order to decide what the government must do except as we decide also how all of us shall be governed. If I may quote again a relevant sentence from the *Letter:* "No individual church has ever taken the position that it is responsible for or bound by the actions of the general council or other wider bodies." I have yet to step inside a Disciple congregation which has officially taken the position that it is responsible for or bound by the actions of any of our conventions. But it is proper mutual dependencies and obligations that must be explored.

The main points of the fifth conception of congregational polity are now clear. It is similar to the fourth in recognizing that some degree of autonomy pertains to every level of ecclesiastical association. In contrast to the fourth, which says that this autonomy pertains because any level of association is to be understood as a congregation, the fifth conception says that these rights and powers originate with the association and have not derived from some other specific association, either more local or wider, higher or lower. Each level of association is to be understood as the highest authority with respect to those churchly functions which it is peculiarly able to carry out. With respect to churchly functions which it cannot fulfill, it must place itself at the service of those associations which can fulfill those functions, though never at the expense of destroying its ability to fulfill its own appropriate functions. In other words, with respect to the religious life there are areas in which a local congregation is "autonomous," and other areas where it is not. The same thing is, in the formal sense, true of a state convention, or a benevolent association, or any other association established to carry out a function that belongs to the church.

It must be clearly pointed out that the fifth conception does what none of the others do in acknowledging that not only local congregations but other levels of association have a place within the church, or participate in it in some way. In this respect it might be very instructive to reread Thomas Campbell's second proposition and recognize that when he uses the term "societies" there is no reason why we need restrict the meaning of the term to "local congregations." Here is Campbell's second proposition:

> That although the church of Christ upon earth must necessarily exist in particular and distinct societies, locally separate from one another, yet there ought to be no schisms, no uncharitable divisions among them. They ought to receive each other as Christ Jesus hath also received them, to the glory of God. And for this purpose they ought all to walk by the same rule, to mind and speak the same thing; and to be perfectly joined together in the same mind, and in the same judgment.

There is no reason to believe that when Thomas Campbell wrote this proposition, he restricted the meaning of the term "societies" to local congregations. That may have been the interpretation that was later put on the term by Alexander Campbell and perhaps even by Thomas, but it is not an original restriction, and there is no reason why we cannot later understand that the term "societies" in this second proposition means local congregations and everything we call agencies. It is in line with the fifth conception of "congregational" polity that the term "congregational" has to go, not because congregations are now to become subservient to some other specific organization, but because our polity in the long run is just as much "associational" or "conventional" or "connectional" as it is "congregational." A true polity is in part congregational, in part associational, in part conventional—but throughout "functional," that is, the powers and authority of any one level of organization pertain to its ability to fulfill a particular function. And all of these participate in "church."

The "church" in which they participate is the whole Church of Christ on earth. But it is erroneous to say that if we add up all the specific local congregations to all the agencies, we will have the whole Church of Christ. The whole Church of Christ on earth is not to be thus misunderstood as a totality of organizations. The whole Church of Christ is, however, not something invisible. On the contrary, it is concrete. But it is to be seen not in terms of organization but in terms of membership, consisting of all those in every place who profess their faith in Christ and obedience to him in all things according to the scriptures, and who manifest the same by their tempers and conduct, and of none else as none else can be truly and properly called "Christians." It is the will of this Church of Christ that is to be fulfilled in all the particular and distinct societies in which it must necessarily exist. This means, for instance, that it is not the function of The United Christian Missionary Society to discover the will of the totality of congregations regarding missions and to effect it, but its function is to discover the will of the church regarding missions and effect it. There may be times—indeed there have been times—when the opinion of The United Christian Missionary Society regarding the will of the Church and the Church's Lord regarding missions has been other than the majority opinion of the totality of congregations. In such a situation the only *honorable* thing The United Christian Missionary Society could do was to seek to give leadership to the churches to show them that understanding of the Lord's will achieved by the Society.

The distinction we have been making above is recognized by the *Letter* from which we have quoted earlier. Paragraph 24 of the *Report* has stated, "The state conference elects . . . a board of directors (or trustees) which functions as an executive committee to carry out the will of the churches as expressed in the conference meeting." In rejoinder the *Letter* states:

> Legally, the will is that of the majority of the members of the Conference and therefore is the will of the Conference. The delegates do not come instructed by the churches, nor do they return for instructions. Therefore, they do not express the will of the churches. The quotations result from confusing the spirit of fellowship with an expression of legal powers and relationships.

When we recognize that the act of association creates new powers and new abilities, we confront the fact that even in instances where a new association may seem to come into existence by the action of "churches associating together" those who form the association have formed a new center of ability, power, and function which has its own rightful sphere of independence and also claims upon those who brought it into being—just as when two parents beget a child, the claims between child and parents run both ways and both in some way are still independent. Because association creates new social entities, the concept of conscience becomes important in social action just as it does in personal action. In religious work, there are a number of people who in the name of democracy and congregationalism deny an independent conscience in bodies wider than local congregations or to federations and councils constituted by particular denominations.

Modern civilization has taken a stand that when a subordinate compromises conscience in order to carry out a criminal order from above, the subordinate has committed a crime. It is equally criminal or sinful for an association or federation to refuse to do something which in conscience its constituent members see should be done because "orders have not come up from below." And this sinful character remains even if the written constitution of the association openly declares that it may do only what is allowed by some units other than itself. The constitution of an association may rightfully indicate the specific functions for which it is responsible, but any constitution which binds one level of association to decisions made by another level is at the outset an immoral document. Indeed, the very fact that churches come together and formally establish a federation or an association is an acknowledgment on their part of a wider authority than themselves. This does not mean that the new association is that wider authority. It does mean that they recognize themselves as part of a wider authority whose will they can fulfill only in part, and that other parts of the will of that wider body are demanding discovery and fulfillment such as can come only through some association other than themselves. An action of churches creating an association is one way within the whole Church of Christ whereby the will of that Church may become discoverable and fulfilled with respect to some specific function. Most frequently, however, in the whole long history of the Christian church, the procedure has been, not that of churches acting to bring such associations into existence, but of interested persons (usually a minority at the time) coming together to form the association.

Just as the Christian person was of importance in the origins of most of our ecclesiastical structure, so he is of great importance today, and a strong word needs to be said for him in the face of the prevailing collectivist trend of all our thought. It has been pointed out earlier that whenever a person is a member of an association, he is primarily responsible to that association. Let us take the instance of Mr. Jones who has been elected as a delegate from First Christian Church to the State Mission Board. An important issue is up in the State Board; a vote is cast—Mr. Jones voting as best he can in the light of his knowledge of all the factors. It later proves that the majority view of the Board is the minority view of First Christian Church. What is Mr. Jones to do now? Is he to "represent" the Board majority against the church majority or vice versa? Suppose the matter comes up for another vote. Must Mr. Jones vote the way his local church majority believes? The answer can be only, "If he is the one to cast the vote, he must do it in terms of his best personal understanding of the functions and obligations of the State Board." He must be the Board's man and vote conscientiously regardless of what majority opinion in either the Board or the church may be. He must vote what he believes to be the will of the whole Church of Christ. In this way, the Christian person transcends the organizational entrapment, and in his Christian freedom serves to continually refashion ecclesiastical organization into an instrument serving the whole Church of Christ.

There is very much more that must be said in very many areas before a polity can be written. The rethinking of Disciple polity is not the work of a single paper. It will be the protracted work of several years and several committees. This paper may have made its contribution more by removing debris than by shaping new timbers. It probably indicates the character of our freedom rather than the law under which we are free. For our Disciple forefathers that law was the New Testament. With the disappearance of the possibility of a legalistic attitude toward the New Testament, we have not really discovered an adequate legislative structure. If the law under which we are free had been as explicitly promulgated by the King of heaven as Alexander Campbell thought it had been, we would not need to confront the task of devising an adequate ecclesiastical legislature, but that is obviously the task before us. Many of the ideas developed in this paper have come from discussions initiated by the Congregational-Christian churches. There appeared in 1959 from the Princeton University Press a book entitled *Authority and Power in the Free Church Tradition*. This book by Paul M. Harrison is a social case study of the American Baptist Convention. At the risk of oversimplification I will report that Mr. Harrison's thesis asserts the American Baptists have given considerable form to power but have resisted giving any form to authority. . . . They have formalized power but not legitimated authority. There is on Mr. Harrison's part a tendency to presuppose that this situation is generally unsatisfactory—and he certainly marshals considerable evidence that the Baptists have found themselves without any authority within themselves to deal with some of their own internal abuses of power. Whatever the ultimate virtues of Mr. Harrison's book, he brings to the analysis of congregational polity yet another set of significant sociological categories.

It is to be hoped that the work of a deep review of ecclesiology which is now under way amongst Baptists, Disciples and Congregationalists continues. There is reason to believe that if it does, the claim made on the dust jacket of Douglas Horton's little book that "Congregationalism holds the key to the future of the Ecumenical Church" will be proved true. Every level of association within the Christian church which is functionally relevant will be seen to be creative of new power, endowed with authority, and, when it is true to its task, properly responsible to the Church of Christ which on earth is One Church.

NOTES

1. *The Report of a Study by the Committee on Free Church Polity and Unity* (New York: The General Council of the Congregational-Christian Churches, 1954).
2. *A Letter from the Counsel of the General Council Concerning the Report of a Study by the Committee.*
3. Douglas Horton, *Congregationalism* (London: Independent Press, Ltd., 1952).

4

A Theology of Denominations and Principles for Brotherhood Restructure

Ronald E. Osborn

THE characteristic form of the ecclesiastical institution in modern society is the denomination. Parallel denominational structures, their true nature hidden as well as revealed by their designation as *churches,* emerged with the grant of religious toleration in the generous world-view of the Enlightenment. Since then denominationalism has increased and multiplied, not only in the United States, where it is seen in extreme form, but throughout the Christian world wherever freedom prevails. Most Christians have accepted the system, and the status of their own denomination within it, more or less uncritically, and few have attempted to speak of it in theological terms. The extremes of unbridled competition and sectarian bitterness have bred uneasiness concerning it, so that one ecumenical prophet termed it *"The Scandal of Christianity."*

Now the emergence of councils of churches, especially the World Council, at a time of great theological self-consciousness, has precipitated new discussions of the doctrine of the church—to such an extent that a new and more justifiable meaning, etymologically speaking, has been assigned to the heretofore little known term *ecclesiology*. Leaders of the World Council have been pleading with the theologians to speak of the councils ecclesiologically, with very little response to date. The near silence at this point may be due to a preference of today's theologians for abstract or historical, rather than pragmatic issues; doubtless it is also due, in some measure at least, to the embarrassing fact that a council is a loose federation of denominations, and we have never really explored the denomination in ecclesiological terms.

I The Ecclesiological Problem

It has frequently been observed that Disciples of Christ launched a movement to do away with denominationalism and ended up by becoming a denomination themselves. Though the irony has become commonplace, it still makes Disciples wince. When Roland Bainton applied the remark to Alexander Campbell in a lecture at Bethany,[1] respected historian though he was, he set off a minor explosion of protests. At no point besides baptism has every previous generation of Disciples received more persistent indoctrination. The very mention of the word *denomination* immediately brings two propositions to consciousness in the mind of the well-catechized Campbellite: (1) denominationalism is sin; and (2) we are not a denomination. All of us have sensed the ripple of displeasure that passes over one of our conventions when a visiting speaker, uninstructed in our mythology, makes a casual and courteous allusion to "your great denomination," and have seen an audience stiffen into resentment at his continued use of the term while the poor speaker wonders what has gone wrong.

Yet the history of Disciples makes it quite evident that we have become a denomination, or two, or three. Indeed, a major cause of the internal tension which has fractured us has been due to varying responses to and interpretations of those influences which were impelling us to recognize our denominational status. Oliver Read Whitley has studied the process in his Bethany Award-winning book, *Trumpet Call of Reformation,* and my colleague Walter Sikes has traced it even more painstakingly from the sources in a major manuscript now nearly ready for publication.

It may be said that Disciples have for a long time accepted in practice most of the rights and privileges pertaining to denominational status, though the old theory was maintained, and it was until recently a rare soul among us with more than ordinary honesty and courage or foolhardiness who would baldly say "our denomination" among a group of Disciples. Yet the attempt to deny our status has been reduced to a semantic dodge, and the well-loved euphemism, "our brotherhood," is nothing more than a synonym for the forbidden word. I even heard Vernon Newland, the apostle of protest against the Disciple "denomination," use the term "other brotherhoods." One of the most ominous moves in recent months, so far as our internal history is concerned, is the organization of a committee among the so-called independents to gain a separate listing in the *Yearbook of American Churches;* in an effort to bypass the Chaplaincy Endorsement Commission of the International Convention, they are willing to accept designation as a separate denomination.

Certainly cooperative Disciples have accepted denominational status in practice, particularly through ecclesiastical involvement in ecumenical processes. The effort to restructure the brotherhood, already proceeding within the states and now about to be launched on a national scale, is a patent if not always acknowledged attempt to devise a more effective denominational institution. Yet Disciples are moving uncertainly in this process, with little sense of direction and few explicit principles other than trial-and-error simply because our ecclesiology is so weak, at least on the pragmatic side, and because we have no rationale of the denomination. Denominationalism has been thrust upon us despite our intentions; we are ready though not happy to accept it, in the absence of alternative; but we do not know what it is.

If we cannot answer the question, here is one place where we are at one with the church of Christ at large, for the whole of

Christendom has tended to evade it. At this point our founding fathers were more sensitive or more honest that most Christian leaders in the early days of American nationality who accepted denominational status with gratitude for religious liberty and with no particular sense of obligation either to define the denomination in ecclesiological terms or to castigate it as sinful. Often the harsh and undefined reality was veiled by such euphemisms as *communion* or *church,* and the problem receded from consciousness. Only recently has it caused even slight disturbance in ecumenical circles. At Lund, Canon Oliver Tomkins, now the Bishop of Bristol, wryly observed, "The World Council of Churches is in fact a Council of Denominations," and at Evanston, in the Faith and Order section, someone proposed that the member churches drop the word *church* from their official titles and frankly call themselves *denominations.* With consternation he could not disguise, Dr. Geoffrey Francis Fisher, the Archbishop of Canterbury, inquired, "Are we being asked henceforth to speak of the Denomination of Sweden?!" Not just among Disciples but throughout Christendom, the field of ecclesiology is weak and evasive. For example, certain ecumenical leaders are much concerned that we be able to say what the World Council of Churches is ecclesiologically; yet scarcely anyone has observed that the difficulty arises from our inability to say in ecclesiological terms what a denomination is. The authoritative treatments of denominationalism are sociological. Troeltsch's typology of churches and H. Richard Niebuhr's thesis concerning the social sources of denominationalism are familiar, as are the names of Wach and Yinger. Church historians have commented on the denomination as the typical pattern of churchly life which emerged in America under the Constitutional guarantee of religious liberty. J. M. deJong has an important essay on "The Denomination as the American Church Form." And Sidney E. Mead has written some suggestive historical essays on the subject, of which the most important is perhaps his "Denomination: the Shape of Protestantism in America."[2] Using the term "free churches" to designate "those churches under the system of separation of Church and State," Mead gives a definition of denomination in historical terms.

> The denomination is the organizational form which the "free churches" have accepted and assumed. It was evolved in the United States under the complex and peculiar situation that there existed between the Revolution and the Civil War.
>
> The denomination, unlike the traditional forms of the Church, is not primarily confessional, and it is certainly not territorial. Rather it is purposive. And unlike any previous "church" in Christendom, it has no official connection with a civil power whatsoever. A "church" as "church" has no legal existence in the United States, but is represented legally by a civil corporation in whose name the property is held and the necessary business transacted. Neither is the denomination a "sect" in the traditional sense, and certainly not in the most common sense of a dissenting body in relationship to an Established Church. It is, rather, a voluntary association of like-hearted and like-minded individuals, who are united on the basis of common beliefs for the purpose of accomplishing tangible and defined objectives.[3]

Other historians—notably Winthrop S. Hudson *(The Great Tradition of the American Churches)* and W. E. Garrison *(The Quest and Character of a United Church)*—have dealt with the denomination as an inevitable product, and probably necessary guarantor, of religious freedom. So far as I have been able to discover, however, little if any serious theological treatment has been given to the reality of the denomination.[4] In preparation for my Hoover Lecture on "The Church of Christ, the Denomination, and the Council of Churches,"[5] I made an extensive effort to discover what responsible thinkers have said about the denomination in ecclesiological terms and could find nothing. Such a book as F. W. Dillistone's *The Structure of the Divine Society,* e.g., essentially ignores the issue. Indeed, with the exception of Garrison's formula, which hardly received hearty acclaim, most of the discussions of the "coming great church" seem to look forward again to one all-inclusive institution within which denominationalism will be done away. The plans of union such as that in South India, seek again to set up a "church-type church"—even though not in relation to the state—and always view with regret the continuance of denominations or sects outside the union. Such thinking is perhaps implicit in most of the drive toward church merger.

II The Charges Against Denominationalism

If the practitioners and beneficiaries of denominationalism have merely accepted the system without rationalizing it in ecclesiological terms, its opponents have been vocal enough, indicting it with the most withering allegations, both theological and pragmatic. The charges against denominationalism lodge deep within the consciousness of Disciples and have been repeated by many another critic. Those most commonly brought forth may be reduced to six.

(1) Denominationalism is divisive, and division is sin. Disciples know this charge by heart, and many another churchman has repeated it. Generally, however, when the presuppositions of the one bringing this charge are analyzed, he is seen clearly in the role of accuser rather than of penitent. The affirmation that division is sin, along with its corollary that the denomination is evil, is maintained with conviction precisely by those Christian communions which believe—or once believed—that their institution is the one true church of Christ. Only rarely does an established churchman speak as discerningly as did Archbishop William Temple when he said: So long as there is division, we are all in sin. And few have asked as persistently as Dr. Garrison, though he has yet to receive a satisfactory answer, just what we are repenting of when we confess the sin of our divisions. The charge surely carries a measure of truth in that divisiveness or alienation among Christians is sinful, and the separate existence of denominations, not to mention their pretentious

pride, doubtless contributes to the sin. In any event, to the extent that we are involved in sin by our denominationalism, Disciples have not escaped it, either by changing the name of it or by permitting only relatively ineffective denominational forms to develop.

(2) Denominationalism is unscriptural. This is evident. The use of the term *church* in a partial and exclusive sense is unjustified, and the New Testament condemns factionalism, ill will, and alienation among Christians. Yet it is by no means certain that *denomination* need be synonymous with *faction, party,* or *sect*. If the objection to denominationalism is that there is no authorization for separate denominational institutions, the answer is that the New Testament simply does not contain clear prescriptions for any ecclesiastical institution at all, united or divided. Yet the church cannot exist in history without them. To deprive the church of any institution which is not clearly set forth in the New Testament is to deny to the New Testament any relevance for the historic existence of the church.

(3) Denominationalism is tyrannical. Our fathers feared ecclesiastical structure or denominational institution because they saw it as an engine of religious totalitarianism. Both Stone and Thomas Campbell had unfortunate experiences with church courts on confessional and practical grounds, and in 1830 the Campbellites found even the loose associationalism of the Baptists objectionable. Yet by Mead's historical definition, denominationalism is associated with religious liberty and offers greater opportunity for freedom than has yet been demonstrated in any one great church. As to the extreme contention that the denomination should have no institutional structure, the answer is that it is inevitable. Meanwhile, the very refusal to develop effective institutions or to impute to them any status of legitimacy may enhance individual or congregational liberty in some instances but denies

it in others and hampers the freedom of the denomination at large.

(4) Denominationalism is impractical. Such a pragmatic charge, shocking to the sensibilities of all Americans, did not characterize the early witness of Disciples but has been repeated in recent years perhaps more forcefully than those listed above. The idea is that denominationalism wastes the resources of the church in competition, in overlapping effort, in expensive overhead, and in the maintenance of parallel bureaucracies which are presumed to exploit the situation to their own advantage. Yet two issues must be faced here. First of all, is the pragmatic principle really to be accepted, or is it being used for convenience? Suppose it were to be demonstrated that denominationalism makes for more effective church work than does ecclesiastical monopoly? This is to introduce the second issue, which is purely factual. Is the denominational system truly impractical? In given instances, of course, it is. And its complexity is confusing, just as that of the American business community must be to a doctrinaire communist or fascist or advocate of any other monolithic system. I know of no serious historical or sociological inquiry into our question, and it would be most difficult to isolate denominationalism from other factors in the American religious scene. Yet I suspect that a major reason for the institutional vitality of American religion today is the variety, the freedom, perhaps the overlapping, and even the competition involved in our denominational system.

(5) Denominationalism is irrelevant. For generations Disciples have urged that Christians shift their emphasis from the peripheral concerns of differences among the sects to the central emphases of the gospel, though it must be admitted that Disciples' own peculiar emphases surely seem peripheral and inconsequential to most other Christians (as well as to many of us when we are quite honest with ourselves). The irrelevance of many of the distinctions made by our Western

denominations has been evident on the mission field from the start and has been largely repudiated by the emergent leadership of the younger churches. It has become almost as apparent in contemporary America, as any pastor discovers when he tries to explain to a newcomer the difference between our position and that of the church to which he belonged in Maine or Iowa; in most instances the newcomer couldn't care less. Harry Emerson Fosdick's rhetoric used justified hyperbole when he said that not a single issue which caused the denominations to separate at the time of their origin has any practical relevance today. Yet all that is being said here is that the traditional self-image of the denomination as the bearer of a unique witness of transcendent importance is distorted. This distortion may or may not involve conscious hypocrisy, as Charles Clayton Morrison has so witheringly charged in *The Unfinished Reformation.* What seems clear is that the denominations are proving to be purposive rather than confessional, as Mead suggests, and that laymen joining churches or transferring membership as they change communities find the center rather than the periphery after all.[6] All of which is to say that while the original distinctions which produced a given denomination may now be irrelevant, the denomination itself continues to flourish because it functions with real relevance to man's religious needs as a bearer of the gospel.

(6) Denominationalism by its "churchism" derogates from the proper dignity of the church as the whole body of Christ. This is the charge pressed home most scathingly by Charles Clayton Morrison in his long and eloquent bill of particulars against the denominational system.[7] The essence of the charge is that the denomination has arrogated to itself, as its own, certain ecumenical functions which pertain only to the universal church. He mentions baptism, Christian education, and ordination. Yet it may be replied that the universal church is a Platonic ideal; it has no way of doing

these things except as they are done by a congregation which cannot do them adequately—or by a denomination. We may regret the necessity of such partial sponsorship of such important functions. But if a denomination makes them possible in the name of and on behalf of the universal church, it serves ecumenical function.

So much for the charges against denominationalism. They are indeed disconcerting, but not final, and we are still left with the fact of denominations. Though we recognize the insufficiency of the denomination and the tendency to corruption which is innate in any historical system, we cannot escape from it.

III Efforts to Evade the Denominational Dilemma

Seldom, however, do the members of the denominations admit the dilemma so forthrightly. Rather have we sought to avoid the issue and have succeeded so well at it that few have felt it necessary even to ask what a denomination is, in ecclesiological terms. There are three common ways in which religious bodies have managed to avoid admitting their involvement in the sin of division or the ambiguity of denominationalism.

(1) One method of evasion is to regard one's own denomination as the whole church of Christ on earth or as the one true church. The Roman Catholic Church makes this claim for itself; so does the Eastern Orthodox Church; so does the typical sect—all in sweeping universal terms. All others are schismatics, heretics, or unbelievers: there is no other true church. The established churches of the European Reformation maintain, at least implicitly, a similar doctrine within the national boundaries, and from these many of our American denominations are descended. Such a denomination in its traditional doctrine tends to define itself as *the* church, blandly ignoring in theory, though not in practice, the existence of numerous other denominations alongside it. Alexander Campbell permitted himself this type of evasion:

While consenting to a missionary society as a distinct object of contemplation, and as a means of diffusing the gospel, I . . . regard it . . . as the church of any given district, in council assembled by her messengers, to devise ways and means for accomplishing this object with more concentrated power and efficiency.[8]

Beguiled by such evasive thinking, each denomination has, in effect, constituted itself as a little self-contained enclave within the totality of Christendom. In practice, for a long time, it recognized the fact of other denominations only to spur itself on to a more ardent witness to the truth; more recently it has begun to cooperate with them. But its doctrine of the church does not tell it what it is as a denomination or what they are.

(2) A second way of attempting to escape the dilemma is the cavalier pretense of a nonexistent unity and of an ecumenical responsibility which few denominations really acknowledge in theory or practice. This is the specious plea that the denominations are like the divisions of an army, all under one command. The inanity of the argument is obvious, and it has no theological dimension; perhaps, however, the sense of a need to rationalize the denomination, even by so flimsy a defense, is significant.

(3) The third attempt at extrication from the dilemma is not evasion. It is a flat denial of the validity of denominationalism and of the propriety of denominational structure, coupled with a serious effort to abolish ecclesiastical institutions beyond the local congregation. This has been the strategy for unity advocated, with slight variations, by Disciples of Christ and Churches of Christ, by the Church of God, by the Community Church movement, and by others. Yet the history of these movements has negated their ecclesiology. In spite of themselves and their most earnest efforts they have developed ecclesiastical institutions; they have become denominations. It is no longer possible for

Disciples to maintain the fiction that this is not true of our case.

Indeed, it may be argued historically that the denomination is inevitable and necessary. For while it institutionalizes division within the church at large, the denomination paradoxically is at the same time an instrument of unity. In the absence of one common institutional structure to express the oneness of all the people of God, the denomination nevertheless serves as a unifying institution for the congregation related to it. It has been an effective device within American Christianity for rendering to the congregation those services which the congregation itself cannot provide and which must come from the church at large—the founding of new churches, the provision of a ministry, the formulation of confessions of faith, the sustaining of the larger fellowship, the spiritual oversight of the churches, the stimulation of missionary and benevolent endeavor and the furnishing of channels for such work, the establishment of schools and colleges, the publication of religious books and journals, the carrying on of the "general work" of the church in all its aspects. All these are important ecclesiastical functions, related to the mission of the church or to its well-being, and congregations cannot live or flourish without them. In America some of these services are available from other sources, but for the most part it is the denomination which provides them.

Institutionally speaking there is no ecumenical church, no all-embracing universal structure in history which includes all the people of God and performs these ecclesiastical functions for all of them. Denominationalism reduces the institutional structure of worldwide Christendom to units of manageable proportions, though its principle of distinction is not geography alone but a complex of confessional, traditional, sociological, and geographical factors. It offends our sense of propriety (which rejoices in well-articulated organizational charts) and outrages our logic that in a situation of such apparent confusion denominations should flourish both spiritually and materially, prospering in their freedom and accomplishing their task with such great effectiveness. The pragmatic argument is of course slippery. One may deduce from the success of the denominations that God has indeed used and even blessed this peculiar system, or one may conclude that the apparent achievements are a delusion of the devil, fashioned to receive the church into acquiescence in sin. In any case the theologian had better take another look at denominationalism and the historic actualities of the system before dismissing it so airily as most of us have done, simply because it does not comport with our ecclesiological theory. I once heard Bishop Angus Dun remark with gracious whimsy to an interdenominational group of ministers: "I am troubled by your success, by the way in which God obviously uses you. I am not troubled by your failures. According to my theology you ought to fail. But in your successes I see God doing through you what my theology says he cannot do."

IV An Attempt to Speak Ecclesiologically of the Denomination

How then shall we speak of the denomination in ecclesiological terms? Let us attempt a definition.

A denomination is a particular historic expression of the organizational life of the Christian institution. As historic it is partial, transitory, conditioned by the relativities of history; it is in no sense ultimate. Rather the denomination—and this means any earthly ecclesiastical institution—*points* to the ultimate, it *bears witness* to the eternal gospel, it carries the continuing (though partial) tradition of those who reach back to the Christ-event, it provides forms for the effective expression of the fellowship among Christians, it serves the mission of the church. Speaking historically—and in the strictest sense, *i.e.,* with reference only to *past* history—the denomination appears to be both inevitable and necessary in the historic existence of the church. No denomination, no particular institutional structure, is of the essence of the church.

In its essence, its nature, its being, we confess that the church is one and undivided, the perfect work of God who through Christ has reconciled hostile men to himself and to one another and has brought into being the community of the elect who are at one with him and with one another. To speak of the *esse* of the church is to speak of the primary deed of God-in-Christ which constitutes the church as the community of the redeemed, but one cannot rightfully speak of any historic institution as being of the *esse* of the church. The one holy catholic and apostolic church, perfect, undivided, uncorrupted, we confess by faith as created by God, but its fulfillment is eschatological. This church is not invisible if that term is taken to mean that there are no evidences of it or intimations of it in history. But the historic existence of the church has never yet manifested the fullness and perfection of the church in its essence.

Yet the calling of the church is to exist in history, for it is within the relativities of history—the sorry career of Israel and the scandalous events of the Incarnation—that God has revealed himself. Existing in history, the church must accept its calling, which is to bear witness to the transcendent God by pointing to him and not to itself, by making use of the relative institutions of history for the accomplishment of its mission, but refusing to absolutize any of these relatives. It is just here that the denomination stands, a relative historical institution, participating in the life of the church, historically necessary to the life and witness of the church, but not determining the *esse* of the church.

If this is a theological statement, Disciples may make the most of it. To attempt to speak of the denomination in scriptural terms—which is the natural way for Disciples to formulate their doctrines—is utterly frustrating, for the denomination as we have known it had not yet appeared in New Testament times. Yet we must confess that most of the texts which Disciples have quoted against denominationalism we have used with a faulty exegesis.

In interpreting texts on the perfection of the church we have not distinguished between the historical and the eschatological.[9] In quoting apostolic denunciation of parties, factions, rivalries, we have failed to discern that the sin is in the spirit of factionalism, not in the existence of historic institutions which are less than universal, namely denominations. One may discern even in the apostolic age, when the church was a tiny minority, incipient institutions which are less than universal but which are not necessarily factional (e.g., Jewish Christians who kept the Law in the Pauline way, and Gentile Christians who did not; the Judaizers were the factionalists).

Disciples have been blinded to the necessity and legitimacy of relative historic institutions by their restorationist dogma, now happily being abandoned. Alexander Campbell, e.g., was completely frustrated at this point, as Walter W. Sikes shows in a most illuminating paper.[10] He was convinced that the New Testament doctrine of the church demanded some sort of general organic structure; he spoke unhesitatingly of the need for general *church* organization; yet time and again he would work through the New Testament in search of the divine pattern for connectional structure, only to be forced to admit that it was not there. Had he found a clear picture of general ecclesiastical institution in the apostolic age—as Calvin was able to find his system and as some find episcopacy—he would have absolutized it. What Alexander Campbell did not see, and none of the others saw, is that the institutional life of the church belongs to its historic existence and so is relative and changing.

One other comment needs to be made about biblical thinking concerning the church. The New Testament uses a number of powerful images to express the oneness of the church with Christ —the figures of the flock under the one Shepherd, the people of God, Israel, husband and wife, vine and branches, the body, the temple growing, and others. It must be admitted in all honesty that these figures all suggest the dependence of the church on Christ and the interdependence of those within the church. They do not, except by the most strained and forced exegesis, describe the structure of the church or imply that any particular historic institution is essential. The argument from the body, i.e., to the essential nature of the episcopacy, is wholly unwarranted.

A pragmatic observation may also be added. If a true doctrine concerning the historic church is its reformability, the denomination renders a most useful service. It is not wholly impossible to reform a "church-type" church, as the history of the Church of Sweden suggests. But the church which seeks to absolutize itself in history forestalls the possibility of reform. The Roman doctrine of infallibility would appear to make it impossible to reverse a papal decision. The Orthodox insistence that reform can be achieved only through an ecumenical council—which by definition cannot be held now or probably ever again—paralyzes the possibility of constructive action. The denominational system, however, makes reform possible in two ways. First, by definition, the denomination is reformable because it is relative. In practice it often becomes static and resistant to change, but by its very theory a Protestant denomination is not only capable of reformation, it demands perpetual reform; and such change does take place. Second, if an existing ecclesiastical institution absolutely refuses to be reformed, a new denomination may be established to carry out the reform, and the new denomination participates equally with the old institution in the life of the church. These are hard words for a Disciple to utter, but I think we must acknowledge their truth.

Now admittedly I have been speaking of the denomination in ideal terms, seeking to set forth principles which rationalize a historic necessity and on the basis of which the denomination may be conceded legitimate existence. It is a well-known fact, of course, that any denomination is not merely partial as a historic phenomenon; it is also sinful as a human institution. Because of the very complexity of the denominational system, the sins of Christians have wrought grave confusion, and the system has been blamed for the sins. We have sought an easy escape from evil by thinking we could abolish the system, an attempt as illusory as the effort in the economic order to eradicate evil by replacing capitalism with voluntary communism. In the foreseeable future, I see no alternative for the church except the denominational system.

The system must, of course, be qualified by certain safeguards. It must be remembered that every denomination is partial and historic. Hence it is not the whole church and must not pretend to be. It is not an essential pattern for the whole church. It is not ultimate. The denomination needs to remind itself of these things. It exists not for its own sake but for the sake of the whole church. It must seek to manifest in its own life that sense of ecumenical obligation, avoiding unseemly competition, resisting the temptation to speak of itself in unrestrained imperial terms (especially at its world conferences), seeking the good of the whole, eagerly exploring every possibility for more adequate institutional expression of the church's nature (see Section V). This means that the denomination must acknowledge the limitations of the system in carrying through the mission of the church and seeking to exert a Christian influence on the culture and must therefore earnestly search for more effective instruments. Certainly the denomination must abjure the spirit of faction, the tendency to operate as an instrument of schism against other Christian bodies, the inclination to unchurch other denominations.

All this describes a difficult path for any institution which is by nature self-seeking and self-protecting. Yet if it is to exist in history the church must take on institutional forms. The denomination, as a necessary institution, partakes of the nature of the church and may rightly be called church—in the historic, though not in the ultimate sense.

One of my former students, Robert Heckard, used to urge that the denomination is nothing more than a sociological phenomenon, that it is a mistake to try to speak of it ecclesiologically.

My contention is that theology must address itself to the historical reality as well as to the eschatological hope, for only so can we impute meaning to and find guidance for our history.

It would be presumptuous to claim to have set forth here an adequate ecclesiological consideration of the denomination. The problem is one of the most difficult of those confronting the church, and few have addressed themselves to the task. Perhaps this is a useful beginning.

V How, Then, Shall We Conceive of Christian Unity?

Nothing that has been said here should be taken as a counsel of satisfaction in the present divided state of Christendom. A recognition of the inevitability of separate institutional structures within the total household of God does not imply an acceptance of the existing state of affairs as the ultimate in Christian unity. How then shall we conceive the oneness of the people of God? The existing denominations may respond to our Lord's mandate for the unity of Christians in at least four practical ways which can only be suggested here.

(1) Every effort should be put forth to reduce the scandalous number of denominations which are the institutional vestiges or forgotten and now inconsequential differences among our Christian forebears. No denomination should be continued as a separate religious body unless there is genuine contemporary reason for it to maintain its distinct existence. The positive statement of this position is to demand that the institutional life of the church always show integrity, that there be real reason for every particular ecclesiastical structure.

The twentieth-century movement for the merger of denominations has given significant expression to the principle here stated. American Methodists, who divided over slavery, realized in 1939 that the issues which led to the schism were no longer pertinent and that their continued separation from one another was a denial of the reconciling power of the gospel. The bewildering variety of Lutherans in the United States was understandable and thoroughly justified within the context of cultural and linguistic diversity in the great century of immigration, but recent and impending mergers testify that in the present situation the common Lutheran tradition is far more significant than the fact of descent from Swedes or Norwegians or Germans or Danes. In Asian lands where missionaries coming from numerous parts of Europe, America, Australia, and New Zealand and adhering to divergent confessions have brought the gospel of Christ, that gospel itself has been revealed to possess a significance for the unity of all believers in Christ, far transcending the incidental distinctions which were transplanted with it but which never took root in Asian soil; in Japan, the Philippines, South India, and North India thrilling unions have taken place on a scale far broader than is immediately likely, or perhaps realistically desirable, in those nations from which the missionaries came.

Ultimately any proposal for merger within or between confessional families must be weighed in the light of our most sincere and conscientious answer to the question: Can the denominations concerned bear witness to the gospel with greater effectiveness and fuller integrity as two "churches" or as one? The question is not easy to answer, and any response to it must be in part an act of faith, springing from a sincere desire for full obedience to the Lord and Head of the church. There is little question in my own mind that a number of significant mergers can and ought to take place in the decades immediately ahead. Yet we must not assume that a progressive series of mergers, one after another, until all the denominations have coalesced into one massive institution, is the key to the problem of Christian unity. Indeed, we cannot consider without some alarm, the potential size of any denomination resulting from a large-scale merger in Protestantism, the massive administrative structure necessary to maintain it, and the danger of a further depersonalized church in our secular society. However, we may answer the question here suggested, it is a safe assumption that for decades to come there will continue to be—and perhaps ought to be—separate Episcopal, Lutheran, Baptist, and Holiness denominations, to name only a few, though we ought to work as ardently as we can for unions within families and even between them where desirable. Indeed, it is probable that a new dimension of unity is profoundly actualized in the experience of Christians when two denominations of quite separate tradition succeed in merging. They are enabled to realize the degree to which we are united *in Christ* and not merely in our inherited historic traditions.

So far as Disciples of Christ are concerned, I confess myself somewhat at a loss with regard to the prospect and desirability of merger. Increasingly in this century, as we have thrown off the legalism of our middle period, we have conceived of Christian unity as the essence of our plea. As denominations all about us have been merging, we have become increasingly frustrated at our inability "to unite" with anyone. Successive attempts at merger with the American (Northern) Baptists have stalled, and efforts to revive them are not likely to evoke much enthusiasm on either side. A vocal minority among us became quite zealous for the Greenwich Plan of Union, but it has been quietly interred. The prospect of successful negotiations with the United Church is by no means clear, and the Blake-Pike Catholic Reformed scheme presents grave difficulties for many Disciples. My own doctrine of the church is such (as is my own temperament) that I can readily find solutions to the problems likely to confront us in discussions with the United Church of Christ, for example; and as an individual I should strongly prefer our casting our lot with such a denomination above our continued separate existence or even our merger with the Baptists. But "we are a peculiar people," as our fathers loved to declare, and it is open to serious question whether the bulk of Disciples are now ready to merge with a denomination which practices infant baptism, adheres to stated confessions of faith, and operates through a connectional ecclesiastical structure. If not, we should not despair or emotionally threaten to leave the brotherhood. There are, after all, important reasons why we have held to believer's baptism and to our relative freedom with regard to creeds and ecclesiastical authority. If we can find no other denomination sufficiently compatible with our convictions to give promise of a merger, we had better continue our denominational life a while longer, seeking the while to bring our institutions under the renewed judgment of God as we find it in the biblical doctrine of the church.

Denominational merger is not likely, after all, to bring us to the end of the road of Christian unity. We need fewer and better, and hence bigger, denominations; they will be better not because they are bigger, but because they have overcome old traditions of meaningless separation and have restored fuller integrity to the institutional life of the church. Even a big merger produces only a big denomination, not the undivided Church of Christ in any absolute sense. It may be hard on our pride to belong to a small denomination rather than a big one, but it is important to remember that when we have gone as far with merger as we can go, Christian unity is something other and further.

(2) The denominations must ever be ready to confess their own historic lack of ultimacy and to honor the larger unity of the church by giving it appropriate institutional expression. The council of churches has assumed dramatic importance in our century as a type of ecclesiastical institution which bears most effective witness to the ecumenical nature of the church at points where the denomination as such is in-

sufficient. By holding membership in a council, any denomination implicitly affirms that the unity of the people of God is greater than its own membership and demands for its expression institutional forms which the denomination, of itself, lacks. Many of the major churches have accepted conciliarism in principle, but the articulation of their conviction is strongest at national and world levels, weakest in local communities. The denomination has not discharged its full ecumenical responsibility by joining the National Council of Churches or World Council of Churches; it must be sufficiently flexible in its demands on its local congregations that they are able to give practical institutional expression to the oneness of the people of God in their own localities.

(3) Another necessary kind of approach toward unity is the removal of barriers which denominational traditions have erected among Christians. This must be carried out in recognition of Christ's deed in breaking down the wall of partition (Eph. 2:14). Any denomination must accept itself for what it is, a partial institutional expression of the redeemed community; its particular practices should be a witness to the gospel as it understands the gospel, not a barrier to other Christians. Peter Ainslie sought a fuller expression of Christian unity through enlisting brethren of many communions to sign a pact of reconciliation:

> We acknowledge the equality of all Christians before God and propose to follow this principle, as far as possible, in all our spiritual fellowships. We will strive to bring the laws and practices of our several communions into conformity with this principle, so that no Christian shall be denied membership in any of our churches, nor the privilege of participation in the observance of the Lord's supper, and that no Christian minister shall be denied the freedom of our pulpits by reason of differences in forms of ordination.
>
> We pledge, irrespective of denominational barriers, to be brethren to one another in the name of Jesus Christ, our Lord and Savior, whose we are and whom we serve.[11]

Separate denominations do not necessarily deny the gospel. Exclusive fellowships do, whether among the Galatians whom Paul chastised so warmly or among contemporary Christians who disfellowship one another by their diverse requirements. It is not always clear how a church in a particular denominational tradition may at the same time bear witness to its own understanding of a particular practice and to the oneness of all the people of God. The denominations will do well to remember that the most holy rituals of the church are sacred, not in themselves, but as they witness to the gospel. When they are used to erect barriers among Christians, then they do not affirm the gospel, they deny it.

(4) We must constantly affirm the spiritual and eschatological oneness of the church which transcends and redeems the partiality of all our institutions. Our confession of the communion of saints and our entering into a sense of fellowship with all believers, past and present, is a spiritual venture as important as anything we do on the institutional level, in declaring the nature of the church. Certain dramatic experiences of international and interconfessional worship help vivify this in our own thinking. Beyond these, we should constantly interpret the sacramental life of the church in this larger dimension. We do not baptize into a congregation or a denomination but into the body of Christ. We do not commune as pious individuals or as members of our denomination but as believers who gratefully accept in faith the saving deed of Christ and await in hope his ultimate victory in bringing into one heavenly community all whom he has redeemed.

So we labor in our various denominations which are significant not in themselves nor in their traditions but in the gospel to which they witness and in the hope by which their partiality is transformed so that they become indeed channels of the grace of God.

Within the context of thinking here set forth, how then does a denomination properly take shape? What principles should rightly guide a denomination like Disciples of Christ as it faces the necessity of rebuilding its ecclesiastical structure?

VI The Disciples Facing Brotherhood Restructure

The problem is particularly acute because of the present painful situation with respect to Christian authority. Disciples have found it necessary to repudiate their original restorationist dogma at the very time their structure has proved inadequate. Thus they cannot do what comes most naturally—simply ask, "What was done about this in the New Testament church?" Disciples may turn their gaze for a moment on other polities, the presbyterian or the episcopal. These structures still appear amazingly sturdy and they may offer suggestions for our edification. Yet they are in no sense mandatory. The authoritative presuppositions on which they were reared must be abandoned along with our restorationism.

Where, then, shall we turn for guidance? Two axioms are implicit in all that has been said above.

(1) Any ecclesiastical institution must seek to manifest its best understanding of the gospel and of the nature of the church to the fullest extent that this is possible through a historic institution. Thus Disciples must search our minds and hearts, read anew the New Testament, study church history, examine our own tradition, enter into ecumenical discussion to come to as full an understanding as possible concerning the nature of the church. Building a denomination is a confessional as well as an institutional task. If there is one cause for alarm in much of the popular attitude among us toward restructure, it is a tendency to shy away from the theological or confessional question, to assume that an effective denomination need not be concerned with com-

mon belief but only with what we belong to.

(2) If a denomination is a historic institution belonging to the church's historic existence, then it must be built of the stuff of history, taking over principles and procedures from its own historic time. Every religious institution has done this, whether it has recognized it or not. Thus the task before Disciples is not to seek some presumed absolute, some divine pattern, but calmly to consider our need and the institutional materials available in our culture to give expression to the nature of the church, as we understand it. With a humble prayer for the power and even the enlightenment of the Holy Spirit we must address our corporate thought to the task before us.

May I suggest, then, certain principles to be found in our culture which Disciples should take into account?

1. *The Effort to Maintain a Constructive Tension Between Freedom and Responsibility.*

   Responsibility rather than autocracy is the proper antidote to license. We seek to devise a structure providing what we do not now have—a recognized procedure whereby congregations may express their responsibility toward the denomination as a whole, the general agencies may be made responsible bodies, and the conventions themselves may be made responsible rather than *ad hoc* assemblies, all within a framework that respects freedom.

2. *The Constitutional Designation and Limitation of Authority.*

   Disciples have had anarchy rather than freedom because they have refused to settle on any constitutional locus of authority. So individuals, journals, organizations have developed as engines of authority, often with no effective means of restraint. A constitution is as important for the power it reserves as for the power it grants, and for the instruments it provides to check unwarranted usurpation of power.

3. *Recognition of the Integrity of the Christian Individual and of the Individual Christian Conscience.*

Disciples emerged in an era of individualism and have entered an era which places much more emphasis on the community. In seeking to correct the extremes of our fathers, we must seek to avoid the opposite extreme ourselves. There appears to be great value, even necessity, in more responsible institutional structure, perhaps in a common confession. If we are wise, however, we shall strive not to ride roughshod over individual conviction but to discover for the church a form for its common life which leaves every Christian free to hear and to obey the voices of God. Any institutional form which impinges on this right ultimately is found to be in denial of the gospel.

4. *A Recognition of the Rightful Integrity of the Congregation.*

The congregation is a company of Christ's people competent to worship, to observe the ordinances, to approve their own ministry, to make decisions affecting their own inner life, to exercise their responsibility toward the the church at large. But channels must be provided whereby their integrity is set within a visible structure of general responsibility.

5. *The Rightful Concern of the Denomination for the Congregation.*

The rightful concern of the denomination for the congregation and its proper involvement through designated instruments of counsel, approval, and participation in matters of general concern. Ordination, the calling of a minister, the discharge of a minister, the relocation of a local church are not purely internal matters; the denomination and the congregation need procedures of consultation and decision in such areas.

6. *Recognition of the Representative Principle.*

   Recognition of the representative principle as truly democratic within a large social organism. In the days of our origin, localism was considered the guarantor of political democracy and republican or representative government was seen as aristocratic. In the church, too, our fathers strove to keep decisions in local hands. We have learned in government the necessity and validity of representation as a sound democratic principle. Freedom in the church is possible on the same basis.

7. *The Principle of Mutual Accountability or Concurrence With Majority Decision.*

   The representative principle of government is founded on belief in the wisdom of the whole or at least in the conviction that it is better to follow the judgment of the majority until further discussion reverses a decision. Acceptance of a denominational constitution implies assent to majority decisions on such issues as are properly referred to general bodies for discussion and vote.

8. *The Affirmation of a Proper Analogy Between the Organization of the Church and that of the Social Order in which It Exists.*

   The church is ultimately judged by the gospel, but in any particular historic period its institutional life, within the demands of faithfulness to the gospel, must adapt the forms of the particular social order. This is necessary for the church's integrity as an institution in history, for its effectiveness in its own time, for its relevance to the lives of its people. A church historian can readily trace the effect of social organization in any period on the life of the church. In the past the church has largely followed political patterns, and these should not be ignored today; however, an equally important organization in our time is the commercial corporation. From it the church may well learn much for its institutional life.

9. *A Recognition of the Churchly Status of Connectional Structure.*

In practice, Disciples have increasingly imputed ecclesiastical character to their societies and agencies; in theory these arose as essentially secular "societies of individuals," while only the congregations were "churches." It has now become common, and it is right, to affirm the churchly character of our common organization, to think of our general workers as being truly ministers. They should have a ministerial title, not just "state secretary" or "national director."

10. *A Recognition of the Genius of our International Convention of Christian Churches.*

By a painful evolution we have achieved a constitutional body which has its house of delegates (Committee on Recommendations), mass meeting (Assembly), and continuous administration (the board of directors and the executive). While the mass meeting is cumbersome, its very great values for fellowship, inspiration, and involvement of the people in the life of the denomination should be carefully weighed before being too easily dismissed. Perhaps the emphasis on mass participation should be channeled more to the state and district level, though it may be questioned whether the same intensity of color could there be maintained. In any case, care must be taken to preserve the values of the present scheme.

11. *Attention to Implications for Christian Unity.*

It is difficult to know just how earnestly Disciples take their repeated votes in convention to enter into negotiations toward merger with the United Church of Christ. If we are really serious about this intention, we would do well to study carefully the organizational structure of this church and to consider the degree to which our new structure can parallel it in form and nomenclature. If considerable similarity commends itself to our people, we may move forward the cause of union negotiations by several years.

12. *Recognition of the Relative Character of Our Organization.*

    Recognition, when all is done, of the relative character of our organization. If the task of restructure goes forward in any large way, as now seems likely, there will be long and earnest discussion, claims and counterclaims, intense debate, and a major effort required to get the new structure adopted by the churches. We shall be tempted to speak extravagantly about the significance of our organization. But however much wisdom and consecration we put into it, it will still be an earthen vessel. It will not be ultimate. We shall still be under obligation to the church at large. We must still be ready to surrender our new achievement to the welfare of the church as a whole. Though we are finally ready to settle for being a denomination, and to devise as effective a one as possible, we must claim no more for it than we concede to any other. Our ultimate concern must be the entire church of God.

Conclusion

Disciples have passed through several stages in their attitude toward denominationalism:

(1) The effort to abolish denominations and be Christians only;

(2) A willingness to work with Christians of other persuasions as individuals in undenominational organizations;

(3) A troubled but growing willingness to work with other

denominations as such, with implicit acceptance of denominational status for ourselves;

(4) The present effort to develop structure for a responsible denomination;

(5) The possibility beyond that of merger in a denomination more adequate to express the nature of the church.

This represents a strange and devious pilgrimage. Yet perhaps a word in the *Declaration and Address*—for which the exegesis is not clear—has real pertinence to our whole discussion: "Although the church of Christ upon earth must necessarily exist in particular and distinct societies, locally separate from one another; yet there ought to be no schism, no uncharitable divisions among them."[12]

NOTES

1. Roland Bainton, "Alexander Campbell and Church Unity," *in* Perry E. Gresham (ed.), *The Sage of Bethany: a Pioneer in Broadcloth* (St. Louis: The Bethany Press, 1960), p. 81.
2. See also Mead's "From Coercion to Persuasion: Another Look at the Rise of Religious Liberty and the Emergence of Denominationalism," *Church History,* XXV (1956), 317ff.
3. Sidney E. Mead, "Denominationalism: The Shape of Protestantism in America," ibid., XXIII (1954), 291-292.
4. For a notable exception—the work of a church historian—see the discussion of the problem by Philip Schaff, as developed by Mead in "A historian's View of the Church and Theological Education in America," *The Twenty-second Biennial Meeting of the American Association of Theological Schools,* Bulletin 24 (June, 1960), 124-132.
5. *Encounter,* XX (1959), 72ff.
6. See "The Influence of Population Mobility," by Hunter Beckelhymer in *The Revival of Churches,* Vol. I: *The Reformation of Tradition,* Ronald E. Osborn, ed. (St. Louis: Bethany Press, 1963), pp. 291ff.
7. Charles Clayton Morrison, *The Unfinished Reformation* (New York: Harper and Brothers, 1953), pp. 48ff.
8. Alexander Campbell, "Reply to James Inglis," *Millennial Harbinger,* (1850), 208ff.
9. See William Nicholls, "The Ecumenical Movement and the Doctrine of the Church," *Ecumenical Review,* IV (1951), 21-23, for useful suggestions at this point.
10. Walter W. Sikes, "Disciples and Their Search for a Constitution," unpublished paper, May 1, 1959.
11. Peter Ainslie, *The Equality of All Christians Before God* (New York: The Macmillan Company, 1930), p. 12.
12. *Declaration and Address and The Last Will and Testament of the Springfield Presbytery* (Indianapolis: International Convention of Disciples of Christ, 1949), p. 16.

5

Ideas for Brotherhood Restructure

WILLARD M. WICKIZER

IT is probably presumptuous for any individual to speak to such a group as makes up the Council of Agencies on the subject that is mine today. Let it be understood, therefore, that I did not ask for this assignment and that I approach the subject with considerable fear and trepidation. Let it be further understood that I alone am responsible for what I say in this paper, for I have not cleared its contents with any group of individuals or with any agency. And yet I would acknowledge a deep indebtedness to many people with whom I have discussed these matters over many years of time. While this paper represents my best thinking to date on the matter of restructuring the brother-

Editor's note: *I hesitated to include this paper for fear its appearance would lead some folk to say, "Ah-ha, here we have at last the 'official' blueprint for brotherhood restructure." On rereading it I realized that there is no better evidence than this paper that there is no such "official" blueprint. Everything presented here is obviously put forward only for discussion; there is no grand design, but only illuminating propositions regarding possibilities in specific areas. The paper was presented originally, not before the Panel, but before the Biennial Assembly of the Council of Agencies meeting at Culver-Stockton College, Canton, Missouri, July 8-12, 1958. W. M. Wickizer, representing the sponsors of the Panel, was a regular attendant at its meetings. This paper owes much to Panel discussions, and brought insight to Panel members. The paper indicates that the lively interaction between the theoretical and the practical already underway in the Panel itself was finding its way into the discussions of the agencies within two years of the beginning of Panel discussions. This paper has not until now appeared in print, but frequent references to it since its presentation have marked it as a milestone in the establishment within Disciples of Christ of a desire for restructure and among them of a climate in which restructure can take place.* W. B. B.

hood, I do reserve the right to change my mind in the future as we corporately face the issues and problems here raised and discussed.

Historical Perspective

It is not necessary, I am sure, to deal at any great length with the history of how Disciples of Christ have arrived at their present state of organized life. As background we need only to refresh our minds concerning a few major trends.

Our founding fathers were *fiercely* congregational and feared all organization beyond the local church. As organization began to grow among us—as inevitably it had to develop—it came about through individuals who recognized a need to be met and who banded themselves together to meet this need. In every instance organizations were born with the support of the few and the active opposition, or at least the indifference, of the many. Many organizations have died along the way, but many of them have lived, for they have been able to attract to themselves an ever-growing constituency. The principle of voluntaryism has always prevailed among Disciples of Christ as far as its organized life was concerned. No individual or congregation has ever been "read out" of the brotherhood for failure to cooperate with this or that organization; indeed, there was no recognized power that could read anybody out.

As agencies and institutions have grown among us in number, in influence, and in loyal adherents there has developed increasing interagency tension and competition. This has given rise to some restructuring, as witnessed by the organization of The United Christian Missionary Society in 1920; but even more it has produced interagency groups designed to promote understanding and cooperation. A few such groups that we might mention are as follows: the Council of Agencies, Unified Promotion, the Commission on Budgets and Promotional Relationships of the International Convention, the Home and State Missions Planning Council, and the National Church Program

Co-ordinating Council. As a brotherhood we have always found is easier to create new co-ordinating bodies than to actually restructure our organized life and thus eliminate overlapping and competition at its source.

At no time in our history, except in very recent days, has anyone dared to suggest that what Disciples of Christ need to do is to look at total organizational structure and attempt a major restructuring that would result in more effective cooperation. Now it would seem that we have reached a degree of maturity as a religious body when such a restructuring might be faced with some hope of success.

Motivation

Before we approach the problem of restructuring the brotherhood, I think we need to face the question of motivation. Why do we want to restructure the brotherhood? What are the fundamental principles that should underlie such a restructuring? What are the historic tenets of Disciples of Christ, if any, that should be safeguarded and preserved?

In recent years I have heard it said with increasing frequency that Disciples of Christ need to bring more *authority* into their organized life. Thus it has been affirmed that we need a stronger International Convention so that this body can speak with real authority in behalf of the brotherhood. We have also witnessed in recent years state organizations built around delegate conventions and some of these state organizations are now claiming authority as far as the churches of the state in question are concerned, passing regulations governing the congregations on the one hand and saying to outside organizations on the other hand that they cannot approach the churches of the state except through the state organization. Is authority what we are after? Do we want to establish greater control over congregations and individual church members?

Personally, I feel that if any considerable number of Disciples of Christ were to get the idea that anybody was seeking to restructure the brotherhood in order to exercise greater control and to limit the local church, the reaction to any new organizational plan that might be put forth would be violent and very negative. We have been strongly congregational from the very first and I am of the opinion that the vast majority of our people are determined that we shall stay that way.

Our founding fathers thought they found the principle of congregational autonomy in the pattern of the early church. Modern scholarship, however, has shown that all of the present patterns of organizational polity originated very early. Our rather extreme congregationalism probably reflects more the spirit of the frontier on which we were born than it does the teaching of the New Testament. Nevertheless, I believe that there is another principle that is basic in Protestant thinking that supports congregationalism as an organizational polity, and that is the idea of the priesthood of all believers.

Protestantism, and certainly Disciples of Christ, has made much of the fact that we are free men in Christ. Each devout believer has free access to God and does not require the intervention of another individual or of an agency to approach God's throne of grace. The basic unit of fellowship and cooperation of these "free men in Christ" is the local congregation and these "free men" bring to the local congregation a freedom that cannot be abridged. This is a fact which it seems to me we must always take into account when we are thinking of organizational structure for our brotherhood, a fact which we should not try to circumvent or to limit.

However, we Disciples of Christ need to comprehend more than we have in the past that congregational autonomy does not mean anarchy and chaos. We must come to appreciate the fact that freedom carries with it responsibility and that the "free man in Christ" must cooperate effectively with other free men in the accomplishment of those things he cannot do alone or which can better be done in cooperation. What I am attempting to say is that I think in restructuring the brotherhood we must preserve the principle of voluntaryism on the one hand but must magnify the principle of responsibility on the other. That in the past we have had too much of the former and not enough of the latter goes without argument, but we must not be guilty of destroying the one to achieve the other. Responsible discipleship within the framework of freedom, then, should always be our organizational goal.

To some it may seem that this is too weak a basis on which to rest an adequate organizational structure for our brotherhood, that to achieve real responsibility we must be willing to abridge or limit our freedom. However, I would like to point out that some of the most significant advances we have made in the past have been made without the weight of organizational authority back of them.

Less than twenty-five years ago we began to foster the idea of functional organization for the local church. Now, approximately sixty percent of our congregations are functionally organized and probably more than eighty percent of our membership is to be found in churches so organized. No convention, state or national, ever took action "requiring" the churches within its sphere of influence to so organize. The only "authority" that has ever been back of the idea of functional organization for the local church has been the authority inherent in a sound and workable idea. On this basis and this basis alone the functional plan of church organization has spread.

Over the past twenty years one of the most influential organizations among us has been the Home and State Missions Planning Council. No convention ever approved this organization. It is a voluntary association of free agencies. Its program releases have been widely used by our churches and have greatly enriched local church program. But the only "authority" that has ever been back of these program releases has been the authority that was to be found in the value of the program material itself.

In recent years much has been said about the role that the state secretary should play in the field of ministerial placement, and more and more our brotherhood has recognized that he should be the key figure in this area, but in any given instance congregations seeking a minister do not turn to their state secretary for counsel and guidance because they feel that they must, or because the state convention has ordered them to do so. They turn to their state secretary, if they do, because he has demonstrated his ability to counsel wisely in such matters and because they have come to have confidence in him.

Do we need to further illustrate how progress has been made without the weight of organizational authority or compulsion back of it? I think not, for each of you can add many illustrations out of your own experience to the three I have mentioned here.

What Disciples of Christ need is not a more authoritative structure that limits the principles of freedom and voluntaryism, but a greater realization of the responsibility that their freedom lays upon them. Too frequently in the past we have wanted to prove our freedom by refusing to cooperate when all the time we could have proved it just as well and far more constructively by cooperating together for the advancement of God's kingdom. Greater efficiency of organization we need. The elimination of some of the wheels within wheels is a desirable goal. A structure that builds upward and outward from the local church without overlapping and impingement, with clear lines of communication and definite assignment of function along the way, is a worthy and much-needed objective. Such a structure must, however, rest upon a sense of responsibility and must protect, not abridge, freedom.

Restructuring at the State Level

Everyone is well aware that there is considerable restructuring going on at the state level. A number of factors have been at work to produce this organizational change. One of these is the fact that so many of our churches are now organized functionally, and states have discovered that if they are to service such congregations adequately, they too must be functionally organized.

Another factor has been the desire to get away from the organizational fragmentation that has characterized state organization in the past. We have had state missionary societies, state Christian Women's Fellowship boards, state educational commissions, state Christian Men's Fellowship organizations, state commissions on Christian Action and Community Service, et cetera. Now there is a growing desire to unify all of this in one comprehensive state organization.

A third factor that is affecting state reorganization is a growing sense of the church. In the past, Disciples of Christ have had little sense of "the church" beyond the local congregation. Now we are beginning to feel that there is a corporate reality beyond local congregations and that this corporate reality should reflect itself in organization structure. Historically our boards, agencies, societies, and conventions have rooted in individual church members who desired to associate themselves together, but now an increasing number of Disciples are feeling that it is the church itself that should be organized.

There are certain dangers involved in what is happening at the state level, dangers that are not necessarily inherent in the new structure that is emerging but which are, nevertheless, very real. In the first place, there is the danger that these unified state organizations may come to feel that they are the church and that if they have spoken, either through state board action or by convention vote, the last word has been said. This attitude could, of course, if carried to its logical conclusion, result in each state being a separate denomination and our fragmentation, therefore, becoming more real than it has ever been in the past. States can restructure themselves on the theory that they are the church organized for fellowship and action, but they must never get the idea that they are the whole church. The kingdom of God knows no state boundaries and the church is larger and more inclusive than the congregations in any one state.

In the second place, states that unify their structure may get a sense of self-sufficiency. In other words, they may come to feel that there is no need for cooperation beyond their own borders; that they are competent to plan their own program, order their own affairs, and go their own way. This means that unified state structures may become barriers rather than channels. Actually, the state that unifies its structure assumes a tremendous responsibility, the responsibility of cooperating fully and effectively with the whole brotherhood; of becoming the medium whereby total brotherhood thinking and planning and programing may reach the congregations for which any given state organization is responsible; of "playing the game" by the rules established by the larger church, the brotherhood as a whole.

Unification at the state level is a desirable end, for only through such a structure can the functionally organized congregation be adequately served. Increasingly our brotherhood should look to the states for practically all service to the local church. National agencies and national staff should be confined to leadership in overall program planning and implementation and certain specialized services. The only direct services that national agencies should ultimately seek to render are those that can be performed better by the brotherhood as a whole, such as church building loans, pensions for ministers, world mission administration, and similar services.

Let me say one final word concerning state unification. In the past there have existed about as many patterns of organization at the state level as there are states. Some of us have been hoping that in the restructuring that goes on in connection with unification a more or less common pattern of organization for our states might result. Such, however, does not seem to be the case, for each state seems to be going its own way so far as a unified structure is concerned. Is it too much to hope that it is not too late even yet to achieve more uniformity of state organization in connection with the restructuring that unification brings about?

Restructuring at the National Level

Much less thought has been given, to date, to the restructuring of our brotherhood at the national level than has been given at the state level, so when one launches out into this area, he is more or less "sailing uncharted seas." Certainly I do not claim to have all the answers as to how our brotherhood should be reorganized nationally. Within the limits of this paper I can only propose certain broad organizational ideas that I feel are worthy of further exploration and consideration.

1. The International Convention

I believe that any restructuring of our brotherhood nationally should place the International Convention at the heart and that all other organizations should stem from it. I say this because I believe that the International Convention is best able to be the *total church,* as far as our brotherhood is concerned, organized for fellowship and action.

In the past the International Convention has been a mass assembly of individual church members, plus a Committee on Recommendations composed of representatives elected in the various state conventions. The basic power of the convention has rested in the Assembly, but the Committee on Recommendations has played an increasingly significant role. The Assembly itself has agreed that all matters of business shall go first to the Committee on Recommendations for consideration and that the Assembly shall limit itself to voting approval or disapproval of recommendations that the Committee on Recommendations might bring to it, or to refer matters back to the committee for further consideration.

Without being fully conscious of the fact we have in essence created a bicameral convention. It seems to me that we should now openly recognize this fact and should strengthen the bicameral nature of the convention by strengthening and dignifying the Committee on Recommendations. For one thing, the committee should be renamed. Perhaps we might call it the Senate or the House of Representatives. For another thing the committee should be restructured and made up of an equal number of ministers, laymen, and laywomen. State conventions should be encouraged to name their ablest leaders to serve on this body. Its meeting schedule should be expanded. Each morning of the convention simultaneous sessions of the Senate and the Assembly might be held. The Senate would be involved in the consideration of business, while the Assembly would have before it only matters of a general inspirational or educational character. Plenary business sessions could then be held in the afternoons when the Senate and the Assembly would sit together.

As to the Assembly, considerable sentiment has developed in the brotherhood to make this a delegate body, each local church sending up its official representatives. Frankly, I have difficulty in seeing how this could be made operative. If each local church —large and small—was limited to one ministerial and one lay delegate, this would mean an Assembly of more than 16,000 people if all of our congregations availed themselves of the privilege of sending delegates. Perhaps the most that can be achieved in this regard is to require local churches to "certify" their members who want to attend and register. It does not seem to me to be too important that we have a delegate Assembly if the Senate becomes a truly representative body.

2. National Agencies

Currently our national agencies are free corporations. Some of them have their boards elected by the International Convention. Some have their boards nominated or confirmed by the International Convention. Some elect their own boards. The International Convention only requires that an agency present to it an audit of its books and a report of its activities and agrees to receive and consider any recommendations the convention may care to make to it.

I believe that national agencies should actually become "arms of the International Convention" to carry forward the program that the convention desires to have projected. This does not mean that these national agencies would lose their corporate identity but it does mean that the boards of the various agencies would be elected by the International Convention and be subject to the will of that body. This would also mean that some of the agencies now reporting to the International Convention would have to sever their relationship or else be incorporated in other agencies, for the convention would not want to have several "arms" operating in the same field.

It would probably mean the greatest difference for The United Christian Missionary Society, for that agency is now a "society" with its own membership. The United Society would have to change from a "society" and become a "board." It would also probably have to give up its Board of Managers, letting the Senate of the convention perform the basic functions now performed by the Board of Managers.

3. Council of Agencies

The Council of Agencies should be incorporated into the basic structure of the International Convention. Its membership should include not only employed executive staff of the agencies but also nonemployed board chairmen. In addition to the present functions now performed by the Council of Agencies the agencies should be required to clear with the council all reports and recommendations they propose to submit to the International Convention and the council should have the power to attach its own recommendations to such reports and recommendations. The Council of Agencies should not, however, have the right to deny an agency access to the convention as regards any matter. If the Council of Agencies is to perform this expanded function, it would certainly require the full-time services of an administrative secretary.

4. Unified Promotion

Unified Promotion should become the promotional arm of the International Convention, raising the funds necessary to support the total organized life of the brotherhood. In this connection the Commission on Budgets and Promotional Relationships and the Commission on Brotherhood Finance should be merged, a single body performing the functions now performed by the two bodies.

5. Program Planning for the Local Church

Over more than twenty years of time I have probably been closer to program planning for the local church than I have to any other phase of brotherhood life, and yet I admit that I am more at sea as to how this phase should be restructured than I am concerning any other phase of our organized life.

Currently some eight or ten bodies are engaged in planning for the local church, the two largest of these bodies being the Home and State Missions Planning Council and the Curriculum and Program Council. The work of these various planning bodies is co-ordinated through the National Church Program Co-ordinating Council.

Of this I am sure, the work of the various planning bodies should be brought together in one overall structure and the National Church Program Co-ordinating Council eliminated, program co-ordination taking place within the basic planning structure.

A number of problems come to mind at once in connection with a proposal to bring together all present bodies planning for the local church. How can we keep such an overall planning body from becoming unwieldy as to size? How can its financing be kept within the bounds of reason? How can its processes be kept simple and direct and not be permitted to bog down in cumbersome procedures? What would be the relationship of state and national agencies to such a body; in other words, how far would agencies cooperating in such a body be bound by the planning released by this planning agency? What should be the relationship, if any, of such a planning body to the Council of Agencies? Would such a body require the services of a full-time administrative secretary? These and many other questions come to mind as we think of a restructuring of our planning processes to bring all present planning bodies into a single overall agency.

And yet, in spite of the serious problems we recognize, I think that our brotherhood needs to face in the immediate future the issue of bringing together its planning processes for the local church and attempt to structure them in a single agency if for no other reason than that unification at the state level makes this imperative.

Conclusion

This paper probably raises more questions than it settles. However, it would be unreasonable to expect one man to have all of the answers. I have here attempted to deal with brotherhood restructuring only in broad outline, realizing that many very important questions are left without answers.

Of this I am sure, it is high time our brotherhood take a look at its organized life in its totality and restructure it according to a basic plan. For too long we have been willing to add patch on patch, never moving according to a carefully worked out master plan. I believe the mood of our people would support such an undertaking at this time.

PART TWO
MINISTRY AND WORSHIP

6

Types of Religious Leaders and the Church's Ministry

D. Ray Lindley

No more difficult bottleneck exists to the entire union movement among the churches than our conflicting conceptions of the nature of the Christian ministry. In our Faith and Order meetings a remarkable oneness appears to characterize us until we come to this question.

The dissident approaches to the nature of the church's ministry can best be understood when seen against the broad backdrop of the types of religious leaders which have emerged historically, and when approached genetically. No religious leader exists in isolation. Every religious leader has always existed in the context of a religious group which in turn is composed of religious individuals. In other words, to understand the religious leader we need to take cognizance of the religious group and of the types of individuals who make up that group.

I *Types of Religious Leaders*

It would be difficult to find a more helpful classification of levels of religious group action, with their correlate types of religious individuals and religious leaders than that given by Geo. A. Coe.[1] He treats of three broad classifications: The religious crowd, the sacerdotal system, and the deliberative group. While there are exceptions, certain types of religious individuals are found in each of these levels of religious group action, and each level has its characteristic type of religious leader.

The Shamanistic

The religious crowd is the excited, unreflective type. It is found in primitive societies and in certain esoteric and primitive levels of modern society. Suggestion, imitation, and repetition produce the cooperation which is desired in crowd action. Frequently a greater or less degree of both self and mass hypnotism is found. This level of religious group life correlates somewhat with what William McDougall describes sociologically as the simple crowd.[2] Here two seemingly paradoxical movements are found.

One is the intensification of the emotions through the reciprocal action between members of the crowd. The crowd impresses each of its members with a sense of power, of unknown capacities, of mysterious and unlimited possibilities. This is greatly increased if all express the same emotion and speak with one voice. "When an orator makes some proposition which the mass of the crowd applauds but which each more intelligent member would as an individual reject with scorn, it is apt to be uncritically accepted by all alike; because it comes to each not as the proposition of the orator alone, but as a proposition which voices the mind of the crowd."[3] Thus the capacity of crowds to arrive at valid judgments by any process of reasoning is likely to be diminished by the heightening of emotion.

The other movement is just the opposite, and that is that fundamentally the religious crowd is held together not so much by any attitude which the individual members hold toward one another but rather by a common attitude which they all hold toward the religious leader. The religious leader who correlates with the religious crowd is what Coe calls the "shaman," more commonly known as the "medicine man" type of leader. The shaman holds the crowd together and maintains his position of leadership by virtue of one thing: his ability to convince them that he is in *possession of mysterious powers* which are denied ordinary men. He may or may not be gripped by this conviction himself, but the degree of his own conviction may have a great deal to do with his ability to convince others. Bearing on his ability to successfully persuade others will be the degree to which he experiences trance more than his fellows, his success in doing the thing which the people desire, and the wisdom which he gathers in his habitual dealing with the public interests. But the essential characteristic of the structural relationship found here is the fact that the lines of flow are not from one member of the crowd to another member, but rather from each member in the crowd to the religious leader. The crowd is saved from dissolution and anarchy by virtue of the belief of its individual members that the leader is in possession of mysterious powers which are denied ordinary men, that he knows the secret formulae by which he can secure control of the god or gods, and that thus he holds the power of good and evil, of fortune or misfortune, of life and death in his hands. Thus the type of individual who characteristically comprises the religious crowd is the *dependent* individual. He depends on the religious leader to tell him what to do, how to believe, how to act. The religious leader secures the desirable social conduct on the part of the members of the crowd through the development of a set of taboos. Among primitive peoples he guided the development of certain tribal rituals, usually connected with the food supply, and intended to help in securing it; certain ceremonies connected with war; and rites related to birth, adolescent initiation into tribal secrets and customs, and marriage. To all of these the medicine man bore a distinctive relation.

It should be noted that the medicine man fulfilled certain necessary functions. He helped make the food supply more stable and social relations more dependable. At any stage of civilization enterprises which do not require discrimination can be advanced by crowd action. And before we are tempted to look at this type of religious leader judicially rather than genetically, we might do well to observe how much of the "medicine man" principle is still with us. Remembering that the key to the Shaman's leadership is his ability to convince the members of the crowd that *he is in possession of mysterious powers which are denied ordinary men,* we do not need to look far to see the vestiges of this type of religious leadership among us today, and even in our own selves. The writer had an unforgettable experience in the spring of 1943 when he attended a meeting in the Rockland Palace on the banks of the Harlem River. Four thousand followers of Father Divine of both black and white hue were jammed into the building. For more than an hour the techniques of suggestion, imitation, and repetition were skillfully used. Finally there was a dramatic pause after which Father Divine slowly rose to his feet. Bedlam broke loose. A huge white man just back of me began to repeat ecstatically, "I knew he was going to get up, I knew he was going to get up." Of course he was going to get up. The most certain thing that was going to happen there that night was that Father Divine was going to get up to speak. But his followers were convinced that it was only by virtue of some mysterious power that he was able to do so.

But we do not need to go to the Harlem River to find modern examples of shamanistic religious leadership. How many of us have had some anxious mother plead with us "pray for my son, for I know that if *you pray* for him, he will get well." Here is the imputation to a modern pastor of a mysterious power denied ordinary men. Not only that, we do not have to look far to observe subtle techniques by which this attitude has been encouraged. The pious look and the holy tone are two examples which, fortunately, are becoming less common, but which can still be found in abundance. We recall Alexander Campbell's classic satire on the young preachers of his day:

> His former classmates, with whom he was once so jovial retain their former jocularity or sobriety—there is no alteration of their visage. But my young priest gradually assumes a sanctimonious air, a holy gloom overspreads his face, and a pious sedateness reigns

from his eyebrows to his chin. His very tone of voice participates of the deep devotion of his soul. His words flow on with a solemn slowness, and every period ends with a heavenly cadence. There is a kind of angelic demeanor in his gait, and a seraphic sweetness in all his movements. With his sunday coat, on a sabbath morn, he puts on a mantle of deeper sanctity, and imperceptibly learns the three grand tones—the sabbath tone, the pulpit tone, and the praying tone—these are the devout, the more devout, and the most devout.[4]

Wherever on the one hand any device is used to imply that a person is in possession of mysterious powers which are denied ordinary men, or on the other, any attitude is reflected on the part of a follower toward a leader that such powers exist, there is a holdover of the principles of shamanism. In primitive societies the religious leader, the political leader, and the healer frequently were one and the same person. When we view the careers of men like Hitler and Castro, and even when we study the techniques of some members of the healing arts today, we cannot but conclude that politics and medicine are no more free of shamanism than is religion.

THE PRIESTLY

The second level of religious group action is the sacerdotal. The shaman fulfilled his role well in the most simple and the most primitive groups. However, as one tribe had increasing interaction with other tribes, or as natural calamities such as drouths and floods required the members of the tribe to scatter more in quest of food, the time came when the shaman could no longer have close enough contact with all members of the group to maintain control of their conduct. A new phenomenon then arose in religious experience known as the fetish. The fetish was the first rude beginning of the sacerdotal system. The essential ingredient of fetishism was the belief that the mysterious power which hitherto inhered in the religious leader was now imputed to an object. By giving each member of the tribe such an object, and requiring that he keep it on his person, the religious leader was thus able to control the conduct of the members of the group even in his own absence. As fetishism grew, it finally developed into a belief that this divine power, presence, or authority which dwelt first in the religious leader, then in a sacred object, now inhered in an organization or an institution. This institution developed its system of rituals, dogmas, codes of conduct, and its characteristic religious leaders. The type of religious leader who correlates with the sacerdotal system is the *priestly*. The essential characteristic of the priest is that he is a *representative of the system*. In shamanism the mysterious power inheres in the person of the leader. In sacerdotalism the priest, the ceremonies, and the physical accoutrements are the sacramental expressions of the power which inheres in the institution. The unity of the sacerdotal group is brought about not by crowd suggestion but by systematized suggestion through sacrifice and ritual, through a code of commands, through dogma.

> The earliest religious rites were . . . actual participation by [the people] in doing the thing that needed to be done . . . in the later temple sacrifice, the thing comes to be done for them. . . . [Rites] are not used because they promote reflection and deliberate action, but because they bring attention back repeatedly to the same point.[5]

The characteristic religious individual who correlates with the sacerdotal system is the *regulated* individual. He seeks rules of conduct and belief as a corrective or restraint of impulse. He gives himself freely to a cause, but the *cause is chosen* for him. As in the religious crowd, he is told what to do, how to believe, how to act. Subservience is required as in all types of domination. Such domination, in the words of Paul Pigors "implies control by a rigidly centralized authority, a heirarchy of functionaries, and obedience."[6]

The power of the priest consists in conserving by institutional means whatever has been obtained. He trains men to law, and trains them to feel and to act together. He makes an immeasureable contribution to the organization of a firm society. "Not self-abandonment to fresh impulse, not intuitive certainties, but the logic of consistency, with an ever-present assumption of the validity of the past—this is priestliness."[7]

It is quite obvious that the most classic of all sacerdotal systems is the Roman Catholic Church. Yet, before we become too complacent, just as in the case of shamanism, it is impossible to ignore the many vestiges of sacerdotalism which are present even in the most advanced of Protestant churches. We are all familiar with the stories of the boys whose lives were saved in battle by the New Testament carried over their hearts, as if the book itself possessed some kind of mysterious power. A more common example of this is the Bible kept on the mantle, gathering dust and never used, as if it would by its physical presence ward evil from the home. Some attitudes of belief regarding the communion service or the physical act of baptism retain strong elements of sacerdotalism. Some attitudes toward the act of stewardship, the formal act of prayer or other experiences of worship, or even of church membership might bear careful study at this point.

Fundamentally, wherever there is reflected an attitude of belief that some kind of mysterious power inheres in an object there is fetishism. Where such power or authority is believed to inhere in an institution, and where such belief shapes an attitude toward an individual as a representative of that institution, there is sacerdotalism. I will leave it to the theologians to demarcate for us where sacramentalism leaves off and sacerdotalism begins.

The Prophetic

With society's growing concept of values, it was inevitable that the day would come when men no longer would be content to have their values defined for them and given to them, but when, with their innate and insatiable curiosity, they would insist on *evaluating their own values*. When that day came, they were no longer content to be told what to believe, what to do, and how to act. This gave rise to the third level of religious group life as classified by Coe, and that is what he calls the *deliberative group*.

Whereas in the religious crowd and in the sacerdotal system the ends are imposed either by instinct or suggestion, in the deliberative group the membership as a whole freely chooses and defines its own functions. Instead of unity achieved through subjection either to an individual or to a system, the unity of the deliberative group is achieved by the heightening and freeing of personality. Through pauses, incitements to reflection, and the pitting of desires against one another, the individual is stimulated to self-discovery, the discovery of what it is that he really prefers.

> Here is the organization of a self, not suppression or mere manipulation. . . . By the same means the individual is stimulated to use the desires of others as data for determining his own preferences. . . .
>
> The distinctive function of the ethical group is the criticism and reconstruction of society itself through the free acts of its members. . . .
>
> . . . Under sacerdotalism an ideal is a pattern to be copied; the idealizing process consists in making the pattern vivid, and faith is acceptance of the authority that imposes the pattern. In the deliberative group . . . patterns are themselves judged, and there is provision for change that implies . . . creative evolution in the social sphere.[8]

The type of individual who most naturally correlates with the deliberative religious group is the *self-emancipating* individual. He seeks to know and to judge for himself. "Deliberation is the search for adequate ends, so that conduct may be controlled wholly from *within* itself; and 'adequate ends' are those that have social validity."[9] Here is aspiration for an inner life, as contrasted with external rightness of all kinds, whether of ceremonial acts or good works.

The characteristic religious leader of the deliberative group is the *prophetic*. Not "What does the system say?" but "What is the Divine Will?" is his criterion. He goes directly to the sources of religious life, setting himself in contrast with the priest who goes to the system. Thus it is to be noted that both the prophetic and the shamanistic religious leaders seek direct access to the divine, but their motivation is quite different. The shaman goes to the divine source in order *to get control of the divine powers;* the prophet goes to the source to become an instrument of the divine purposes. His leadership, while it is continuous with shamanism, thus transcends it and contrasts with it.

> Here is a transition point in religious leadership, the rise of a fresh conception of the leader's intercourse with the god. Inspiration or divine possession is now evidenced by *ethical fervor.*
>
> . . . Paul actually attains the notion of sitting in ethical judgment upon anything that offers itself as a divine message.[10]

Pure prophets are rare indeed. It is important to be aware of the strains of both shamanism and priestliness which infiltrate the prophetic impulses of most of us. Yet when we consider how most religious bodies today contain a commingling of the dependent, the regulated, and the self-emancipating individuals, we might do well to pause before we discount too much the shamanistic and the priestly roles of the average religious leader.

II The Church's Ministry

In Christendom, with minor variations, the approach to the nature of the church's ministry can be understood against the background of these three major types of religious leaders. While certainly a blending of these elements is to be found more often than not, the important fact is that the dissident groups in the Christian church take their point of departure from one of these three basic presuppositions in their approach to the definition of the church's ministry: (1) that the ministry consists of persons who are set apart by a mysterious divine call which is withheld from other people, with the implication that they thus are in possession of either knowledge or power which is their exclusive possession; (2) that the ministry is created by a sacerdotal system to serve as representative of that system, and whose function is to conserve by institutional means the values of which the institution is the exclusive trustee; (3) that the ministry is functional, emerging in a deliberative group as a result of a sifting process which is guided by the criteria of ability to perform and readiness of dedication. To put it another way, various groups in Christendom would hold that the *call* to the Christian ministry is either (a) by direct, arbitrary intervention of the Holy Spirit, (b) by the ecclesiastical machinery of the church, or (c) by the people.

The Shamanistic Approach to the Christian Ministry

There can be no doubt but that some of the earliest leaders in the Christian church were believed to be in possession of mysterious powers which were denied ordinary men. The apostles are reported to have spoken in "other tongues" on the day of Pentecost;[11] Peter to have healed the lame man at the gate of the temple,[12] to have raised the dead,[13] and by implication to have brought about the death of Ananias and Sapphira;[14] the apostles as a group were believed to possess the power to heal the sick;[15] Stephen to have performed many "signs and wonders";[16] Philip to have performed miracles;[17] and Paul to have possessed such power of healing that his power was imputed to have been transferred to handkerchiefs and other garments which touched his body.[18]

The extent to which the first Christian leaders claimed these powers for themselves or to which the powers were imputed to them by their followers is a question for biblical scholars to decide. But the fact that this faith has been the authority by which later leaders have claimed similar powers is a matter of history. Esoteric groups in our own day have their Aimee Semple McPhersons, their Fathers Devine, and their tent and radio evangelists with healing cloths. These groups possess a kinship with the primitive religious crowd not only in that they believe the leader to be in possession of mysterious powers denied ordinary men, but also in that it is this common way of believing about their leader, rather than any common relationship which they bear toward one another, which holds them together. But they have ignored the profound difference between their leaders and the leaders of the early church, and that is the difference of motivation. The early leaders went directly to the divine source *in order to become instruments of the divine purpose* rather than to get hold of the divine powers for human purposes.

A far more worthy and profound level of the attempt to conceive of the ministry as being in possession of mysterious authority is to be found in the approach made by many Protestant groups, particularly in the more Calvinistic bodies. According to this idea, the call to the ministry is by means of a direct call of God through some kind of miraculous intervention of the Holy Spirit. The one called thereby is in possession of a type of inspiration which is withheld from the ordinary layman. He, therefore, is set apart both by mysterious knowledge and by mysterious power.

Second only to his denunciation of the doctrine of "apostolic succession," Alexander Campbell took sharp issue with this conception of the call to the ministry.[19] It was not the ministers, but this conception of the ministry which he questioned:

> Although I feel myself as able to demonstrate and prove that both the one and the other of these positions is false, as I am to prove that there is a God, the Creator of heaven and earth; yet, I cheerfully admit that there are now, and there were formerly, many good men who have advocated the necessity, and expatiated on the importance, of a special call of the Holy Spirit to the work of teaching the christian religion.[20]

Those who hold to this conception of the ministry without doubt have acted upon the same judgment as that expressed by Bishop Headlam when he said: "The Church always acts through its regular and duly constituted ministers. . . . There never is wanting a regular ministry, and the Church never acts but through them."[21] But having rejected his thesis of a continuity of the ministry, and desperate for an evidence of divine sanction in a sense they have moved backward through history and have adopted something of a shamanistic presupposition in their approach to the church's leadership. While there likely are both adequate scientific and defensible theological grounds on which to question this conception, perhaps the most telling blow is its conflict with the basic Protestant doctrine of the priesthood of all believers. Certainly it is foreign to Luther's thinking:

> . . . according to Luther ordination is simply a rite of the Church by which a minister is installed to discharge a particular office. He receives no indelible character, is not exempt from jurisdiction of the civil courts, and is not empowered by ordination to perform the other sacraments. At this point what the priest does any Christian may do, if commissioned by the congregation, because all Christians are priests.[22]

THE SACERDOTAL APPROACH TO THE CHRISTIAN MINISTRY

The early spread of Christianity was coordinated and spearheaded by what Alexander Campbell called "officers plenipotentiary."[23] Local church officers consisted of "bishops" and "deacons." The former, either because of their direct association with our Lord, or because they enjoyed close fellowship with those who had been his associates, occupied positions of special authority. The work of bishops and deacons was local and largely administrative. The bishops gradually began to assume episcopal roles due to two things. One was the gradual passing off the scene of the apostles, prophets, and teachers who had been close to the primary sources in the historical development of Christianity, and the other was the rising threat of heresy, particularly the Gnostic errors. To erect safeguards against the corruption of the faith, the church began to take on a "catholic" nature. A "rule of faith" was adopted. The New Testament scriptures were canonized. The authority of bishops was increased so that in many quarters they began to be looked upon as successors to the apostles. From the old Jewish economy and from heathen religions the idea of a priesthood was borrowed, and there was the spread of the idea that the ministry were possessed of the attributes of a priesthood. The movement toward sacerdotalism was in full sway.

> . . . This . . . had the effect to exalt the clergy, especially bishops, in the popular estimation, and to separate the ministry, as a high order, from the "laity." Episcopacy at the outset was a *governmental*

arrangement. The sacerdotal theory does not make its appearance prior to the end of the second century.[24]

In the Western church, as early as the middle of the third century the sacerdotal theory had advanced to the point where confirmation had become the exclusive prerogative of the bishop. The evolution of the sacerdotal system is described succinctly by Fisher:

Clement of Rome tells us that the apostles set over the churches presbyters and deacons, and provided that their places should be filled by other worthy men to be appointed by them with the *concurrence of the church.* The design is represented to be to prevent disorder by keeping up an unbroken succession of officers. This idea of succession was familiar in municipal administration and in private corporations. To Irenaeus and Tertullian, the chain of Bishops —link within link—had come to be the guarantee of the transmission of genuine apostolic teaching in the churches. There is even a "gift of truth"—a *charisma*—qualifying them for the service. Earlier, we find in the Epistles of Ignatius that it is not the bishops, but the presbyters, who are the successors of the apostles; and later, in the school of Cyprian, when the sacerdotal idea has taken root, this new element modifies the theory of succession. The privilege of proposing names for election caused the clergy to exercise more and more agency in the choice of their successors, until nothing was left to the people but the expression of approval.[25]

While initially the idea of succession presupposed an authority on the part of the church's ministry which would protect and save the church, in time it came to mean that the ministry owed its authority to the church and that they held their authority by virtue of being representatives of the church. Bishop Headlam quotes and interprets Cyprian at this point:

His writings make it clear that if the Church depends upon the bishop, the bishop himself depends upon the Church. He is their representative, elected by their suffrage. Cornelius had been made Bishop of Rome "according to the judgment of God and His Christ, on the testimony of nearly all the clergy, by the vote of the laity who were present, and with the consent of bishops, men of age and character." What did this mean? The judgment of God was believed to have been shown by the voice of the Church.[26]

The sacerdotal theory had now come full circle. Bishop Headlam, a moderate Anglican seeking common ground with the evangelical Protestant churches in the ecumenical movement, outlines three different interpretations of the doctrine of apostolic succession:

> 1. The Gnostics claimed to teach a more profound Christian doctrine, and asserted that they had received it by a secret tradition from the Apostles. To meet this claim, Iranaeus and other theologians appealed to the open-tradition of the great churches. It was no secret, unknown succession of obscure teachers that had handed on the true Apostolic tradition, but the open succession of well-known bishops. . . . These had handed on the true tradition of Christianity, its Scriptures, its faith, its rules of life, and its Church order. . . . This open tradition was a strong testimony to the *truth of their teaching.*[27]

Bishop Headlam asks what this implies, and in replying, outlines this theory of apostolic succession:

> It implies no more than a succession of rulers, each lawfully appointed to his office, or a succession of teachers in a school. It does not imply any succession by ordination. The bishop was properly ordained, no doubt . . . but there is no idea that the validity of his ordination depended upon this succession, or that the succession depended upon any spiritual gifts received at ordination. If the manner of appointment to office had been without any religious ceremony the succession for this purpose would have been equally valid. *The important point was correct and public appointment to the office.*[28] *(Italics mine)*

(2) At a somewhat later date the bishops began to be spoken of more directly in their personal capacity as the successors of the apostles. This meant that they performed the *functions of the apostles.* This theory is analogous to a succession of kings in which each one fulfills the functions and inherits the privileges of his predecessor, and these can be traced back to some historical founder.

(3) For the third signification of the term "apostolic succession," Bishop Headlam quotes from Bishop Gore:

"It was intended that there should be in each generation an authoritative stewardship of the grace and truth which came by Jesus Christ, and a recognized power to transmit it, derived from above by Apostolic descent."[29]

This succession, says Bishop Headlam, is not merely a succession of office but a succession of ordination. The apostles transferred their spiritual gifts to the first bishops by the laying on of hands, and they in turn on those who came after them, and the coming of the gifts *depend on this fact of transmission.* Thus, this theory holds that for a valid ministry, and the due performance of the sacraments this succession and transmission by ordination is necessary. This essentially is the theory held by Roman Catholics and high church Anglicans.

Of these three conceptions of the doctrine of apostolic succession, Bishop Headlam says:

> From a period shortly after the middle of the second century, and very probably earlier, the idea was prominent in the Christian Church that there had been a regular succession of bishops in the principal sees since the days of their Apostolic founders. This belief was probably well established, and it was held, and, within certain limits, probably rightly held, that it was strong evidence for the claims of the Catholic Church to teach truly the Christian tradition. It was further held . . . that these same bishops might be looked on as the successors of the Apostles in the sense that they performed the same functions that the Apostles had exercised in their own times. Of any idea, on the other hand, that their spiritual gifts depended upon transmission from the Apostles, or that they in ordination transmitted grace to others which had come to them from the Apostles, there is no evidence at all.[30]

In general we might say that the third of these conceptions is held by the Roman Catholic Church, the first two by many Anglicans, the Church of Sweden, and probably most of the Eastern churches. It is doubtful that any evangelical Protestant groups would go any further than the first, i.e., correct and public appointment to office. Of the third conception, Alexander Campbell, in his debate with Bishop Purcell, had this to say:

To adopt the positive and dogmatic style of my learned opponent, may I not say that *I have fully proved*—

1. That the office of pope, or supreme head on earth, has no scripture warrant or authority whatever. Indeed, that the whole *beau ideal* of a church of nations, with a monarchical head . . . is as gratuitous an assumption as ever graced a *romance,* ancient or modern.—

2. That it cannot be ascertained that Peter was ever bishop of Rome nay, it has been shown, that it is wholly contrary to the New Testament history, and incompatible with his office.

3. That Christ gave no law of succession.

4. That if he had, that succession has been destroyed by a long continuance of the greatest monsters of crime that ever lived; and by cabals, intrigues, violence, envy, lust, and schisms, so that no man can believe that one drop of apostolic grace is either in the person or office of Gregory XVI.[31]

Whatever our position theologically with regard to sacerdotalism, as a matter of historical record, it has fulfilled a conserving, regulating, and organizing function on the one hand, and has been a deterrent to freedom, initiative, and creativity on the other.

The Prophetic Approach to the Christian Ministry

The career of Martin Luther initiated a new level of understanding of the nature of the Christian ministry. His doctrine of the priesthood of all believers set the stage for what Coe called the "deliberative group" in religious experience and a milieu favorable to the "prophetic" type of religious leadership.

When Erasmus read Luther's tract on *The Babylonian Captivity,* he ejaculated, "The breach is irreparable." "The reason," says Bainton,

. . . was that the pretensions of the Roman Catholic Church rest so completely upon the sacraments as the exclusive channels of grace and upon the prerogatives of the clergy, by whom the sacraments are exclusively administered. If sacramentalism is undercut, then sacerdotalism is bound to fall.[32]

By excluding confirmation, marriage, ordination, penance, and extreme unction, Luther reduced the number of sacraments to two, leaving only baptism and the Lord's Supper. He based this on the principle that a sacrament must have been directly instituted by Christ, and must be distinctively Christian. The repudiation of ordination as a sacrament demolished the cast system of clericalism, and provided the basis for the doctrine of the priesthood of all believers. Bainton quotes Luther at this point:

> All of us who have been baptized are priests without distinction, but those whom we call priests are ministers, chosen from among us that they should do all things in our name, and their priesthood is nothing but a ministry. The sacrament of ordination, therefore, can be nothing other than a certain rite of choosing a preacher in the Church.[33]

As Protestantism grew, however, its competing sects unconsciously retained many elements of priestliness in their concept of the ministry. The doctrine of the "priesthood of all believers" was rarely grasped in its full implications, and when it was, there was a tendency to abolish the ministry altogether. In his youthful iconoclasm Alexander Campbell yielded to this temptation until he saw the religious atomism and congregational anarchy to which it led.

> . . . While we contend that every citizen has a right to be heard as well as to hear, in the christian community . . . yet we have no idea that every disciple is to become a public preacher, baptizer, teacher; critic, commentator, at his own volition, option, or solicitation, by virtue of his discipleship.[34]

Campbell, thereupon, began a study in depth of the doctrine of the priesthood of all believers, with the result that it is at this point he made one of the finest of all his contributions. He developed Luther's concept of the priesthood of all believers and of the nature of the Christian ministry with their full implications, and in so doing came nearer than any before him to Coe's ideal of the deliberative religious group with its self-emancipating members and its prophetic leaders. His concept of the nature of the religious group rooted itself in his understanding of the nature of man himself:

". . . Man exhibits himself as possessing the right of suffrage anterior to his coming into the social compact. It is not a right derived from or conferred by society, for it is a right which belongs to him as a man. Society may divest him of it, but it cannot confer it. But what is the right? It is that of thinking, willing, and expressing his will. . . . God has given to man the power of thinking, willing and expressing his will, and no man ever did, as a free agent, enter into society without willing it. And, we may add, no man could enter into a social compact without first exercising what we must call the right of suffrage. It is a right *natural* and *underived,* to the exercise of which every man has by nature as good a reason as another."[35]

When individuals so endowed came together in a social body, the inevitable result, according to Campbell, would be a deliberative group:

The spirit and soul of all reformations is free discussion. Every reformation in society has been the offspring of free investigation. . . .

Along with this, and kindred to it, is the doctrine of equal authority in all persons.[36]

In his concept of the church as a deliberative group Campbell excluded no vestige of sacerdotalism from the resulting inquiry:

Neither the evidences of the gospel, nor the solemnities of religion; neither the constitution of the church, nor the rights of its members; neither the divine right of bishops, nor the value of holy orders; neither the spirituality of the soul, nor the materiality of the body, can escape the ordeal of free and full discussion.[37]

It was within this framework that Campbell set the concept of the priesthood of all believers:

Jesus . . . establishes the doctrine of personal liberty, of freedom of choice, and of personal responsibility, by commanding every man to judge, reason, and act for himself. . . .

There are now no more fleshly or family distinctions. There are now no hereditary rights and honours as respects access to the person of the Messiah.[38]

These positions caused some, like Bishop Purcell, to question whether Campbell believed in the setting apart of any man or set of men for priestly functions. While undoubtedly there was an evolution of his thought on the ministry of the church, there was no time in his career that he did not believe in the setting apart of designated leaders for designated functions in the church. While he denied any right of apostolic succession and while he further repudiated any doctrine of a special and miraculous operation of the Holy Spirit in calling men to preach, he was just as definite in opposing the type of "independency" which led some to insist on preaching without the proper credentials:

> It is not . . . of the wisdom which comes from above, nor of even human prudence, to countenance every one who wishes to be heard in the church or in society, or to employ all the members of the community, either at one time or in rotation, to preach, teach, or exhort.[39]

Campbell insisted that all who were to officiate or function in any capacity in the church's ministry do so only when armed with the proper credentials. Only those who were called were to serve. And in what did that call consist? He was clearer and more consistent on no subject than this. THE CALL TO THE MINISTRY CONSISTED NEITHER IN A PERSONAL AMBITION ON THE PART OF THE ONE CALLED, A MANDATE FROM THE HOLY SPIRIT, NOR A TRANSMISSION OF AUTHORITY FROM A SACERDOTAL SYSTEM, BUT IN A SOCIAL COMPACT WITH THE CHURCH. The office of the ministry was in the nature of a social relationship, and call, appointment, and ordination were all integral to a social compact with the church:

> . . . Every thing essential to appointment, call, or ordination was vested in the minds of the brethren. Their desires, however expressed, gave the office to the candidate, however he was announced. . . .

. . . No instance can be found in the inspired writings, where the circumstances are detailed, of the call and appointment of any brother to any office, where the call and appointment is not distinctly represented as the act of the brethren, and in no cases is an ordination or appointment made without them. But their call is what, in all cases, gives the right to officiate.[40]

The call to the ministry as a social compact Campbell held to be functional in nature. It was not the office but the work to be done which was to be considered.

Little men in office are great officers. They have much to say about official duty and official power. Great men in office lay much less stress upon the office than upon the qualifications necessary to the discharge of its duties. They regard the duties above the office, and the office for qualifying them for discharging its duties, rather than as imparting any virtue to their acts.[41]

These functions to be served became, then, the only occasion of the social compact, and apart from such functions, no "call to the ministry" existed:

. . . The only call which any man could urge with either scripture or reason on his side, was his competency to instruct, and the need for it. The same call which the rich man has to relieve the poor when he discovers them, is that which an intelligent christian has to instruct those ignorant of God.[42]

On the part of the church, the selection of those who were to be "called" was to be guided by (1) the nature of the functions to be performed, and (2) the qualifications of those called to perform them:

. . . The qualifications for any office are always found in the nature of the office. They are generally detailed, but not always, because the *work to be done* is the best guide in ascertaining the qualifications of the doer of it.[43]

Ordination, then, was not to be confused with the call to the ministry. Ordination was the formal and public act of the church which signified that he had already been called. It actually was more of an inauguration. This idea fits in very well with the current practice of an "installation" service of the ordained minister in each new congregation to which he is called.

When confronted with the charge that this conception made the call to the ministry a purely human thing, and left God out, Campbell's reply was "vox populi, vox dei," that the grace of God attached to the service in that God had granted to the church the right to "call" its ministry.

In the last quarter of a century Disciples of Christ have been moving away from the local congregational toward some type of consociational method of ordaining men to the ministry, but there has been no essential change in our basic conception of the nature of the Christian ministry. Further, perhaps it is not being too brash to say that Protestantism generally, including even those who hold to the doctrine of apostolic succession, have moved in the direction of a functional approach to the ministry. These are times when one is inclined to believe that some of these groups, while clinging to their historical forms and tenets, are more considerate of the functional requirements of the ministry in their selections than are we.

Conclusion

When we consider the history of religious experience and the levels of religious development, as well as the individual psychology and types of individuals who are identified with our religious groups, we cannot but be a little less arrogant in our own religious assumptions, and more tolerant of those who differ with us. While their contributions have been and must always be limited, the shaman and the priest have and are filling important roles in human history and religious development. So long as there are the "dependent" and the "regulated" types of individuals who need religious leadership, there will be a place for a certain measure of shamanistic and priestly religious leadership. Possibly it is at this point that the one who would be a "prophetic" type of religious leader might do well even to heed the words of Apostle Paul when he said, "I am become all things to all men." This does not imply any insincerity or compromise with the status quo. But who among us, when approached by a distraught mother with the request "Pray for my son, for I know that if you pray for him, your prayers will be heard" would take it as an occasion to lecture her on the nature of the Christian ministry? Quite likely there will always be those to whom the prayers of the minister will bring a comfort which no others could bring.

On the other hand, men like Luther, Campbell, and Coe have helped create for us an *image* of the ideal level of religious development toward which we all must move. The pivotal factor must be that while we take each individual at the point of his own religious needs, and each religious group at the level of its own development, in every instance our guiding principle is the prophetic one which asks the question, "What is God's will for me here and now in this situation as a minister of this individual or to this group." It will be to spurn the temptation to exploit the faith of any with shamanistic or priestly practices. It will ever be to be guided by the desire to lead this individual from dependence on the religious leader to dependence on God, this other individual from being a "regulated" person, relying on a system to tell him what to do, how to believe, and how to act, to an emancipated, creative, and free Christian.

NOTES

1. Coe, George Albert, *The Psychology of Religion* (Chicago: University of Chicago Press, 1916), Ch. 8-11.
2. McDougall, William, *The Group Mind,* Ch. 2 (New York: G. P. Putnam's Sons, 1920).
3. *Ibid.,* p. 59.
4. *The Christian Baptist,* Vol. 1, p. 35.
5. Coe, *op. cit.,* p. 127.
6. Pigors, Paul, *Leadership or Domination* (New York: Houghton Mifflin Co., 1936), p. 69.
7. Coe, *op. cit.,* p. 181.
8. *Ibid.,* p. 133.
9. *Ibid.,* p. 136.
10. *Ibid.,* p. 184.
11. Acts 2:4-8.
12. Acts 3:1-10.

13. Acts 9:36-43.
14. Acts 5:1-11.
15. Acts 5:12-16.
16. Acts 6:8.
17. Acts 8:4-13.
18. Acts 19:11-12.
19. Lindley, D. Ray, *Apostle of Freedom,* pp. 51ff.
20. *The Christian Baptist,* Vol. 1, p. 19.
21. Headlam, Arthur, *The Doctrine of the Church and Reunion* (London: John Murray, Albemarle St. W, 1920), p. 87.
22. Bainton, Roland, *Here I Stand—a Life of Martin Luther* (Nashville: Abingdon Press, 1950), p. 137.
23. Campbell-Purcell Debate, p. 51.
24. Fisher, George, *History of the Christian Church,* p. 54.
25. *Ibid.,* pp. 54-55.
26. Headlam, *The Doctrine of the Church and Reunion,* p. 118.
27. *Ibid.,* pp. 124-133.
28. *Ibid.,* p. 126.
29. *Ibid.,* p. 127.
30. *Ibid.,* pp. 128-129.
31. Campbell-Purcell Debate, pp. 139-140.
32. Bainton, *Here I Stand,* p. 137.
33. *Ibid.,* p. 138.
34. *Millennial Harbinger,* 1832, p. 501.
35. Richardson, Robert, *Memoirs of Alexander Campbell,* Vol. 2, p. 311.
36. *Millennial Harbinger-Extra,* 1837, p. 577.
37. *Ibid.,* 1845, Vol. 16, p. 50.
38. *Christian Baptism,* p. 109.
39. *Millennial Harbinger,* 1832, p. 501.
40. *Christian Baptist,* Vol. 1, pp. 260-261.
41. *Millennial Harbinger,* 1840, p. 507.
42. *Ibid.,* 1831, p. 114.
43. *Christian System,* p. 82.

7

The Christian Task and the Church's Ministry

W. B. Blakemore

THE aim of this chapter is to provide a renewed understanding of the relationships which appropriately pertain between the Christian churches and their ministers. At the outset there will be a brief section presenting in the most general terms the criteria by which a Christian church should judge whether or not it is really doing "the Lord's work." But general terms must always be interpreted into practical terms, and the second and much longer portion of the chapter will discuss how the Christian churches have arrived at their present understanding of ministries, and in what way these ministries may be renewed in their Christian character.

A Brief Dialectical Introduction: Theological and Practical

A. The Theological Voice in the Dialogue

When, amongst men, there is a common loyalty which transcends their potential for divisiveness, they become a community.

A religious association is any group within a community seeking to give expression by confession, ritual, and ethical teaching to their understanding of the character of that transcendant loyalty.

A Christian church is distinctively a religious association in which men specifically proclaim the Lord Jesus Christ as the foundation of their community. Within the church the relation of Jesus Christ to the church is recognized as Lordship. He is the ground of faith whom we worship and whose ethical guidance we trust; we adore him and we follow him. In and by him we know God and in his cross we know the measure of God's costly love to all mankind. We know whom we have believed, and we seek his will for our lives as men and nations—and as a church.

We are still speaking in very general terms when we say that Jesus Christ lays upon his followers a ministerial charge. The Apostle Paul characterized this charge as a ministry of reconciliation. Matthew 28: 19 and 20 summarizes the ministry in terms of making disciples of all nations, indicating in whose name they shall be admitted to the Christian community and whose teachings they shall receive. At many another New Testament point there is a general indication that the church has a work to do. It must therefore constantly ask itself, "How adequately is this charge being fulfilled now; with what words and worship can the church express its faith and accomplish its work today; in what organized form and with what personnel can the Christian ministry be carried out; how can it be translated into action?"

B. THE PRACTICAL VOICE IN THE DIALOGUE

The actions of any American Christian congregation and its employed personnel are amazingly varied. The possibilities of their degeneration into "busy-work" is frightening, yet their potential for accomplishing Christian ministry is enormous provided the tasks are never done out of routine habit but are constantly judged for their Christian efficacy. These numberless activities include: baptisms, prayers, visiting the sick, building churches, preaching, organizing women's societies, conducting Sunday church school classes, constructing worship centers, conducting summer camps and daily vacation Bible schools, consoling the bereaved, electing officers, attending conference or synod or convention, calling committee meetings, installing officers and ordaining clergy, hymn singing and choirs, scripture reading, getting guests to sign the register in the foyer, passing collection plates, making a budget, burying the dead, reporting to state secretaries or bishops, teaching confirmation classes, counseling parishioners, publishing a congregational paper and worship bulletins, consulting comity commissions, addressing Kiwanis, celebrating anniversaries, issuing letters of transfer, receiving new members, and a thousand and one other details which, taken in their totality, constitute the actions of the church. But the question is whether these actions are a translation into action of the ministry with which Christ charges his church. As a matter of fact, in any particular congregation do these activities all contribute to one objective, or would careful examination disclose diverse if not even contradictory aims? If they do fulfil a single aim, is it commensurate with the great commission received by the disciples? Does it constitute what Paul called a ministry of reconciliation? If it does not, what changes need to be made?

A plus B. The Theological-Practical Consensus

Church may be defined as a religious association which succeeds in translating our Lord's ministerial charge into effective practices. Any particular religious association deserves to be called a church only when its practices have integrity with Christ's ministerial charge.

Approaching from the direction of our Lord's charge we ask, "By what activities can we carry out the commission?" Approaching from the direction of existing activities we ask, "What integrity, what general character do our activities display?" But it is only at the junction point of these two approaches that there is enlightenment. Apart from its embodiment in practices, the various ways of stating the charge remain formal and general theological statements whose meaning is not yet apparent. Apart from discipline in terms of appropriate aim, the practices of the church degenerate into meaningless busywork.

Christian Ministries Among the Christian Churches

When the Christian Churches (Disciples of Christ) emerged into history following the unification of the "Campbellites" and the "Stoneites" in 1832, they had already a tradition regarding the ministry in relation to the churches. Both tributaries to the new unity believed that it is to the church as a whole, and not to its "clergy," that the charge of ministry is given. It is both a gift from Christ to his church and a command defining the task of the church. Whatever "ministry" may be performed by individuals is derivative from the ministry Christ has given his church to perform. The Christian Churches (Disciples of Christ) continue in this doctrine, affirming as did their founding fathers the priesthood of all believers.

Both "Stoneites" and "Campbellites" believed that from the pages of the New Testament they could derive a precise scheme for the offices of congregations. Their descendants by no means continue unanimous in this doctrine. As a matter of fact, while the founding fathers may have agreed unanimously on this general doctrine, they never reached unanimity regarding the several different schemes which they severally read off the New Testament pages.

In 1832 the two streams brought together somewhat different heritages regarding a "paid ministry." In earlier years Alexander Campbell had preached against a "hireling priesthood" who had established a "kingdom of the clergy" by appropriating as their possession powerful ecclesiastical organizations interlocked with the state. Mr. Campbell certainly did not deny that a man might be called to preach and evangelize, but Mr. Campbell in his earlier years believed such a man ought not be paid for such ministry. By 1832 he had modified his position enough to admit that "evangelists" who itinerated among the churches should be paid, and by 1832 he was about ready to recognize the significance of a "settled" (and paid) ministry. At the time of the union of 1832, the Stoneites had always had the tradition of a settled ministry, but they were already stating that there was no sacramental distinction between "clergy and laity." The descendants of Campbell and Stone in the Christian Churches (Disciples of Christ) agree that a Christian congregation needs a "settled pastorate."[1]

Both the Stoneites and the Campbellites agreed originally that the only manifestation on earth of the Church of Christ was local congregations. Admitting that a charge to minister may, in one respect, come directly from God to the individual, they agreed in theory that in so far as the church received a ministerial charge from her Lord, it is laid only upon congregations. Their polity was strictly congregationalist. On this point, their descendants have many questions.

We come now to a point on which the vast majority of their descendants do not even understand what their forefathers' doctrine was or what it meant. Both the Stoneites and the Campbellites, within their congregationalist polity, had a tradition of a threefold order of the ministry. The orders comprised deacons, elders, and evangelists or pastors. Originally these were understood as the three *ministerial* offices of the local congregation. Later generations have fallen away from this understanding, and now, despite their insistence in the priesthood of all believers which should disallow any distinction between "clergy and laity" they think of their deacons and elders as "lay" officers, and only the pastorate is thought of as a "ministerial" office. To all intents and purposes, the Christian Churches (Disciples of Christ) today stand for a single *order* of the ministry though, as we shall see, they think of varieties of ministerial specializations.

Through the early stages of their history, the Christian churches looked upon deacons and elders as indispensable officials in the structure of the congregation. Originally, and for some time thereafter, they did not consider the pastorate a necessity. (In other words, deacons and elders were indispensable because weekly communion was essential to the existence of a Christian congregation; since preaching was not essential, the pastor was not indispensable.) Today the situation is reversed. Some churches no longer have deacons and elders at all. In the majority of congregations the concepts of deacon and elder have relevance only to waiting upon the table of the Lord's Supper. In some congregations in which the elders had already been stripped of all functions except that of prayer at the Lord's table, when the manner and content of their prayers fell below the qualitative desires of the congregation, this last function, too, has fallen to the pastor except as the elders may still be used to lift the patens and cups from the table and place them securely in the hands of the deacons.

To a great extent the lowering of the esteem accorded the elders may be due to the way in which a former generation of elders with dogmatic ways and dictatorial manners became "ruling elders." The "anti-elder" attitude of the twentieth century has many resemblances to the nineteenth-century "anticlericalism" which was a reaction against earlier abuses of clerical power.

What has happened is that functions formerly belonging to the elders and deacons have been redistributed amongst a new and rapidly multiplying group of offices known as "functional offices." Certainly deacons and elders used to perform the duties now fulfilled by these functional offices. What has happened is that a former ministerial work of the eldership has been virtually lost to memory. This ministerial work of the eldership was originally a responsible participation in a spiritual concern for the spiritual welfare of the congregation. All of this concern has now devolved onto "the minister," and it is the rare elder who understands himself as sharing a general ministry of spiritual oversight. In too many churches the question has become, "Now that we have functional officers, what are the elders supposed to do?"

The continuing tendency has been to focus the expectation and responsibilty for "ministry" upon the one office still popularly recognized as a ministerial office, namely the pastorate. This movement from a three-order ministry to a single-order ministry is fundamentally a "devolution" and not an "evolution" for at heart it has been a misunderstanding of the nature of the eldership, and part of the renewal of church must be a re-establishment in congregations of all the functions formerly appropriate to elders even if the eldership itself is not restored. These matters will be dealt with later in this chapter.

Originally the program of activities of the churches was quite simple. In 1832 there was no instrumental music in worship, and therefore no paid musicians. The Sunday school movement was barely begun. There were no state societies, much less "foreign" societies, and therefore no women's fellowships nor men's fellowships as such. There were no benevolence agencies nor church colleges, and no "special days" except those of a puritanically modest Christian year which included Christmas but not Advent or Epiphany, Easter and Good Friday but no Lent, and, occasionally, Pentecost. Often there was no settled pastor or other paid workers and therefore no budget and no financial officers. Deacons and elders comprised the "board" of the congregation, and one of the elders probably served both as chairman of the board and as president of the congregation when gathered for purposes of ritual (i.e on Sunday mornings). In the early days the church board served as the legislative and the executive branch of the church and even as a board of discipline (a function now lost even to the congregation). Whatever powers it exercised, such a church board often went directly to the congregation with specific items as well as for election of its members. Organization could hardly have been more simple nor democracy more direct, but program was simple.

By midcentury the programs of local congregations began to proliferate rapidly. Individuals began to cooperate through agencies established to carry out good works. Officers in local congregations began to multiply, and such officers as Sunday school superintendents and Christian Endeavor leaders were added to the elders and deacons to comprise an "official board." Sometimes these became "general boards" including not only those elected to some specific office but also members at large who provided a sort of general representation of the congregation. Activities have proliferated to the astounding extent indicated in the introductory section of this chapter. Many congregations have taken the steps which give their boards a "functional" character. The emergence of the concept of "function" as an attempt to deal with the proliferation of church activities will be analyzed later in this chapter. As congregational activities have expanded, the ministerial responsibilities of the pastor have been magnified until he has emerged, as Richard Niebuhr indicates in *The Nature and Purpose of the Ministry,* not primarily as a preacher or pastor in the classical senses of these terms, but primarily as the director of a congregational or parish program—as an impressario rather than soloist or conductor to use operatic terms, as production manager rather than company president or director to use industrial terms.

What are some of the factors that have accompanied the historic development of church activities during the past century?

The proliferation of activities resulted in a division of labor. Early instances of program expansion were instrumental music and choirs, and Sunday schools. The church organist or choir director appears in Christian Churches (Disciples of Christ) history about the same time as the Sunday school superintendent. Originally these were "volunteer" workers available because of their great personal interest in these areas. But this volunteer assistance was all too often bought by a congregation at a high though hidden price. The choir became primarily a means of personal expression for the organist or director, or a means of expression of the musical tastes of the choir. In either instance the choir might no longer express the religious concerns of the congregation, but being "volunteer" it defied being "fired." This self-expressive choir learned how to defend its niche with arguments about the Christian superiority of the volunteer spirit to the spirit of "paid professionalism." A similar circumstance often characterized the Sunday school which became the preserve of a superintendent and his teaching corps. These volunteers often learned the arguments that defended their vested interests and distracted the congregation from the fact that in return for volunteer work it often paid the price of allowing these "volunteers" to do what they wanted irrespective of the general aims appropriate to a Christian congregation. Many a time there developed the circumstance in which the Sunday morning worship, Sunday church school, Boy Scouts, and women's society no longer were a single religious association or church, but four distinct associations sharing only a roof in common.

One answer to such a situation has been to pull leadership back into a single focus by reducing the scope of volunteer activity in favor of professional guidance.

Another factor which tends to place guidance in the hands of the professional ministry is the sheer growth of an enterprise. In many churches the musical program, requiring highly specialized skills and considerable time, went into the hands of paid musicians at an early date. When the church school became too extensive for any volunteer to accept full responsibility, the Sunday school superintendent was followed by the Director of Religious Education. (Sometimes both titles were still used; actually there had come a division of labor within this educational area. Usually the director had the larger supervision and the superintendent the more visible role on Sunday morning; but the division of labor between the two titles differed from congregation to congregation). The move toward "professionals" was often deplored as obscuring the priesthood of all believers. At the same time, the centralization of parish-program guidance in a paid staff promised greater efficiency, effectiveness, and integrity of congregational purpose. After all, the livelihood of a paid staff, unlike volunteers, depended on disciplining tendencies to self-expression in terms of congregational intentions. Gradually, not only the "pastor," but the whole paid staff came to be looked upon as "the ministry" of the church. In so far as this ministerial image grew in the minds of the congregations and the staff, the latter began to explore their rights to "ministerial" status. Was there not justification for the change of image implicit in the change of title from "choir director" to "minister of music"? Would not the congregation and the director of religious education alike have a better conception of his role if he were called "minister of education"? In large congregations situated in neighborhoods of high population mobility the full-time "minister of membership" has appeared. Where the business and financial involvements of a congregation have been extensive enough the "minister of church management" has emerged.

Sex difference has played its confusing part. Many women "directors of religious education" have preferred that title to "minister of education." Many a feminine choir director has not cared for the connotations in the title "minister of music." The basis of these predilections regarding title are often vague and resist articulation.

Every time someone has become a "minister of (something)" the question of appropriate ordination, if any, has arisen, and often has been pushed hard.

As these divisions of labor have occurred, it has sometimes been questioned whether they can rightly all be termed "ministries." The term "church vocations" has appeared, particularly in relation to recruiting high school and college students whose commitment to full-time church work might be deterred by their stereotyped conceptions of the character of "ministers."

Once a term is devised and adopted, its use somewhere will persist even though other terms—presumably more appropriate synonyms—come into use. Something of the proliferation of "ministries" is evident in a list of monographs on "church vocations" now available. The Christian Churches (Disciples of Christ) issue monographs covering:

The pastoral ministry
Home mission ministry
Church music
Christian education
Military chaplaincy
World mission ministry
Institutional chaplaincy
Social work
Campus ministry
The ministry of teaching
Religious journalism

Recently the terms "Radio and TV ministry" and "Counseling ministry" have come into use. There is constant pressure on seminaries to provide in each of these areas curricula leading to advanced degrees.

In one sense the proliferation reflects a laudable flexibility, but it also threatens chaos unless there are operative principles for evaluating emergent activities in terms of an integrating objective commensurate with Christ's charge to his church.

The need for standards and standardization is often expressed by those who carry out in the church tasks which have warranted extensive education and training. Such persons rightfully resent the use of titles by some one scantily trained. Yet, when no "professionally trained" person is available, a congregation may employ some one whose education has been in an area other than that of religion, but who is obviously gifted for the available situation. Should the difference in education actually be reflected in a difference in titles—or should it be noticeable only in the degrees listed after one's name? And should certain titles require certain specific degrees? Must the word "minister" require the Bachelor of Divinity degree? Is the distinction between director of religious education and minister of education a matter of degrees, of sex, of size of the job, of ordination, of local church preference, of local church habit, of self-understanding on the part of the worker, of different job description, of geographical region, or of social class? It is obvious that all of these factors, and probably others, have played into specific decisions regarding the title for the educational supervision of a local congregation. The same circumstance pertains to many another title attached to church vocations.

Furthermore, will not the "church vocations" prove as dynamic and changing as many other "vocations" are proving to be in our highly dynamic society. A recent estimate indicates that in the immediate future the average person will go through more than one "vocational retraining" in a lifetime. Until recently it has been expected that before adulthood a person makes choice of a "vocation" which will be his for life. This idea has been accompanied by the attitude that it is in one's "vocation" that the securities for his adulthood are established! But what is the circumstance in this new age in which vocations rapidly become obsolete, in an age where even a new technological vocation may appear, flourish largely, and become obsolete in fifteen to twenty years. In such a society the idea of "vocation" as a life calling becomes meaningless. Another paper in this volume indicates that the idea of "vocation" can find fundamental meaning only in the very ground of existence and not in any particular job or profession. In the new kind of technological society we have entered even the traditional concept of "call to the ministry" has to be rethought.

There are frequently found in churches certain titles which have not yet been mentioned. One group of them has appeared in connection with what is now referred to as "multiple ministries." Sometimes the work of a congregation has grown beyond the powers of one minister and a second man is needed. Perhaps there is no one area (education, membership development, etc.) which is large enough to warrant a man's full time, but all the areas together warrant the time of two men. In other words, it is not easy to make a clear-cut division of labor. A typical response is to employ an "assistant" or "associate." These terms allow the pastor and associate to come to agreements regarding each other's working area without making the judgment in terms of what has been done elsewhere. Or, such terms may indicate that the second man, like the "minister," is available for the work of the church generally though in some defined relationship to the first man. Sometimes the term assistant implies a much younger person with relatively little experience. The less the age gap and the experience gap, the more likely is the term to be "associate." The term "assistant" is likely to carry the implication of a junior partner under direct supervision. "Associate" tends to carry the implication of freedom for creativity under a mutually accepted policy. The congregation, in its turn, will probably expect more of an "associate" than of an "assistant," though they will expect most from "the minister."

Another term is "copastor." This term implies equality, with the further implication that either man is the pastor of the church. Under this conception the pastorate of the church is equally shared in all areas by as many "copastors" as the church may see fit to employ. This notion of several men sharing "equally" has appealed to many as being "democratic," and the term "copastor" has often been used when the relationship was anything but democratic. That does not mean that the situation was not Christian. One thing that many Christians need to do is to ask in a sophisticated way in what degree the political term "democratic" has relevance to the structures of the Christian church. The fact that "democracy" is a criterion of government does not mean that it is a criterion of religion.

Actually, there are connotations to the terms "assistant," "associate," and "copastor," but there is no precision of meaning. (In contrast, in any university and throughout the academic community as a whole the terms "assistant professor," "associate professor," and "professor" have well-understood meanings.)

In the ministry, one has to look at the realities of a situation in order to discover what they are. Titles are used so variously and for such different reasons that looking at titles tells very little about the relationships which pertain. There are situations in which two men are about each other's equal, and treat each other in egalitarian fashion—yet the terms "pastor" and "assistant pastor" are used. There are other situations in which the relationship between two men is, upon examination, hierarchical, but the term "copastors" is used.

It is necessary in order not to compound our confusion more than it is already compounded that "free" churchmen untangle in their minds several sets of terms:

1. Types of political order
   - Totalitarian
   - Monarchical
   - Aristocratic
   - Democratic
   - Socialist
   - Communist
2. Elements of organization
   - Hierarchical (Sometimes called "line")
   - Egalitarian (Sometimes called "staff")
3. Styles of interpersonal relationship
   - Personal
   - Impersonal
4. Personality types
   - Dominant
   - Submissive
5. Types of church polity
   - Papal
   - Episcopal
   - Presbyterian
   - Congregational
   - "Presby-gational" or "Congreterian"
   - Connectional
   - Conventional
   - Conciliar

Unfortunately, too many of us are so imprecise in our use of words that we speak as if "congregational," "democratic," "egalitarian," and "personal" were synonyms. For instance, when it is said that a man's behavior to his subordinates is "real democratic" what is meant is that his behavior toward his subordinates is personal, i.e., he takes their personal feelings, characters, and ideas into account in dealing with them. If a man is a submissive personality type he will feel he is being treated impersonally if he has to operate in an egalitarian relationship in an organization—and he will feel that he is being handled impersonally, no matter how nice to him is the man who tries to deal with him in terms of their places within that egalitarian aspect of organization. The first and fifth lists above should remind us that in this twentieth century we have outgrown, or should have outgrown the thought forms of the seventeenth century. In the seventeenth century the three terms "monarchial, "aristocratic" and "democratic" were sufficient to describe all the political realities that existed at that time. Socialism, communism, and totalitarian Nazism describe later-appearing realities which any list of types of political order must nowadays include. Similarly, the terms "episcopal," "presbyterian," and "congregational" were adequate in the seventeenth century to take into account all types of ecclesiastical order then extant. By midtwentieth century at least three more terms must be added. I have heard a number of Lutherans describe most American Lutheranism as "presbygational." Methodists often describe themselves as "connectional." There are at least two brotherhoods which, within the last century have devised a new kind of structure by which to give practical expression to their brotherhood. These two denominations are the Baptists and Disciples of Christ; their new invention on which they have been making improvements in every generation since their invention began is the "convention." The development and use of this instrument has gone so far that it is certainly no longer correct to speak of either the Baptists or Disciples, and not even the Congregationalists, as being "congregational" in polity. It seems closer to historic reality to describe both Baptist and Disciple polity as (alas and alack, considering other connotations of the term) "conventional." However, the Christian Churches (Disciples of Christ) cannot be characterized as a "pure" conventionialism because they are more and more involved in the conciliar patterns used by the ecumenical movement. Among the Baptists, the American Baptists are most like Disciples of Christ; the Southern Baptists are different in that they have no element of conciliarism in their behavior, though much earlier and more rapidly than either the American Baptists or the Christian Churches (Disciples of Christ) the Southern Baptists became Conventionalist. This they would still deny fiercely because among them the term "congregational polity" is much more of a shibboleth than it is among either the American Baptists or the Christian Churches (Disciples of Christ).

Perhaps most of all we need to unscramble the terms "monarchical," "aristocratic," and "democratic" from the two terms "hierarchical" and "egalitarian.' Unfortunately, the designation of the Roman Catholic officiary as "the Hierarchy," has blinded many Protestants to the fact that all organization (whatever its political character) involves both hierarchial and egalitarian elements. Papalism, which culminates in one man, makes much greater use of hierarchy than does world episcopalianism which culminates in an egalitarian Lambeth Conference of bishops and archbishops from around the world sitting as equals. That Conference is slightly more hierachical than the Lutheran World Federation which is a sort of great presbytery, and more hierarchical still than the World Convention of Churches of Christ. On the other hand, papalism is egalitarian in the internal structure of its Curia in which no one "congregation" has superiority over another. Episcopalianism in America culminates in an egalitarian House of Bishops. The Christian Churches (Disciples of Christ) use egalitarian structure in such co-ordinating bodies as the Council of Agencies, and the Home and State Missions Planning Council, but the executive operations inside most of our state and national societies, our church-related colleges, and our benevolence and publishing operations are hierarchical. Wherever the delegate convention has appeared in our state conventions, a hierarchical element between churches and the convention has been introduced—though it seems to be a very limited hierarchy since everywhere it is still asserted that the actions of the convention are "only advisory" to the churches. Between the delegate members of a state convention the relation is egalitarian, as it is between the members of the Committee on Recommendations, though the Committee is in a hierarchical relationship to the International Convention. Oddly enough, the hierarchical superiority of the International Convention is limited in two different ways. Relative to the Committee on Recommendations the Convention is limited (self-limited, by the way) in terms of what it may do with the recommendations the committee sends to the floor. The Convention is also limited relative to the churches by the "advisory" character of its actions. But these limitations do not belie the obvious hierarchical supremacy of the Convention to both its own Committee on Recommendations and the local churches. Whether or not the Convention is "politically" superior depends upon whether our brotherhood continues its flight from the proven inadequacies and incongruities of "congregationalism" toward a "conventionalism," but even if we are to remain strictly and radically congregationalist, any wider body such as a state or international convention will be organizationally in hierarchical relationship to local churches. (This is the organizational state that actually pertains between the North American Convention and the "independent" Christian churches.) Hierarchy is not to be confused with monarchical or papal authoritarianism. Hierarchy is one inevitable element of organized existence and it is a usable and serviceable and indispensable instrument within a democracy as well as within a monarchy. But that is another matter from the decision to use it in church organization. If church organization employs some elements of hierarchy, it should do so not because hierarchy is either democratic or papalistic—in and of itself it is neither—but because it is appropriate to the church's task in a particular historic moment and place. If church organization makes some use of egalitarian structures, it should be doing so not because they are "congregational" or "aristocratic"—in and of themselves they are neither—but because they are appropriate to the church's task in a particular historic moment and place. A man should not deal with his subordinates personally because it is either "democratic" or "becoming to a benevolent despot"—in and of itself it is neither—but because it is the fundamental law of human relationships, though every administrator, even a minister, knows that within limits set by this fundamental law, impersonality has its occasional positive uses.

Oddly enough, when a dominant personality within the limits of decency dominates a submissive personality and succeeds in freeing the latter into prolific activity, both will feel that the relationship has been deeply "personal" and spiritually satisfying. They will tell you that they see eye-to-eye, that it has been a great experience in teamwork and co-operation, and that the relationship is beautifully "democratic." Others may know better and decry the extremes of personality type which experience dominance-submissive relationships as if they were encounters between men of equal ego-force. But these critics, before they discount the personal satisfactions and general good achieved by such relationships, better ask themselves if they are prepared to pay all the psychiatrists' fees involved in ridding the dominant man of his domination and the submissive man of his submission.

Several years ago I was involved in a conversation with one of the leading and most effective ministers among the Christian Churches. This man is a magnificent church leader. He makes decisions quickly, and executes them firmly. He schematizes and charts the operations of his church aptly. He knows what should be done, and his congregation knows that he knows what should be done. They have shared his views, and he has listened to theirs, and they want the kind of ministry he maps out. But it is far more than any one man can accomplish alone. If this minister finds assistants who share his ministerial ideals (even though the assistants could not themselves have projected those ideals,) they will together have a tremendous sense of freedom. The relationship will in actuality be hierarchical with "orders" emanating from the top down, though under the circumstances they will not feel like "orders"; they will feel like the natural thing to do.

Now it so happened that this minister was, as are many Christian folk, so prejudiced against the term "hierarchy" that this prejudice kept him from an honest understanding of what relationship with his "associates" would have to pertain in order for every one to operate well in the situation. The result was that in talking to prospective associates he used all the language of political democracy and none of the language of organizational hierarchy in order to engage a man for a position in his church. On one occasion at least this led to an acceptance of the position by a young man remarkably capable of operating within the egalitarian aspects of an organization, but with enough ego-force of his own to prevent him from being easy in a hierarchical relationship with dominance-submission overtones. Needless to say this effective minister and this promising young man were incompatible. Unfortunately, what others could recognize as a personality clash was, to the end, interpreted by each of the principals involved as a failure on the part of the other man to live up to the terms of the original contract.

The success of the elder man's ministry continues because our young man was succeeded by another who finds perfect liberty in a hierarchical situation. Our first young man is now out in his own church, fighting his own battles—and he has some tough ones to fight. But he is experiencing that perfect liberty known to such a man who is never more free than when his back is to the wall and he knows that he and he alone will decide on the next parry and thrust.

My only disappointment is that the older man never did understand the situation. How could he? He lives in a communion which tends to be deeply prejudiced about "hierarchy" and willing to accept only what can by some device be labeled "democratic." But that communion has been using some hierarchical structures throughout its history, and continues to do so—though most of its members are blind to the fact that the relationship which they acknowledge should pertain between elders and deacons is a "hierarchical" relationship which is even visibly acted out every Sunday morning in their communion services.

Theoretically, "multiple ministries" might be of two types. Practical experience indicates that while one of these types can be successful, the second is usually unsuccessful.

Obviously, multiple ministries can be hierarchical in character and succeed. Such a structure requires in its personnel those kinds of responses in which the relation of "superiors" to "inferiors" all up and down the line can be exercised. Persons who cannot exercise such a response should avoid being drawn into this type of multiple ministry.

What is not yet proved is that "multiple ministries" of an egalitarian type can actually succeed, whether a situation which is in truth "copastoral" can actually work. The evidence so far seems to be to the contrary. Several attempts have been made across the nation to use the copastoral procedure in its literal meaning. Does it not seem that such a procedure would be a grand example of the democratic principle at work? The evidence is that the outcome, instead of a congregation served by several ministers, is a gradual division into as many distinct congregations as there are ministers. This division may be in existence many years before any conflict occurs. Often, before that point is reached, the emerging congregations reassert themselves into a unity, and, moving away from the multiple copastors, find a lead shepherd. They may allow him to have "assistants," but they will insist that he is the lead shepherd.

Several years ago, one of the most popular magazines in America gave extensive coverage to a church in a suburb of one of our great metropolitan areas. The church had four coministers and was held up as a model of "democratic teamwork." Even as the publicity was being prepared, the results of the attempt to cominister were being visited upon that church, and two years later the program was over and done with. Unfortunately, the allurement to this kind of multiple ministry provided by favorable nationwide publicity was not balanced by the caution that might have been provided by information regarding the sequel.

Some points with respect to the multiple ministry may now be summarized:

1. The number of multiple ministries will increase. The "little brown church in the vale" like the "little red schoolhouse" is, by virtue of sociology, the automobile, and the very limited ministries afforded by a small church, replaced by consolidation into middle-sized churches. There may be little increase in the number of massive churches requiring four or more ministers, because massive churches have their own kind of built-in spiritual handicaps. The optimum size for a Protestant church seems to be one requiring two or three ministers, and the number of such churches is increasing.

2. The relationships within a multiple ministry should be clearly and accurately understood, and should take into account personality factors, the nature of organization, and the needs and opportunities of the particular local church.

3. There is not at present (and there may never be) a standardized set of titles accompanied by implicit "job descriptions" applicable in all situations.[2] In each situation, the multiple ministry must be designed in accordance with that particular situation, its needs and opportunities, and the personalities actually available for ministerial staff. Each change in ministerial staff warrants a review of the relationships within the multiple ministry.

4. In moving into "multiple ministries" the idea of "job description" should be used with exceedingly great caution. The term is borrowed from the field of industrial production. It can be nothing more than a metaphor in relation to the professions (ministry, medicine, the law, teaching, dentistry, etc.) with their

essentially personal activities which require creative judgment and practical flexibility and versatility at every moment and in every situation, and in relation to the particular persons to be ministered unto. Nonetheless, within the multiple ministry there must be a clean understanding of "division of labor."

5. The labor which is divided should be Christian ministry. But how can we know whether it is Christian ministry? How do we secure integrity when several ministers are involved? We shall be returning to that question again after we have seen ways in which the church has, in the past, sought integrity, wherein those ways have proved inadequate, and the current attempt among the Christian Churches to achieve "functional" integrity.

Congregational "Functions" and the Christian Task

Time and again throughout history, it has been asserted that in the New Testament there is a model of the church adequate to provide integrity to the faith and order of the church in any age. This preferred model is "the apostolic church."

Undoubtedly the earliest Christians and the Apostles in particular had a deep apprehension of the nature of Christian ministry. They had vivid memories of the life and teachings of Jesus of Nazareth. They felt themselves to be possessed of the same spirit. Because they had experienced the resurrection and Pentecost, the Apostles, and after them the apostolic community, carried out a responsibility no later age could exercise. The apostolic community had the first responsibility for working out an effective proclamation of the gospel facts and Christian faith. The responsibility grew into the task of recording that proclamation of facts and faith, and compiling it into a body of Holy Scripture. The apostolic witness in scripture continues throughout all time to provide the directive within Christian history. When any community can no longer be understood as fulfilling the aims that the apostolic community sought to fulfill, it is no longer a Christian community. This does not mean that a particular community may not "do things differently." Indeed, each community must do things differently, doing them in accordance with its particular place and time in history. But all Christian communities, each doing things differently, must not be doing different things. They must be doing the same things.

How are these common tasks of the churches everywhere, and the whole Church, to be identified?

During most of church history, men have sought to define the unity of the church in structural rather than in functional terms. The New Testament was supposed to provide a model of church organization. This supposition became, within Protestantism, a presupposition which blinded men as they examined the Scriptures for direct answers to detailed problems of church order. The presupposition led them to read more into the biblical record than is warranted. As a result claims have been made that the New Testament provides a model for orders as various as episcopalianism, presbyterianism, and congregationalism. In addition it has been asserted that while the New Testament does not provide a model of a mature church, it does provide church order "in embryo." This way of stating the case implies that it is of the nature of the church to change over the centuries—or at least to "develop"—and therefore we should not expect the church to be the same age after age. Roman Catholic apologists at one time made extensive use of this argument over against those Protestants who sought to restore and maintain an unchanging order.

Over against such diversity of interpretation, the present generation of biblical scholars has moved to a different understanding. The move has been in two stages. First it was acknowledged that the New Testament reflects a variety of forms of church organization. This position was expressed by the late Dean Frederick Kershner in his presidential address before the International Convention of Disciples of Christ meeting in San Antonio in 1935. The second stage has come with a more precise recognition of the organizational primitivity of the primitive church in which there were such fragmentary elements of organization that even the word "embryo" is too definitive.

A third stage of understanding is achieved when it is recognized that the presupposition that there is only one form of church government which is valid is an unexamined assumption. Furthermore, to approach the New Testament with the three categories of "episcopal," "presbyterian," and "congregational" is also to bring to the first century a set of categories which made some sense in reference to the early Reformation period but has made sense neither in earlier or later church history. It is now recognized that the three "classical" forms of church polity are a great oversimplification of the much greater variety of orders actually established by the churches, most of those orders being so varied that they defy identification by such simple terms as "episcopal," "presbyterian," or "congregational."

In the face of these newer understandings of the variety of church order, it has become more valid to believe that what is given first to the church is not its structure but its task. It then becomes the responsibility of the churches to discover what organization, at any particular place and time, will accomplish its Christian duty, enable it to do the things it should do.

Within the past twenty-five years, one communion which was formerly dominated by the idea that for the local congregation there is only one valid form of church order, has witnessed within its churches an almost universal acceptance of the principle that structure must serve the tasks which are the Lord's command to the church. Disciples of Christ, in a short generation, have seen most of their congregations move from an organization supposedly based on a New Testament model to the position that local church order must be judged on its functional effectiveness. This "functional" principle has in more recent years been adopted in the re-examination of area and state organization. It is becoming an inalienable principle in the general study of "restructure" which the communion has initiated. This functional principle is bound to lead to a recognition that what the New Testament affords is a definition of the work of the church, but what history affords is a dynamic continuum within which adjustments and reforms and restructures have always been necessary in order to accomplish the work of the church. Organizing and reorganizing must become a continuing work of the churches. What gives the church its stability is not its organizational forms, but the work of ministry set by its Lord, a work to be carried on amidst all the changes and vicissitudes of earthly existence.

Actually, the church has succeeded through history by virtue of an amazing flexibility which has gone unacknowledged. This flexibility is evident in the practice of both the "free churches" and the older, and supposedly more rigid, church bodies. It is especially obvious if, instead of reading history denominationally, we read it from the standpoint of the whole church and recognize its many forms as many adjustments on behalf of effective obedience. What the church has lacked is a consciousness of the positive significance of these continuing adjustments. Therefore there has not been written a polity which adequately acknowledges the necessarily dynamic character of church organization as it has constantly adjusted to give the eternal gospel effectiveness in the face of changing conditions.

What does the church discover when it turns to the Bible for the definition of its task? It finds on the one hand, such general definitions of its ministry as that provided by Paul in the term "reconciliation." On the other hand, the church finds a considerable number of specific indications of things to be done, and a wealth of instruction regarding personal conduct. Christians must not neglect the gathering of themselves together. They must observe the Lord's Supper, practice baptism, care for the widows and orphans, be hospitable, and so on. We shall, in a few paragraphs, indicate the ways in which these duties may be considered systematically. It is important to recognize at the outset, however, that it is only at the most general level that a full definition of duty is available from the New Testament. As Alexander Campbell long ago recognized, when Christianity supplanted Judaism, God replaced rule by precept or statute with rule by principle. Perhaps there is no greater contradiction in Campbell, than his ability to state clearly at one time the fact that in the New Testament God has respectfully treated us as mature sons to be ruled by principle (leaving to us the work of deducing the meaning of those principles for particular occasions) and, at other times, seeking to bind the churches with the doctrine that nothing can be enjoined upon them for which there cannot be found an express precedent or a "thus saith the Lord."

In the New Testament it is only at the most general level that full definition is found. The definition of ministry in terms of "reconciliation" is a definition of the work of the church as a whole: all specific ministries must be conceivable as "reconciliation." At the level of such an instruction as "neglect not the gathering together of yourselves," while the corporate character of Christian worship is undeniably established, nothing is said regarding the frequency or hour of meeting. In the specific ordinances to observe the Lord's Supper and baptism the grand outlines of Christian worship are discernible, but no rigid prescriptions so bind down Christian worship that in new times and new places it could not move forward from the obsolescence of forms that had previously served the gospel to new ways which will serve the gospel in the new situation. This is not to deny the dangers inherent in such forward movements. In such transitions the expression of the gospel may become perverted. But it is equally a perversion to suppose that transition is unnecessary. "Modernizing" is always right in principle, and always involves the risk of falling into some form of "modernism." It is, indeed, a most interesting fact that the canon of the New Testament does not provide any manual of worship forms. Such manuals were in existence when the New Testament canon took shape, but the early church did not make any of these manuals binding upon the later centuries. This fact places a severe caution sign before any contemporary use of such manuals as the *Didache* (which has a certain contemporary vogue) or any other historic forms, however early. This is not to deny that these early forms were an effective Christian worship for their circumstances. It does mean that we can appropriate the meanings of those early forms of worship only by moving back from their detail to the eternal principles to which they gave a particular historic witness, and then moving forward from the eternal principles to our own day before moving down from those principles to decisions regarding the forms of worship which will be effective now.

Whenever a group has access to generalizations on the one hand and unorganized lists of activities on the other hand, it must employ some conceptual schemes, some categorical schedules or lists, in order to handle the wealth of detail—"rationalizing" it in order to think about it, or be rational about it. With respect to any body of detail, there are various reasons why it must be thought about—and various schemes have to be applied to the same materials. For instance, a generation ago, seeking a way in which the vast detail of a church program could be divided into manageable units, some Disciples of Christ developed what they named "functional organization." It divides church program into units of a size convenient for committee management. Furthermore, by making each committee accountable to all the committees acting together as a "board," an alternative was found to the traditional board composed of "elders" and "deacons." Bringing the chairmen of the functional committees together with the minister provided a cabinet for efficient coordination of the program as a whole. This functional organization commended itself rapidly and has, on the whole, been effective in reviving church program in so far as it superseded an inefficient and tradition-bound structure. As we shall see later, such a functional organization does not guarantee that a church program will actually provide for the fulfillment of the Christian duties of a church. However, the list of functional committees is a comprehensive list, and exceedingly valuable as a scheme for the division of program labors. Among Disciples of Christ, the following program areas are identified:

1. *Worship,* involving all the devotional and ritual activity of the congregation.
2. *Evangelism,* the winning of men to the gospel of Jesus Christ. Evangelistic preaching is only one among very many evangelistic activities in the program of a typical church. Interestingly enough, the "revival," a highly effective form a century ago, is today so generally ineffective that it is only rarely included in church programing.
3. *Stewardship and property* (sometimes separated into two functions). Stewardship education takes place in both church and church school activities.
4. *Christian education,* includes not only the church school, but the "educational" aspects of the pulpit, stewardship programs, etc.
5. *Membership development,* by which the Christian character of the membership is constantly strengthened—an older generation might have said "edified" or "upbuilded." In today's established congregations the greater part of pulpit utterance will be "edifying" in contrast to the evangelistic emphasis which dominated the pulpit of the expanding frontier and its newly established congregations. Second, "membership development" is greatly enhanced by occasions of fellowship: churchwide, large-group and small-group, "cottage" group, "colony" group, "face-to-face" group (and every other kind of "group" devised by the experts in group dynamics). Third, a great deal of membership development must be done in work with families and individuals. Every church must have some program of counseling, pastoral calling, etc., however informal. Membership development includes not only the edifying of those already strong, but the cure of those souls who have fallen into sin or despair or some other predicament.

6. *World outreach,* involving planning for program by which the congregation participates in the world mission of the church and in the wider ranges of the ecumenical movement.
7. *Christian action and community service,* providing for Christian involvement in one's own civilization, and for involvement in responsible action in the immediate community, and the closer ranges of the ecumenical movement.

(In small congregations, the full spread of program activities can be covered with fewer committees by combining some of the above: for instance, Evangelism and Christian Education, World Outreach and Christian Action and Community Service, etc.)

This scheme provides a basis for the division of well-defined labors and responsibilities between the members of a congregation available for committee work. On occasion it has been used as a basis for the division of labor between the members of a multiple ministry, or for the program areas of a state or area association. But in these latter uses, the scheme is inadequate. It is tailored in terms of a congregation's program, which is something other than a minister's program or that of a state convention. Whenever a list of program functions is developed or used, it should be exhaustive of the activities in the total program involved. The importance of the above list is that relative to congregations it is comprehensive, exhaustive, all-inclusive. In other words, every single detailed activity that goes on around a church can be placed under one of the above-listed departments. Each department may have to break down in further committees and subcommittees to get all its work done, but no more departments need be added—perhaps. This "perhaps" must be put in because we live in a dynamic world. But whenever new "departments" are suggested, careful scrutiny must be made. The functional system breaks down when items which are containable under an already-existing department are allowed individual status within the structure. The main purpose of the above paragraphs has been to illustrate the way in which task must be given primacy in the devising of structure. Church organization should not be primary but derivative, derived in terms of work to be done.

What Disciples of Christ did with respect to the congregation's program a generation ago, churches more generally did a century ago with respect to the program of the professional minister. The list of categories is not identical with the functional departments of a congregation, but it is similar. This list has traditionally been known as the "offices" of the ministry, but it is important to note that the offices are defined in terms of tasks to be done.

1. Preaching: evangelistic, edifying, educational, etc.
2. Worship: leading in worship on the basis of a disciplined study.
3. Religious education: overseeing the educational program of the congregation.
4. Pastoral care: "shepherding the flock" by enriching its occasions of fellowship, and by counseling with its individual members.
5. Church administration: overseeing all the business of the congregation as congregation.
6. Congregational relationships: leading the congregation in its relationships to its community, other churches, and the world mission of the church.

So useful is this catalogue that it has been used to establish some of the areas of study for ministerial education:

1. Preaching—homiletics
2. Worship—liturgics
3. Religious education—catechetics
4. Pastoral care—poimenics
5. Church administration—ecclesiology (more properly "ecclesiastics")

6. Congregational relationships: Christian social ethics.

Half of these names for subject areas have gone out of style, but the areas persist in seminary teaching under other names.

This catalogue is also fairly useful as a basis for dividing the labor within a multiple ministry, though caution should be exercised lest its suitability for rationalizing the work of an individual minister hides flaws with respect to its applicability to a multiple ministry.

Another way of analyzing the minister's work stems from the fact that the church is an organization that must be administered. Less than any of the above, the following list provides a basis for dividing labor, but in its third point it brings to light the crucial problem for the church as it confronts its task. As organization, the church will collapse unless the following functions of administration[3] are carried out or cared for.

1. Provision is made for the maintenance of communication of all the parts of the organization with each other. (Note that this is a task different from that of the preacher's work of "communicating" the gospel. However, it ought to remind the minister that his task is to keep the church he serves in touch with congregations throughout the earth, and also throughout the ages—the "communion of saints.")
2. Procurement of personnel, goods, services, and funds necessary to the maintenance and functioning of the organization.
3. The articulation of the general morality of the organization: the provision of definitions of the work of the church as a whole.

The constant threat to any organization is that instead of being a unity moving toward common objectives it will become a loosely knit collection of enterprises leading in different directions. Of all the kinds of organizations subject to diffusion, the church is most susceptible. Many a congregation has become a series of groups (women's work, youth work, Boy Scouts, men's sports club, a group that worships at 11 A.M. Sundays, a church school, etc.) sharing the same building but lacking any unity of purposes. It is only the existence of definitions of the work of the church as a whole which may prevent or overcome such a lack of organic integrity. Unless there are ways in which the members of the church, despite the diversity of their particular tasks, perceive themselves as working toward the same objectives, they are no longer a church. The organist and the couple doing evangelistic calling, the kindergarten assistant and the financial secretary, the ladies who prepare the communion elements and the young people planning a caroling party—each of these must ultimately be motivated by the church's work rather than by enjoyment of a particular activity, or the church will fall apart. The organist loves to play, and the financial secretary gets great satisfaction out of keeping detailed financial records. If the church does not command these loyalties on behalf of a more transcendent duty, the organist will go wherever the opportunities for performance are greatest and the financial secretary will find the place where records are handled with the greatest skill. It is the statement of the transcendent tasks or functions upon which the unity and integrity of the church program depends. The program functions are indispensable, but they are not the general functions which give the church its meaning. The program functions provide a method by which the work of the church can be divided into different activities. They do not define the way in which these different activities achieve the same objectives. These objectives are given in the definitions of the general functions which everyone in the church, no matter what his program responsibility, must be achieving. The general functions are the responsibility of every member and of every program department. These general functions are not "program," but they are the aim of every element of the church's program, otherwise each program element becomes an end in itself.

How shall we define the general or transcendent functions of the ministry that is Christ's gift and command to the church as a whole? It has already been suggested that they may be defined in the most general way by such a New Testament term as "the ministry of reconciliation."

It is useful also to find categorical schemes by which these tasks may be identified. Here is such a four-point scheme. It is not presented as final, but as a means of pointing out the difference between a list of program functions and a list of general functions.

1. *Evangelical witness.* The church, in all its parts and in every individual member of the church, must find its meaning in its witness to the gospel. It must always be "telling the old, old story" in word and deed. Every church member, by his words and the way in which he walks through this life does bear witness to the faith that is in him, and he must ever be seeking to assure that by his life he does bear witness, however imperfectly, to the God made known to him through Christ.

2. *Remembrance of the Lord.* The activities of every department and of each member must be shot through and through with the remembrance of him through whom we know God. While this remembrance may occur pre-eminently in connection with the communion, it must nevertheless pervade the whole consciousness of the church and its membership. Otherwise the church loses its grasp upon that element of its subjective life through which God communicates what he has made objectively known through Christ Jesus. The loss of Christian memory is as fatal to the Christian community as the loss of the memory of the mighty acts of God on behalf of their forefathers was to the Hebrew community.

3. *The establishment of Christian fellowship.* The function of the church is not to celebrate congeniality, conviviality, comradeship, fellowship in the ordinary human sense, delightful and valid as they are. The function of the church is to establish that fellowship in Christ whereby every middle wall of partition is broken down. It is to establish that kind of fellowship in which every barrier is transcended, and in which there is neither Jew nor Greek, Scythian nor barbarian, slave nor freeman, male nor

female. The church does not fulfill its function when it provides only opportunity for the enjoyment in each other of free and independent spirits all capable of standing on their own two feet. It finds its meaning in creating that fellowship in which men are given to each other in a true interdependence in which they are responsible for each other body, soul, mind, heart, and spirit.

> Blest be the tie that binds, our hearts in Christian love:
> The fellowship of kindred minds is like to that above.
>
> Before our Father's throne we pour our ardent prayers;
> Our fears, our hopes, our aims are one, our comforts
> and our cares.
>
> We share each other's woes, each other's burdens bear,
> And often for each other flows the sympathizing tear.
>
> When we are called to part, it gives us inward pain;
> But we shall still be joined in heart, and hope to meet
> again.

4. *Commitment in Christian service.* Christian service is not to be confused with charity and almsgiving which are commanded in every religion that has ever existed. As the *Report on Service* of the Third Assembly (New Delhi, 1961) of the World Council of Churches points out in its opening sentence, "Christian service, as distinct from the world's concept of philanthropy, springs from and is nourished by God's costly love as revealed by Jesus Christ." At New Delhi indeed, the word *koinonia* or fellowship which the churches have favored as a term of self-definition was being replaced in favor by the term *diakonia* or servant. *Diakonia* from which the term "deacon" is derived, is the Greek term meaning "a slave waiter." The church, its departments, and its members, must cease thinking of themselves as free men who may voluntarily give a portion of their goods and time to Christ, in order to find themselves as slaves to Christ, men responsible for bringing about that complete reformation

of life and civilization which is Christ's kingdom. It was further emphasized by many delegates at New Delhi that the church must be ready, if called upon, to accept the definition of *martyria:* faithful unto death.

The point regarding the above list can be made by saying that the work of Christian service is not the responsibility of the deacons alone, but of the church as a whole: collectively, departmentally, and individually. Christian fellowship is not the objective of the department of membership cultivation alone. The minister's sermons, the congregation's financial integrity, the restoration of the spirit of a member through counseling, all have their part in building the quality of fellowship in the congregation. Remembrance of the Lord and witness to the gospel are inalienable functions of the church if it is to be Christ's church. If these general functions are not accomplished, the church degenerates into an unprofitable and busy bustling that exhausts instead of builds, which rapidly loses meaning and drags its members and society down into the degradation of a deadly dullness.

The claim is not being made that the above list of four general functions is complete. Perhaps "teaching" should be added, but my impression is that the central content of the church's teaching is contained under the point of evangelical witness, and the method of teaching is a program item contained under Christian education in the listing of program functions.

A very important instance of seeking to discover the integrity and meaning of the church in terms of general functions has recently emerged in the ecumenical movement. The New Delhi Assembly of the World Council of Churches concurred in a statement which had first been worked out a year earlier at St. Andrews, Scotland, during a meeting of the World Council's Commission on Faith and Order. This St. Andrews statement, as slightly modified at New Delhi, seeks to indicate the character of the church's unity. Notice that it points to that unity, not in terms of a common body of scripture, nor a common form of worship or order of ministry, nor a particular creedal tradition, but almost entirely in terms of general functions. These functions are at the heart of the Statement and are made obvious by the following matter of setting them out:

We believe that the unity which is both God's will and his gift to his Church is being made visible as all in each place who are baptized into Jesus Christ, and confess him as Lord and Saviour are brought by the Holy Spirit into ONE fully committed fellowship,
holding the one apostolic faith,
preaching the one gospel,
breaking the one bread,
joining in common prayer, and
having a corporate life reaching out in witness and service to all, and who at the same time are united with the whole Christian fellowship in all places and all ages in such wise that ministry and members are accepted by all, and that all can act and speak together as occasion requires for the tasks to which God calls his people.

Nothing will revive the life of the church at center so much as a renewed grasp of its general functions. The St. Andrew's statement and many another listing of those general functions provide guidance to renewed understanding and revived life for our congregations.

The final section of this paper will deal with the character of the ministry in the revived churches.

When Disciple of Christ congregations moved from boards composed of "elders" and "deacons" to boards made up of functional departments, many a church came upon the question, "What do the elders do now?" In many churches it seemed as if the only task left for the elders was to hand the trays from the communion table to the deacons and to receive them back. In many churches, of course, the elders still fulfilled a traditional duty by offering the prayers for the communion elements. But in a vast number of churches the only task left for the elders seemed to be these simple ritual duties. What had happened was that in years past the elders had already defected their principal duty as elders, but since they carried program work later turned over to functional departments, their defection had gone unnoticed amidst their busyness.

The recovery by a congregation of consciousness of its general functions once again brings the true and biblical duties of the elders starkly into view. The general functions are everybody's business. That means they are nobody's business unless it is somebody's business to see that these general functions are being carried forward. The oversight of these general functions belongs to the overseers—to the *episcopoi* or presbyters or elders, to give them three names by which these overseers have been known in the churches.

The tragedy in our churches has been that with the emergence of the professional ministry, we have fallen into a "one-man" concept of the ministry, and as a consequence the elders have lost their understanding of themselves as overseers of the general ministerial functions. The professional minister has often been left all alone as the one person bearing responsibility for the spiritual life of the congregation—and it is an absolutely untenable position.

A professional minister alone cannot succeed in bringing a congregation to the fulfillment of its general ministries. If he alone seeks to discipline the unruly or niggardly spirits who are destructive of Christian fellowship he is accused of exercising "his" personal preferences. If he alone challenges the stewardship level of the congregation, he is pushing "his" program. If he alone is seeking to bring his congregation to ready articulation of the gospel, he is trying to get others to do "his" preaching for him.

It is particularly at the level of the spiritual life and temper of the congregation that the elders are responsible. Congregations are peculiarly susceptible to the inroads of aggressive and destructive spirits unless there is within the congregation a substantial spiritual leadership exercised with wisdom and love. Program will not move if it is captive to exploitative personalities. Zeal will not rise if it is being struck at by mean and gossipy criticism. Charity will take itself outside of the church if it is accused of being political in its motives. The young spirit flees from the indolent spirit which protects its own laziness by defining the situation as one in which nothing can be done. A congregation dies when the five deadly sinners—the prideful, the slothful, the wrathful, the envious, and the avaricious—forever get by with their false outcry that the only deadly sinners are the lustful and the gluttonous.

The place of the elders—and the deacons—at the communion table defines the high importance of their place in congregational life. Serving at the communion table is not just another job among many around the church. It is participation in that central act of worship in which the whole meaning of Christianity is set forth. Communion is not a self-contained action, but an action whose meanings spread out through the whole life of the congregation and its members as they participate in church, family, and community. The elder's place at the table is the focal symbol of his ministry to the congregation. A man has no place as an elder or deacon if he is not the kind of man whose actions have embodied spiritual service and imparted spiritual energy to his fellow Christians. He has no right to be a distributor of the emblems of Christ's loving energy whose own life has not strengthened his own family and community by the outpouring of his own life's energies in strong and compassionate devotion.

When a congregation relaxes the spiritual standards of the eldership and finds itself electing anyone who will take the job, it is already out of business as a Christian congregation. The focal symbol of the eldership—service at the communion table—is a symbol and goes empty if the life of the elder in church, family, and community does not provide content for that symbolic action. The bread and wine are emblematic of the Christ. The service of those who wait upon the table destroys that emblematic power if their own lives are a travesty or a feeble instance of striving after Christian integrity. To handle the sacred emblems is to accept both spiritual responsibility regarding the example one's own life affords, and responsibility for the spirit and temper of the congregation as a whole. Such responsibilities cannot be "programmed." They cannot be made the work of a "functional department." They can be fulfilled only by prayer and constant concern, by precept and example of life. Here is the most important work to be done in any congregation. When it is well done, the congregation has spiritual guidance adequate to the fulfillment of those ministerial duties which alone give Christian meaning to the busy activities of our churches: the gospel is given witness, our Lord is remembered, Christian fellowship is established and lives are poured out in service in the measure of God's costly love made known to us in Christ.

NOTES

1. To all intents and purposes they "agree unanimously," but the word "unanimously" is withheld from the body of the text because there must be somewhere (hypothetically at least) some one whose "pet heresy" is the settled and paid ministry. Every Disciple of Christ has a pet heresy—otherwise he might not be exercising his rights of individual conscience. As a result, there is probably not a doctrine in all of Christian thought that is not, among us, someone's heresy. Therefore (theoretically at least) "no one can speak for us" because there is nothing about which we are unanimous!!!

Needless to say, as long as anyone continues to entertain this kind of travesty of the doctrine of the rights of individual conscience (a doctrine the writer staunchly supports), he condemns his brotherhood to irresponsibility to the whole Church of Christ, if, indeed, he is not even blaspheming against the Holy Spirit which seeks to unite us in truth with all Christians.

2. There is confusion even at the level of the retired ministers. In their desire to honor their former pastors and give them in their retirement years a title that implies some level of continuing ministry, congregations have bestowed such designations as "senior minister," "minister emeritus," "minister ecumenical," "minister-at-large," "honorary minister," etc.

3. See Part IV (especially pages 217 to 234) of C. I. Barnard *The Functions of the Executive* (Cambridge: Harvard University Press, 1948).

8

Toward a Theology of Baptism

STEPHEN J. ENGLAND

THIS paper makes no claim to complete coverage of a theology of baptism for Disciples of Christ or for any other Christian group. Complete coverage would ultimately include every aspect of a Christian theology, with special impingements on soteriology (the doctrine of salvation), ecclesiology (the doctrine of the church), and a theology of sacraments in general. The attempt here is to illumine some of the factors of special importance to Disciples of Christ. In it, we shall propose the following:

A. That while in baptism the response of faith by the individual is an essential, the primary act is that of God: a position far more "sacramental" than Disciples have usually held.

B. That it is the church's rite that is administered, with the result that "membership" is conferred rather than chosen, although not apart from the response of faith.

C. That in baptism, the act of God creates or brings about unity, although unity can never be empirically realized without the response of faith by which the baptized enters into that relation with others.

The paper will also point out that while the New Testament meaning of baptism must always be normative for the church, the present scene introduces factors not operative in the beginning days of the church, in the light of which any theology of baptism must be considered. It is perhaps needless to say that in one of the most significant traditions of Disciples of Christ the aim of this paper is not an authoritative statement of meaning intended to become binding upon the consciences of ministers or members in Christian Churches. Rather, it hopes to point the way for further study and deeper understanding of what was, in the beginning of the church, a deeply significant act of worship.

Introduction: Issues Involved

Disciples of Christ have been noted for "majoring in baptism." They are still "majoring in baptism," but in two directions that seem quite divergent, and supported by two groups, each of which is confident that it alone represents the authentic line of theological descent from the founding fathers. The two agree in administering only immersion to believers as baptism. They disagree on the terms on which persons who received sprinkling, or were christened in infancy, can be accepted into the fellowship of the local congregation.

The "conservative," taking his stand with Alexander Campbell, insists that immersion is the sole basis upon which such persons can be accepted. To many a "conservative" the practice is a proud symbol of orthodoxy, bearing a symbolic importance greater than the instrinsic significance of the rite.

The "liberal," claiming to stand in the line of Barton Stone, advocates accepting into the fellowship those who are members of churches, whatever the basis upon which such membership was attained. The "liberal" is likely to regard "open membership" as the badge of true liberalism, attributing to his rejection of immersionist practice an importance greater than the significance of baptism itself.

Both "conservative" and "liberal" have been led into inconsistencies in practice, in part because the practices have been unreflective. The diverse practices have been popularly equated with the unfortunate division, overt in many places and possibly irreversible, that has separated Disciples into "Independent" and "Cooperative." The designation is not completely accurate, for although all "Independent" churches reject open membership as completely heretical, their accusation that all "cooperatives" practice open membership does not rest upon a basis of fact. The fact is that a considerable number of cooperative churches are uneasy about open membership, and the anomalous situation has developed that there is no longer a free exchange of members even among cooperative churches. This situation cannot endure permanently; out of this kind of tension further division could be expected.

One obvious purpose of the present paper is to study the meaning of baptism in the hope of bringing Disciples to such an extent of agreement that this tension may be relieved and the threat of division averted. An added purpose relates to the posture of Disciples in the ecumenical movement. Those who have attempted to solve the problem of the relation of baptism to unity by ignoring it must feel considerable uneasiness as they observe the increasing discussions of baptism within the World Council of Churches. That issue will certainly emerge into the full light of debate in the next decade. Up to now, the principal contributions have been made by the Pedobaptist bodies that form the vast majority of the World Council. It seems incumbent upon believer-baptism groups to make their witness in such discussions, and Disciples are one of the two major bodies in America in a position to bear this testimony. It would be regrettable if the failure of Disciples should help create the impression that only Pedobaptism is worth consideration, and thus foreclose the possibility of solving the intricate problem of baptism in relation to union by failure to bring up the issues in discussion at this stage. It would also be most unfortunate, at a time when Disciples are seriously considering merging with a Pedobaptist group (The United Church of Christ), if the impression were conveyed that all our churches would readily accept the Pedobaptist position. In the end they may do so, but at the present it is unlikely that all of them would, and it would be tragic to negate the possibility of a comprehensive union by failure to discuss the theological meaning of baptism at this stage.

Any discussion worthy of the name must of course be consonant with the heritage of baptismal thought and practice of Disciples. It must also be agreeable to the total heritage, and if agreeable, it cannot eventuate in a statement that claims "authority," official or otherwise, as a position which all Christian Churches must accept, or as the sole basis upon which a union can be entered.

Perhaps the most that can be hoped for this paper is that it may clarify some of the issues, and generate irenic discussion that will lead to deeper understanding and firmer union.

I Historical: Baptismal Concepts Among Disciples

Disciples have held theological views about baptism, but some of them have gone unperceived, and most of them have remained unexamined, because Disciples have approached baptism pragmatically rather than reflectively. We may take three items as characteristic. In the first place, Disciples are a part of the believer-baptism group: they refuse to administer the rite to infants. Second, they are basically nonsacramental: their typical generic term is "ordinance" rather than "sacrament." Third, they have held historically to "baptism for remission of sins" as the correct interpretation of its meaning.

Disciples, originating among the Pedobaptist Presbyterians, entered the ranks of believer-baptism advocates because of their reading of the New Testament, and in part (especially in the career of Alexander Campbell) out of their debates with Pedobaptist opponents. The original desire to "restore the ancient order" of practice as seen in the New Testament—an ideal shared by both Stone and Campbell—led to the practice of believer-baptism. In his debates with two Presbyterians, Walker and Macalla, Campbell developed the doctrine that baptism as administered in New Testament times was for the remission of sins actually committed, therefore inapplicable to infants who had committed no sins. No doctrine was more distinctive of Disciples. Barton Stone shared it, and Walter Scott's enormously effective evangelism made full use of the doctrine. It had the merit of simplicity: it could be understood, if not theologically comprehended. It was based on clear and obvious New Testament passages, such as Acts 2:38 (known to every Disciple of earlier generations), Acts 9:17; and Mark 16:16. Strong emphasis on this explanation of the theological meaning of baptism led to the accusation of Disciples by their opponents that they were "sacramentarians" or "water dogs" who believed in "baptismal regeneration," as if the water had some magical property. The accusation was due to a misunderstanding on the part of the opponents, and even on the part of Disciples, who vigorously rejected any "sacramentarian" implications, while vigorously quoting the New Testament in support of their position. To them, baptism was not a "sacrament" but an "ordinance."

The term is characteristic of Disciples. Its use cannot be explained on the ground that it is "scriptural." While the word "ordinance" occurs in the Bible, it is not used in reference to either baptism or the Lord's Supper. Probably its use reflects the desire to avoid the implications of the term "sacrament," with its extreme emphasis on the passivity of the participant. It also betrays a basic conception characteristic of Disciples: baptism and the Lord's Supper are things "ordained" or "commanded," and are to be observed forever in the church for this reason.

This view of the nature of the church's rites is not inconsistent with a high view of their spiritual value. In a notable passage in the *Christian System,* Alexander Campbell wrote:

In the Kingdom of Heaven, faith is, then, the *principle,* and ordinances the *means,* of enjoyment; because all the wisdom, power, love, mercy, compassion, or grace of God is in the ordinances of the

Kingdom of Heaven; and if all grace be in them, it can only be enjoyed through them. What, then, under the present administration of the Kingdom of Heaven, are the ordinances which contain the grace of God? They are preaching the gospel-immersion in the name of Jesus into the name of the Father and of the Son and of the Holy Spirit—the reading and teaching the Living Oracles—the Lord's Day—the Lord's Supper—fasting—prayer—confession of sins—and praise. To these may be added other appointments of God, such as exhortation, admonition, discipline, etc.; for those also are ordinances of God; and, indeed, all statutes and commandments are ordinances; but we speak not at present of those ordinances which concern the order of the kingdom, but of those which are the primary means of enjoyment. These primary and sacred ordinances of the Kingdom of Heaven are the means of our enjoyment of the present salvation of God. . . . Not one of them can be dispensed with; they are all necessary to the full enjoyment of the Reign of Heaven.[1]

The number of "ordinances" surprises us as much as the exclusive means they provide for enjoyment of the "grace of God." It is noteworthy that they are "statutes and commandments" of God. As such, they are to be obeyed implicitly, and the blessings of divine grace follow obedience. But there is no hint that there is any direct action of God in the observance of the rite.

That obedience is the way to receive the promised grace of God can be illustrated copiously in the literature of the last century. One of the most eminent preachers, Benjamin Franklin, developed this in a sermon, "Positive Divine Law," the general idea being that there are commands of God which have no rational justification, but are to be obeyed for no better reason than that they stand there:

Who can see why any man should be immersed? No man can see that it can do any man good, in a religious, or a spiritual sense, to immerse him. What, then, is there to impel a man to be immersed? Nothing to the rationalist. He can see nothing in it, *in itself,* to lead him to be immersed. Indeed, he can see pretty clearly that there is nothing in it, in itself, for soul or body; that, in itself, it can have no tendency to produce or bring about what the sinner is seeking—the salvation of his soul or the remission of sins. . . . Why must the sinner be immersed? Not because he can see any virtue in water, immersing a man in water, or in all of it together; but because the supreme and absolute authority has appointed it. . . .[2]

As a religious motive, obedience to God must not be underestimated; but the assertion that baptism is nonrational, if not actually irrational, echoes strangely to Disciple ears. It is in the light of Franklin's discourse that we must understand the typical doctrine that "baptism is for remission of sins." This is not sacramentarianism, nor is it baptismal regeneration. It casts the whole in the framework of command joined to promise, and receiving of the promise joined to obedience. The familiar comparison of "remission of sins" to the receiving of a pardon from the governor of a state lies at this point. When the terms for pardon are completed, the pardon is issued; until that time, it is not. The theory assumes that baptism brings one into a legal relation to a governing authority rather than into a personal relation to a Father. It may become as subpersonal, hence non-Christian, as the sacramentarian view that makes baptism an *opus operatum*. As a doctrine, however, baptism for remission of sins is clearly in the New Testament.

Speaking in general terms rather than in those of specific concepts, Disciples have regarded baptism as nonsacramental, thereby reflecting the influence of the Baptists; as individual rather than ecclesiastical, thereby following the highly individualizing soteriology of Protestantism; and have, in the present century, both localized and denominationalized the rite.

Strangely for those who have held so high a doctrine of the church, Disciples have tended to regard baptism as the business of one person with God, in which the church is a spectator. This is a drastic change from the concepts of an earlier generation that held that baptism is into Christ, therefore into his Body, the Church; and that therefore there is no salvation outside the Church. The tendency to individualism in the concept of the meaning of baptism has issued in the increasing practice of private baptism, elimination of the baptistry from the chancel, and minimizing the importance of the rite. Increasingly, Disciples have both denominationalized and localized baptism. It becomes more and more the means of entering a local congregation, hence under the control of that group, subject to their changing ideas—or more accurately, subject to the ideas of their changing ministry. Such localizing also rejects the sense of responsibility of each congregation to the entire fellowship in the receiving of members. To many, also, the practice of baptism has become a badge of the denomination. Success in convincing some member of a Pedo-baptist group that he should be immersed is too often regarded as a denominational victory.

The general attitudes we have mentioned rest upon unexamined theological assumptions, the more influential and potentially the more noxious because they are unperceived, or at least unstudied. These, as well as the more overt expressions, must be considered.

II The Theological Basis of Sacramental Worship

The question whether sacramental observances are essential to the present-day church is one that must be considered in the attempt to formulate a theology of baptism. The emergence of such nonsacramental church groups as the Friends and the Salvation Army, whose individual adherents frequently display a dedication and character far above that of their sacramental neighbors, points up the issue. The casualness with which the average church member regards his church's sacraments indicates that he attaches slight value to their observance.

The tendency toward nonsacramental religion among the intellectuals in all churches comes out at the same point. An increasingly rationalizing approach to Christian faith may see the value of reading of the sacred record, preaching, praying, and even the use of music in praise to God, but may be repelled at the thought of such nonrational practices as immersing a believer in water, or sprinkling a few drops of water on the head of an infant, or eating a fragment of bread and drinking a few drops of wine, all to the intonation of solemn words.

This raises the question fairly before the modern church member: why does the church observe any sacraments? Is there an adequate reason? Admittedly, the tradition of the church since its beginning records sacramental observance, and if we would remain in the tradition, we must continue the practice. But it seems no easier to hold that the church can be transmitted only by an unbroken series of sacramental acts than to hold that it can be transmitted only by an unbroken series of episcopally ordained clergy.

No longer is it enough to hold that we should observe the sacraments because the Lord of the Church commanded them. This criterion would not be universally acceptable, on the critical grounds that the words of command may not be authentic words of the historic Jesus. Even if we could be sure of the genuineness of the words, this would not warrant imposing upon the church for all time customs and practices for which there is no intelligent purpose. We feel rightly that no Christian is obligated to obey unintelligently; to do so is (as Donald Baillie points out) at best formalism and at worst a form of magic.

This requires us to face the question: is there intelligible foundation for sacramental observance of any kind? Baillie phrases the question clearly:

> What is there in human nature and human needs and our human situation, what is there in the Christian faith, the Christian Gospel, the Christian salvation, what is there in the nature of the divine grace and its ways of working, to demand this strange visible, tangible expression, in material things and in perceptible actions, which we call sacramental?[3]

In reply to his question, Baillie holds that we live in a "sacramental universe." By this he means

> that because nature is God's and He its creator, it lends itself to His use, and He can make its natural elements to speak sacra-

mentally to us; . . . God by His Word can use, and therefore we by our faith can use, natural objects . . . as sacramental expressions of His mercy and faithfulness.[4]

He answers the ancient argument, that a truly spiritual religion does not need material aids, by rejecting the opposition between spirit and body, in the language of the New Testament, and by holding that in the New Testament, the idea of "spiritual" is close to the modern idea of "personal." The goal of true religion is to bring man to live as a real person, in personal communion with other persons and especially in relation to God. That is unspiritual which is impersonal or subpersonal; and

God is spirit, but we are spirit-body, because God has so created us; and for us, who live in the body, there is nothing unspiritual in the use of material aids, sacramental symbols, so long as we use them in a way which *personalizes* (instead of depersonalizing) our relationship to Him.[5]

It can also be maintained that worship in the form of actions is congruent with our understanding of the nature of revelation as set forth in the Bible. The view held for many generations, that the Bible itself, as a written record in verbal form, is God's revelation, lent itself to the concept of worship in rational patterns and in verbal forms. So long as revelation is thought of as the imparting of doctrines or truths—that is, as propositional—the actual words of the Bible are supremely important, and may come to be revered as constituting the Word of God. In this view, the actions recorded, although they may be considered the actions of God, are valued chiefly for their doctrinal or theological meaning, not as in themselves revelatory. Worship, for those who hold this view, lays heavy emphasis on the verbal aspects and the rational understanding. Sacramental worship, comprised in acts, is minimized in importance. Such acts may be continued because the verbal "revelation" records the command of Jesus Christ for their beginning as well as the practices of earlier generations of Christians. It does not necessarily follow that the ceremonies in themselves have intrinsic significance, or that they serve to bring the worshiper significantly into the presence of God.

At present, it is common to hold that God's self-revelation was in his gracious and mighty acts in and through history for human redemption. In the Old Testament, these acts were such as the release of Israel from Egyptian bondage, the exile of the Jews, and their return to rebuild the temple.

In the New Testament, the climax of the self-revelatory activity of God was the coming of Jesus Christ, his birth as a human infant, his gracious ministry, his redemptive death, and his resurrection by the power of God. In the light of this concept (set forth in an excellent paper before the Panel of Scholars by William Baird), the Bible becomes, not itself the revelation, but the record of the revelation, the witness of those to whom the historic revelation came, and the instrument of the revelation to later generations.

Those who hold that God's self-revelation was given in acts may well feel that worship in acts has a certain consistency; particularly if the actions performed in sacramental worship are linked in form and as a matter of continuity with the revelatory acts of God to which they bear witness. This is the case with both the Lord's Supper and Christian baptism. Those who hold that God's self-revelation in Jesus Christ climaxed in his redemptive death, his burial, and his resurrection (1 Corinthians 15:1-4) will see in the symbolic repetition of these acts that which is meaningful, apart from the rational understanding of Christian doctrines of salvation. It may also be established that the significance of the Christian sacraments inevitably links them with the career of the historic Jesus, in whose life God revealed himself. So Donald Baillie observes:

> The sacraments of the Christian Church are not arbitrary symbols chosen from time to time against the background of a sacramental universe. They are something more. It has always been regarded as being of their very essence that they go straight back historically to episodes of the incarnation, to the words and work of Jesus Christ in the days of His flesh.[6]

The Christian sacraments have an inseparable connection with that historical fact.[7]

This view of sacramental worship implies that the performance of the acts, in worship, may, like the reading of the Scripture or the preaching of the Word, bring the worshiper to confront God in Jesus Christ. As we shall see below, the New Testament seems to support this view.

What we have just said concerning the inescapable connection of the Christian sacraments with the historic events of the life of Jesus indicates the importance of their "institution." In Protestantism, since the days of Luther and Calvin, the tendency has been to reject the Roman Catholic listing of seven "sacraments" by limiting the number to those that carry "dominical institution." By this is meant the discovery of an overt command of Jesus for his followers to repeat the sacramental actions, indicating that they have some kind of sacramental meaning. More importantly, however, the "institution" of the sacraments by Jesus deals with the fundamental concept that Christianity is a historical religion. As Donald Baillie points out, it is not merely a system of doctrines, whether these are regarded as divinely imparted or developed by men, but having no essential relation to any historical events. If it were, then conceivably Christianity might evolve symbolical rites as it grows, with no limit on the number or their significance, so long as they express the timeless truths held by the Church. But if Christianity tells of something that once-for-all happened in history, its rites must be linked to that event. Hence, the "institution" of baptism and the eucharist by Jesus, in the sense that they are linked to his career in history, is of vital importance.

III Some Views of Baptism in the New Testament

The practice of baptism in the church, in any era, must be grounded in the New Testament practice and also in the New

Testament understanding of the ceremony. To our Disciple forebears, the practice was far more significant. That baptism was universally practiced in the Christian communities from the beginning is now acknowledged by scholars of every theological view. In the earliest church, no one ever questioned whether baptism should be administered, and its importance is both asserted and implied. In the Judaizing controversy, for example, the initial focus was on the question whether the non-Jew should be admitted to baptism without prior fulfilling of the requirements for proselytism to the Jewish position; and the heat generated by the controversy was doubtless intensified by the importance attached to baptism, both as the initiatory act to the organization called "the church" and its deep religious meaning. It is also agreed by scholars that the descriptions of baptism in the Book of Acts either specifically link the rite with a prior profession of faith, or seem to imply such a profession. It was this obvious point that was cited by the Campbells, Stone, Walter Scott, and others as final proof that only believer-baptism is commanded in the New Testament, hence still to be required in the modern church. Against this obvious fact, asserted by (e.g.) Karl Barth and admitted (e.g.) by such Pedobaptist scholars as Cullmann and Flemington, the attempt has been made to oppose the "household" baptisms of Acts 16:15, 33, a feebly supported position; and somewhat more impressively, the argument from the silence of the New Testament record. It is pointed out that the New Testament engages in no denunciations of infant baptism; nor does it record (as pointed out, e.g., by Cullmann and by Lampe) that in the second generation of Christians, any adult who had grown up in a Christian home was admitted to baptism, following a profession of faith. The argument from silence is always precarious; here, the silence may imply the practice of infant baptism, or it may imply the continuance of the practice earlier recorded, that baptism was administered to believers.

Such scholars as Cullmann and Flemington, of the Pedobaptists, and Neville Clark, of the British Baptists, feel that the New

Testament record of practice is inconclusive, and that we must turn to the theology of baptism expressed or implied in the New Testament for its definitive witness. Cullmann believes that this favors or even requires the baptism of infants in Christian homes, a conclusion by no means universally accepted, even by Pedobaptist scholars. If this conclusion could be established, then infant baptism would be established as the normative Christian rite, with believer-baptism reserved for mission lands wherever the Church was being established. It should also be noted that the theological analysis of baptism in the New Testament may minimize the importance of the form of the ceremony. It was customary a century ago among Disciples to emphasize that the command to baptize employed the Greek verb *baptizo*. Since the meaning of the word can be established by etymological and lexical studies as "immerse," it can be argued that the Lord commanded immersion as the only acceptable form of the rite. This is the approach of a book by Lawson, *Did Jesus Command Immersion?* issued in 1915 and reprinted in 1948. Theological study of the New Testament might indicate that some other form is equally acceptable, although not so ancient as immersion. William Robinson in 1937 asserted that the primary objection of Disciples to infant baptism is not because it cannot claim to be the most ancient practice of the church, but because of its significance. The same conclusion may hold good for immersion as over against affusion.[8]

References to baptism in the New Testament are so numerous that a brief discussion such as the present one cannot undertake to treat them all in detail. For our purpose it will be sufficient to consider indications of the meaning of baptism as seen in the origin of the rite, and in a limited number of references to effects that were believed to issue from the act. In the latter category we shall consider baptism in relation to the conversion of the individual, in relation to "membership," and in relation to unity. In both the origin of baptism and its practice in the early church, the basic issues will be sought rather than a description of the actions performed. One of the basic issues is whether in baptism, including the baptism of Jesus as well as the rite administered in the church in his name, God is thought of as the primary or perhaps the sole actor. A related issue is the extent to which the voluntary response of the one baptized is in any way definitive of or limiting upon the results expected.

We have no clear statement of the origin of the practice of baptism in the New Testament Church. Since it was a universal custom from the beginning, we must suppose that there was some overriding conviction that it was in accord with the will of God.

The New Testament records that Jesus submitted to baptism at the hands of John (Mark 1:9-11 and parallels), and that after his own baptism and while John was still at liberty (John 3:26; 4:1f.) he practiced baptism under circumstances that are not clear. In view of the later difficulties between the church and the surviving group of Baptists who traced their origin to John, it is inconceivable that the church invented either story. It is clear enough that Jesus did not require baptism of any of those who followed him, probably in order to differentiate between his mission and John's. Had he required baptism, it is inexplicable that the church should have failed to cite his practice as the warrant for use of the rite in his name. The difference between the Church's rite of the Lord's Supper and baptism at this point is distinct. Apparently the followers of Jesus had engaged in common meals with him prior to his death, and continued the custom, with deepened meaning, afterward.

Baptism did not stand in the same kind of continuity. For this reason, we must seek the "institution" of baptism in something other than a specific command of Jesus during his lifetime, such as we have for the "institution" of the Lord's Supper in the Synoptic narratives (Mark 14:22ff and parallels) and in Paul (1 Corinthians 11:23-25). The "institution" of baptism as a command of the risen Christ is found in Mark 16:15f and Matthew 28:18-20; this is the "dominical institution" held necessary by Protestantism, and considered as sufficient authority for the requirement of the baptism of all believers by Stone, Campbell, and those who came after them.

Attempts to include the command to baptize in the authentic text of Mark face insuperable objection on the basis of textual studies. No such difficulties surround the textual tradition of Matthew; the words in question are as ancient as the remainder of the gospel. The use of the trinitarian formula suggests a date later than the origin of the gospel, especially when we note that in Acts baptism was administered in the name of Jesus (as, e.g., Acts 19:5). The trinitarian concept, however, is not necessarily inconsistent with an early date, appearing in Paul (2 Corinthians 13:14).

Whatever our decision as to the originality of the command and formula as part of the text of the gospel, its presence in the gospel reflects the conviction of the church in the last half of the first century that the practice of baptism as a means of "making disciples" (as the participial form indicates) was in accord with the will of their risen Lord and the Head of the Church. Some such dominant conviction is required, as we have seen, to account for the universality of the practice from earliest times.

Some scholars would trace the origin of Christian baptism, and its "institution," to the baptism of Jesus at the hands of John. Certainly the understanding of the church's rite is subject to our interpretation of the significance of that event as Jesus experienced it. John's baptism, in the opinion of many modern scholars, was not simply the Jewish rite administered to proselytes, but a new ceremony, with a new and richer meaning. "Proselyte baptism," then, is not determinative for the significance of the baptism which John administered, nor is it determinative of the significance to Jesus of his submitting to immersion at John's hands.

Present-day discussion of the meaning of baptism as "instituted" by Jesus in his baptism turns on interpretation of the phrase "it becomes us to fulfill all righteousness" (Matthew 3:15). Cullmann, assuming the historical genuineness of the account, explains the meaning of the phrase by taking the term "righteousness" as equivalent to the Pauline "justification"; in the Greek, the words are the same. The purpose of Jesus in submitting to baptism was to "fulfill," or work out, "all justification"; that is, the salvation of all. Thus Cullmann is able to equate Jesus' baptism with his death, supporting his view with references to baptism in Jesus' teaching as indicating his death (as, e.g., in Mark 10:39 and Luke 12:50). Apparently Cullmann's interpretation is based upon a Lutheran type of soteriology, in which "justification" is principally a transaction between the divine Father and the divine Son, objectively accomplished without the need of human response. In this way, Jesus' baptism becomes a scene between Father and Son; the element of real human response by a really human Jesus is minimized to the point of disappearance.[9]

Cullmann's interpretation faces insuperable obstacles. It rests upon a Christology that is almost docetic. It speaks of Jesus in his baptism accomplishing "a general baptism for all" that becomes effective for each when he actually is baptized in water. But the concept of vicarious baptism appears nowhere in the New Testament, though there is a New Testament doctrine of vicarious suffering.

Neville Clark, a British Baptist, bases his interpretation of the meaning of Jesus' baptism upon an orthodox christology that holds to the true divinity and true humanity of Jesus. God sent his Son for human redemption and the Son willingly submitted in obedience. This, Clark holds, is the corollary of the joining of the human and the divine in the person of Jesus Christ. To leave out the action of a truly human person as Cullmann seems to do—is as erroneous as to make it chiefly or exclusively the action of a man, and rests upon a faulty view of the nature of Christ. Clark applies his view of the baptism of Jesus to the meaning of Christian baptism in these words:

> Just as the baptism unto death of the Lord is constituted by the conjunction of divine action and human response, so the baptism

unto death of his followers demands for its reality their ratification of his response in obedience to the word proclaimed to them.[10]

It is easier and far more consistent with acceptance of the true humanity of Jesus to see in the words of Matthew 3:15 Jesus' explanation of his submitting to baptism as his humanly willed act of obedience and dedication. "To fulfill all righteousness," then, means "to meet willingly the rightful demands of God," by submitting willingly to baptism at the hands of John, whom he regarded as God's messenger.

Unless Jesus' baptism was his real self-offering to God, in which God accepted him, it was docetic, a mere pretense, and can never be an example for us.

In general, the synoptic narratives agree in their accounts of the baptism of Jesus. John, God's messenger, called for obedience to God in baptism. Jesus, the man, willingly responded. In the word heard by Jesus and in the sending of the Spirit upon him, God granted his approval of the act of dedication.

By his submitting to baptism, and in the concomitants of his baptism, Jesus transformed John's rite. As we shall see below, the same elemental features appear in Christian baptism: the *kerygma,* in which God calls for obedience and offers forgiveness, is followed by the act of obedience on the part of the hearer. The baptism of the believer is thus "to fulfill all righteousness" as he meets God's rightful demands, which include far more than submitting to the rite. To the believer, as to Jesus in his baptism, God completes the ceremony by his conferring the gift of the Holy Spirit upon those who obey (Acts 2:38).

In the Church during New Testament times, baptism was (as we have seen above) universally practiced; all were baptized as the rite of initiation to the Church. In the thought and experience of that day, what was accomplished in the act? The same basic issue appears here as in the case of the baptism of Jesus. Was it regarded as primarily (if not exclusively) the act of man, responding to the gospel and primarily (if not exclusively) as the act of God doing something for man?

Disciples of Christ have traditionally been counted chiefly on the side of those who see in baptism something which man is commanded to do and which he can do, something which is then followed by God's fulfilling his promises. Baptism is "for remission of sins"; but the remission is God's act, following after baptism, which is man's act. The proponents of infant baptism and such Calvinists as Clark and many British Baptists see in baptism chiefly the act of God. So Clark says, while safeguarding himself slightly by insisting that "faith is indissolubly connected with the New Testament rite":

> Baptism is a sacrament of the Gospel, not of our experiencing of it; of God's faithfulness, not of our faithful response to Him; any theological formulation which lends itself readily to an interpretation of the rite primarily in terms of a public confession of faith must at once be suspect.[11]

Clark's somewhat one-sided emphasis grows out of his Calvinism, with its asumption of human helplessness to respond to the divine offer of redemption. The tradition of Disciples, developed in large part in opposition to Calvinism, has led often to an equally one-sided emphasis upon what man does when he submits to baptism. It is significant that the passive of the verb *baptizo* is regularly employed in the New Testament. So Peter, on Pentecost, advised his hearers "be baptized"; the Ethiopian asked Philip, "What hinders me from being baptized?" In the New Testament baptism is regarded, not as something which one does for himself, but as something that is done to him. What is done is not ultimately the act of one man (the baptizer) to another (the baptized), but the act of God upon one who in faith and with willing obedience makes his response to God's offer and call.

In the New Testament this is related to the obvious fact that the Church's sacraments were kerygmatic in character. This is overtly stated concerning the Eucharist in 1 Corinthians 11:26: eating the bread and drinking the cup "proclaims" the Lord's death. Baptism, so Paul observed (Romans 6:3f), depicts the death, burial, and resurrection which constitute "the gospel"

(1 Corinthians 15:1-4) by which men are saved. So Eric Dean writes:

> Baptism, like preaching and the sacrament of the Lord's Supper is a form of Christian witness. . . . What is celebrated in baptism . . . is that which constitutes the Church.[12]

The kerygmatic sacrament of the Lord's Supper in its form is related to what is proclaimed: the redemptive acts of God in the death of Jesus Christ. So in baptism, the form is related to what is proclaimed, setting forth what God did in the death, burial, and resurrection of Jesus Christ.

We must observe, however, that in the New Testament, kerygmatic preaching did not consist simply in words uttered. To Paul, "the word of the cross," which he characterized as "the folly of the kerygma" was "the power of God" to those being saved (1 Corinthians 1:18ff). In the proclamation God was acting. But without the response of faith, nothing really occurs in the life of the hearer. The revelatory act of God in Jesus Christ, which is the content of the kerygmatic offer, must be completed by the faithful witness of those whom God called for that purpose. So the kerygmatic act of baptism must be completed by the response of faith, in which again witness is borne to the redemptive power of God. Baptism thus sets forth the divine proffer and redemptive action, and includes the human response to that offer.

It must be emphasized again that in baptism, as seen in the New Testament, baptism is more than an act of man, although it is this; and more than a laying hold on what God has offered, although it is this. Paul points out that baptism is self-identification of the believer with Christ. In his death, Christ died *for* sin; the believer, by identifying himself with Christ in his death, dies *to* sin. Christ rose from death to a new life; the believer, identifying himself with Christ, rises also to a new life which is empowered by God in the gift of the Holy Spirit.

Because baptism is thus a dying to sin, the leaving behind of the old life, it becomes the mark of forgiveness. In its true meaning, forgiveness is not merely a legal transaction in which God makes a bookkeeping entry or issues a pardon to a guilty person who is unchanged as he leaves the prison door. The pardoned criminal may go out to the same kind of life which brought him into the prison; but in the Christian understanding of forgiveness, the pardoned one leaves the old behind. The past is dead. He can now live for and into the future. It is only as baptism really results in death to sin that it can result in forgiveness of sins.

Let us now reflect that such a death as this can never take place by the act of man, no matter how resolute. Paul can call upon the Colossians (3:5) to "put to death" their members that are upon earth, but, in the deeper sense, only God's power can put evil passions to death, although man's willing acceptance of that death-dealing power is essential. No more can man, by his own power, rise to a really new life. Death to sin must precede rising to new life, but it is only by the power of God that a new life can result from baptism, although again man's acceptance and response are essential. Brunner states the dual conclusion clearly and forcefully:

> In baptism, it is God, first and sovereign, who acts, who forgives sins, who cleanses man and regenerates him. But man acts too in baptism. He allows this cleansing of himself to take place, he lets himself be drawn into the death of Christ, he confesses his faith and his attachment to Christ. Baptism is not merely a gift to man, but also an active receiving and confession on the part of man. Indeed baptism, precisely as this free confession of man, is the stipulation for the individual's joining the Church. Baptism is not only an act of grace, but just as much an act of confession stemming from an act of grace.[13]

The sacramental act and the kerygmatic word, the deed and the understanding, the divine action and the human response are inextricably linked. Entering "a personal relationship with God" requires the voluntary response of a person to the gracious act of God who discloses himself in the redemptive event.

In the New Testament, baptism was held to result in "membership." The same correlation between offer and response, between the willing submission and the act of God, that we saw above in relation to the conversion of the individual applies to the relationship of the individual to the body of Christ and to other individuals.

As Arndt & Gingrich point out,[14] the word *mélos* in the New Testament refers basically to the parts of the human body, such as the eyes, hands, arms, and by a figure commonly used in New Testament times outside the New Testament, referred also to the relation between individuals and the group to which they are related. Specifically, in the New Testament the word is used of the relation of the individual Christian to the Christian community, the church. So the individuals are "members" of the same body (Romans 12:5), whether Jews or Gentiles (Ephesians 3:6), and the "membership" is that of individuals as such, not that of names on some roster. "You are individually members of the body," says Paul (1 Corinthians 12:27).

The New Testament also sets forth the concept that individuals are "members of one another" (Romans 12:5); it is for this reason that we should "speak truth to one another" (Ephesians 4:25).

The means of this coming into "membership" with the one body, and with one another, is the act of baptism: "By one Spirit you were baptized into one body" (1 Corinthians 12:13), says Paul, or again (Galatians 3:27f.) he links baptism with the blotting out of the distinctions of race and class within the church, a concept repeated in a baptismal context in Colossians 3:11f.

It seems quite clear that persons are *made* "members" in the act of baptism, and not simply by the fact that they have submitted to the rite, for it is the Spirit that acts (1 Corinthians 12:13). Voluntary going beneath the waters does not of itself bring the person "into Christ," or make him truly a "member" of the one body, or join him indissolubly to other individuals.

Just as the Lord, in the Last Supper, gave the cup of the new covenant in his blood, thus creating a new people of God, so, in baptism, God must act to unite those baptized with Christ as "members" of his body. Without the intervention of God, the ingrafting of an individual into the one body is no more possible than is the transplanting of organs from one person's body into another's, by the modern surgeon.

This seems to be reflected by the use of the passive voice in baptizing. As we have pointed out above, the baptism which makes one a "member" of Christ's body is something done to him, although it cannot be done against his will. It is God who acts in baptism, though it is the church that administers baptism, in the stead of God. Disciples have understood this kind of sacramental action in the case of the Lord's Supper; they regularly and proudly insist that the rite is not that of the congregation or the denomination, but that of Christ, for whom the church acts in spreading the table. Disciples have not, however, so readily extended the same interpretation to the administration of baptism. The New Testament seems clearly to have moved in this direction. In Acts 2:47 it is God who adds to the group those being saved and in this context, they must have been baptized (2:41). Believers "were added"—the passive is significant—to the Lord; they did not add themselves. Evidently, some vital transformation must have taken place in those baptized, with the result that they became in reality "members," joined to one another and to Christ's body. This is the kind of change which, as we have seen, took place in the individual's dying to sin and rising to a new life. Only as God acted in the rite could "membership" result.

At the same time, the New Testament kept distinct the need for the individual to respond in faith, also no baptism (in this sense) could occur. This grew naturally out of the nature of the relation into which the baptized entered: it was personal, not organizational. So Robert Dobbie remarks, in words which are directed primarily against the collectivism of infant baptism:

In his own ministry Jesus . . . demanded personal loyalty, the total moral orientation implied in *metanoia,* not an unresponsive participation which makes no primary moral demands on its initiates . . . collectivism . . . may apply to the notion of a church but it does not commensurately apply to that of the kingdom of God, where one's relation is to a Person, not to a group.[15]

To phrase it differently, even though the individual submits to a required ceremony in which it is held that God acts through the act of the church that administers the rite, true "membership" has not empirically resulted unless the individual has responded with such faith that he really enters the status. This was the point to which Paul wrote. The Corinthians had received immersion, and we may suppose that he held God had been potentially active in the rite. But, in fact, they had refused the status of "membership"; each still felt that he had individually received something, not that he had been merged into the one body, vitally related to every other "member." The division in Corinth grew out of the failure of response, not the failure of God to act.

The church in which "membership" was attained by baptism was the Body of Christ. While the exercise of *koinonia,* or fellowship, must have been then, as it is now, chiefly a local experience, and while the act of worship was obviously then, as now, a local phenomenon, the larger concept of "membership" prevailed. The effectiveness of local "membership," as a uniting of individuals, rested ultimately on their having been joined personally to the one body. Thus, the New Testament states nothing of membership in a local congregation as the result of baptism, although, as we have seen, such "membership" is implied. It need not be mentioned that "membership" in a denomination was not thought of. Yet these features—membership—membership in a local congregation, and in a denomination, are the prevailing concepts in our time, even (surprisingly) among Disciples.

What we have said about baptism and church membership implies the relation of baptism to unity. As I have pointed out elsewhere, the New Testament regards baptism rather than the

Lord's Supper as the sacrament of unity.[16] The concept apparently is that in some sense unity is effectually the result of baptism. This can result only if God acts upon the individual so as to join him to other persons. The uniting of such diverse elements as the Jew and Greek, the bond and free, even male and female, into a single body (Galatians 3:27f) where Christ is all (Colossians 3:11f) can be only the evidence of God's power at work; this is the implication of the effectual making of a person into a "member" of Christ's body, which is more than listing his name on a "membership" roll. Recognition of this fact in the New Testament concept underlies the emphasis in the modern ecumenical movement upon unity as "given," rather than "achieved"; although it is not common to find the "given" unity linked with baptism. Some pious nonsense is evident at this point. Unity is not "created" by the act of baptism, after the way in which a machine is "created" by its inventor, apart from the response of persons precisely because in baptism the entering of a personal relation is involved, and this requires the response of the individual who willingly submits his stubborn prejudices to the will of God in an act of solemn acceptance of the proffered grace, and in an act of serious dedication that allows him to enter a new relation of unity with others who are also "members" of the one body. Even though it sounds iconoclastic, someone should arise in ecumenical gatherings to insist that there can be no "given" unity in the modern church, as an empirical fact, any more than there was a "given" unity in ancient Corinth. Realization of what God offered, by the deliberate acceptance of it, must precede realization of the practical ideal of unity.

IV Formulating a Theology of Baptism in the Twentieth Century

The formulation of a theology of baptism in the twentieth century, for Disciples of Christ or for any other Christian group, must be based not only on the normative New Testament meaning of the rite, but also on realistic appraisal of the actual situation. The procedure in discussing baptism among all groups is substantially the same. Beginning (as this paper has done) with an exposition of the meaning of baptism as set forth in the New Testament by men of deep spiritual perception who were moved in a special way by the Holy Spirit and who related their own experience of baptism, the assumption is then made, more or less unconsciously, that this significance describes what happens to every person, infant or adult, who is baptized in a church today. This transfer can be achieved only by the neglect of the changes that have taken place in baptismal practice, and therefore in thought, in the long history of the church. This leads to infinite confusion of definition of terms. How is it possible to unite groups in the practice of baptism when those proposing to unite mean different things by the term, and when each group is confused further as to what it means? This is the point of an article by A. L. Haddon in *The Ecumenical Review* for July, 1960: "The Two Baptisms and Christian Unity." What Haddon says about infant baptism applies in some degree to all modern discussion of baptism. He points out that while Paul spoke of "one baptism," modern theologians describe two, without themselves being aware of their confusion. First they describe what the New Testament says about the relation of baptism to the new life in Christ, a concept which we have briefly set forth above. They then assume that the same description applies to infant baptism and apply the term "baptism" to both. But infant baptism rests on a different theological justification. Haddon observes: "to attach the same name to two such different things is misleading and has unfortunate results." The same kind of confusion, in differing degrees and applied to different areas, can be discerned in most Christian thought today.

Some of the new factors in the practice of baptism have arisen since New Testament times, while others were existent then and have continued with enlarged influence. So far as the overt record goes, the form of the ceremony in New Testament times seems to have been an immersion in water. Now, this form is still employed, but sprinkling of water and pouring of water are also common. In the New Testament, so far as the recorded baptisms are concerned, baptism was administered only to those who were able to make a profession of faith. Now, the rite is administered to infants. In addition, there has grown up a non-sacramental Christianity including such groups as the Friends, who abjure any form of sacramental worship. The same term, "baptism," is employed by all the groups in relation to their practices. Confusion is inevitable.

Some of the difficulties which we face in regard to baptism existed in New Testament times, although many commentators seem unaware of this, or, in their overidealizing of the New Testament period, are unwilling to admit their presence. For example, the New Testament clearly speaks of baptism as a dying to sin and a renewal to life by the power of God, but this deep experience was not attained by all, or most, of those in the churches. This is what Paul is disturbed about in Romans 6 and in Colossians 3. His readers had received baptism, but had not actually died to sin or risen, empowered; they had not "put to death" their members upon the earth, nor experienced the reality of a "life hid with Christ in God." In the New Testament not every baptism grew out of or resulted in an "experience of conversion." That this condition remains today is not news to anyone.

In the New Testament "membership" was a result of baptism —a uniting of persons whose lives were transformed to Christ, to his Body the Church, and to one another. But that this did not always occur is the burden of much of Paul's admonition to the church at Corinth, where internal dissension threatened to destroy the group. Those whose lives were substantially unchanged were spoken of as "baptized," and those who displayed little or no sense of being members of Christ's body were regarded as "members." In the New Testament the terms had their high and ideal meaning, and they were also employed in a lower and looser sense. A "member," in practice, had doubtless come to mean "one who habitually associates with the Christian community." That this is distressingly modern is no secret.

In the modern world, furthermore, the term "membership" has been extended more widely, and at the same time has been limited in its application. The sociological feature of the modern church is the development of the denomination. It is only in and through a denomination that anyone now can hear the gospel proclaimed, can profess faith in Christ and become obedient in baptism, and can engage in worship and the practices of fellowship. The result has been the extension of the term "membership" beyond the New Testament usage. It now includes those who regularly associate in public worship and social relations within a local group (which is one of the New Testament meanings), and also includes those outside the local group, with whom most individuals may never meet, who are committed to the distinctive beliefs and practices which mark their denomination. But this extension has operated to limit the term. "Membership" in a denomination makes it the more difficult for any individual to think of himself as part of the one great Church which is the body of Christ—a concept that stands clearly in the New Testament, especially in the later books. Yet "membership" in a denomination is—or may be—a valid concept in our time. Each denomination originated because some aspect of vital Christian truth and practice was overlooked or distorted. If any denomination has theological justification for continued existence in separateness, it will be its continuing witness to what God has given it to see. This kind of witness, however, must not be allowed to obscure or efface the view of the Church as the Body of Christ which is more than any denomination.

In framing a theology of baptism, a starting point is the definition of the term. Christian Churches (Disciples of Christ), like other Christian groups, are not agreed as to what ceremony is required, or what matters of belief beyond a ceremony are required, to make the rite real baptism. To some among Disciples, the form is all important: only immersion in water is baptism. Defense of this view by reference to the New Testament practice and the meaning of the Greek *baptizo* creates an embarrassment, however, not because the New Testament evidence is inadequate, but because it proves too much, and convicts most Christian Churches of improperly observing the Lord's Supper. If only the repetition of the exact ceremony employed in New Testament times is valid, present-day modification of the Lord's Supper proves that it is not the Lord's Supper. We have not hesitated to change from one cup to many, from one loaf, broken in the presence of all, to minute fragments of a breadlike substance, from Saturday night to Sunday morning, from wine to unfermented grape juice, often eliminating the solemn words of institution originally used. The fact is that antiquity is not the only—or perhaps the best—test of proper observance; rather, as William Robinson points out, the question is the meaning of the form employed. Immersion in water as baptism can be supported on the basis that this form best represents what the rite is intended to signify, but on the analogy of our change in the form of the Lord's Supper, some other form might conceivably be recognized as baptism. Prior to formulation of a theology of baptism should be a study of the relation of the form to the meaning, in baptism as well as in the Lord's Supper. Christian Churches might be willing to recognize as baptism a ceremony other than immersion if it was received after a profession of faith.

Disciples of Christ have insisted on believer-baptism, but this general qualification still leaves the definition vague. Belief *of* what, or *in* what? The example of the Philippian jailor, baptized "the same hour," has been cited as the norm, assuming that anyone who hears the preacher will comprehend what baptism signifies. In fact, many adults regard the ceremony as something like the initiation requirement to a lodge. While it would be foreign to the heritage of Disciples to require adherence to a fixed creed prior to baptism, it would be appropriate to insist upon a profession of faith in Christ and adherence to him personally, rather than a profession of *a* faith or *the* faith. Prebaptismal instruction directed to this personal commitment of life, and baptism regarded as, at the very least, the expression of sincere desire to become obedient to the will of Christ, would seem to be a minimum definition.

While Disciples of Christ have been resolute in rejecting baptism of infants, they have been hazy as to the age when infancy is left behind and "belief" is possible. The practice of infant baptism ideally calls for a period of instruction following the rite, culminating in confirmation and formal assumption of full membership in the early teens. The practice of Christian Churches somewhat irregularly follows the same pattern, while vigorously rejecting infant baptism. It is not uncommon for churches to administer immersion to children as young as six years if these are in homes of the church. The usual justification, aside from the child's ability to verbalize the "good confession," is that otherwise the child may be lost to the church. It is hoped that the attainment of chronological age, spiritual sensitivity, and emotional maturity will bring the child to comprehension of the meaning of the rite, and to meaningful church membership. In substance, this is not far different from christening and confirmation by Pedobaptist bodies. It leaves unanswered the question of the age when immersion becomes baptism.

It would be helpful if we could understand the reasons why the baptism of infants has had such currency in the practice of the church. Cullmann would base it on a theology of baptism which, he insists, requires this ceremony. This is less likely than the view of Neville Clark that the custom arose quite early in response to a widespread popular demand. Parents in Christian homes feel deeply that their children are not little sinners, requiring drastic conversion and wrenching experience of forgiveness, but stand, rather, in a special relation to God because they are in Christian homes. Clark observes that infant baptism has been a practice in search of a theology, and that the practice among British Baptists of "infant dedication" is its counterpart:

"It arose in response to popular Christian demand. Again, it has been, more or less unsuccessfully, in search of a theology ever since."[17] Among Christian Churches, a comparable ceremony, "the blessing of infants," is widely practiced—and almost as widely denounced by sturdy "conservatives" who regard it as infant baptism by subterfuge. Both those who practice and those who denounce are equally without any reflective explanation of the status of the infant in relation to the church. Theological study of the nature of Christian marriage is the basis of a theology of the status of the infant. Clark suggests a new ritual expression of that relation, when it is determined. Baptism, he holds, is not the correct ceremony. It is of more than incidental interest that Dr. Kenneth Kirk, the Anglican Bishop of Oxford, suggests something similar. Viewing the serious difficulties faced by the Church of England in regard to baptism of infants, he proposes that instead of infant baptism the child should be enrolled as a catechumen or learner. Later, after a period of instruction and attainment of maturity, he should be admitted to baptism and communicant membership. A. L. Haddon suggests that among Christian Churches a ritual service be devised to be employed at the time of "blessing" of an infant; it would acknowledge the operation of the grace of God in the Christian home, as well as unitedly pledge both home and church to the Christian nurture of the infant. This would be followed by an actual profession of faith at a later time, baptism into Christ, and entrance into communicant membership. It is certain that Christian Churches cannot come to a satisfactory definition of baptism, or move toward a solution of the problem of union in practice, until the question of the status of the child is determined and embodied in the ritual practices of the church.

Karl Barth, who vigorously attacked infant baptism, admitted that persons had been brought into Christ by that ceremony. It is also obvious—a point to which Barth did not address himself—that the same result has followed the nonsacramental practices of the Friends. Lest we be misunderstood, let us insist that a similar result can be observed among believer-baptism groups, such as the Christian Churches (Disciples of Christ): The bearing of these facts upon the definition of baptism, and upon baptismal practice, has not been realistically considered.

A correct interpretation of the phenomena is not that infant christening is baptism or that the nonsacramental custom of the Quakers is baptism, but that whatever God intends to accomplish by baptism he is actually accomplishing without baptism. This interpretation, however, does not force us to conclude that the modern church may properly disregard baptism, or that either the form or its relation to the faith of the individual is irrelevant. It is still true, as Christians have held through the centuries, that God is not limited by his sacraments—fortunately for us and for everyone. It does not follow that the church is not bound to faithful witness in its sacramental observances, whether in the Lord's Supper or in Christian baptism. Unless the church is to become completely nonsacramental in worship—an unlikely event—it must fashion its observances as nearly as possible to its understanding of the meaning of what is done, gratefully acknowledging that the grace of God moves outside all our human inadequacies to touch the hearts of the penitent and bring them into Christ.

Out of my boyhood in a Christian Church, I well recall hearing evangelists who called upon their hearers to be baptized (i.e., immersed) in obedience to the command of Christ. This would bring them "into Christ" or into the Church which is Christ's body. After this, they were told, they could "join any church" they chose. While the evangelist doubtless hoped that such persons would see the light and "join the church" for which he was preaching, the invitation was not pressed in these terms. The fundamental concept behind this preaching and practice was sound. It rested first upon the idea that immersion in water following profession of faith in Christ is certainly baptism and therefore will be universally recognized. A second concept was that baptism does not lead to local but to universal "membership"; it is not primarily baptism into the congregation but into the Church Universal. This concept has been all but lost among Christian Churches; it should be restored—if the idea of "restoration" is not too offensive! To accompany it, the ritual of baptism should be revised, separating the baptismal act from reception into the local group. The latter depends solely upon the choice of the individual; the former depends almost entirely upon the act of God. Distinction between "membership" in the body of Christ and "membership" in a local group would relieve the excessive "localism" that has beset Disciples throughout much of their history.

In the New Testament, those baptized were in a local fellowship, regarded as individually members of one another, and were also "members" of the body of Christ, the Church Universal. In our time, interposed between the fellowship of the local group and the Universal Church, stands the denomination, a sociological fact and a stubborn one. Realistically, baptism as currently practiced by all groups brings persons first of all into a local congregation, which recognizes itself as a unit in the denominational group; and next, baptism confers such a status that when persons move to other communities, they will be readily received into the local congregations there that bear the same theological and sociological marks. Baptism, as thus administered, becomes a part of the witness of the denomination to its reason for existing separately rather than merging with the total Christian community. This fact bears on the phenomenon of vastly mobile populations in America, and on the trend to Christian unity.

Christian Churches, like other Christian groups, have held in general this view of baptism. While baptism of believers by immersion is not all that they have stood for, nor the most important item of their distinctiveness, it is certainly a part. For Christian Churches, two vital questions emerge. Christian unity requires them to consider the practical question of merging with other groups. The most immediate possibility is probably union with the United Church of Christ, a pedobaptist body. Shall the witness, in practice, of believer-baptism by immersion be maintained, or dropped in favor of such a merger? The fact of mobility of population forces to the fore the question of transfers of persons into the fellowship of local Christian Churches. Shall those who became members of churches by infant christening be baptized upon transfer, or accepted on the basis of the rite already administered to them?

The final decision in both these matters will not be pragmatic but theological, not whether a given practice looks superficially "liberal" on the one side or "orthodox" on the other, but whether in the first place the traditional witness of Disciples is to be maintained, and if so, in the second place, by what method in practice it is to be maintained. The consensus of thought among Disciples at present is that the witness is valid and must be kept alive.

One of the unsolved problems obstructing the way to union is whether and how pedobaptist practice and believer-baptist practice can be united in the same group. It is not a question whether the believer-baptist groups—a minority in total number—shall impose their practice upon a merged group. It is rather whether the huge pedobaptist majority will allow effective witness to the believer-baptist position. If this cannot be maintained, then either believer-baptism will be lost in the merger, or we shall face the dolorous prospect of two union groups, one based on pedobaptism, the other on believer-baptism.

The proposed United Church of North India–Pakistan, which hopes to bring together great pedobaptist bodies (such as the Methodist and Anglican) and small believer-baptist groups (such as British Baptists and Disciples of Christ) suggested a solution. The former pedobaptist churches would continue their practice, but no person would be accepted into full membership until after an actual profession of faith and voluntary acceptance of the baptism administered in infancy. The former believer-baptist groups would also continue their practice. But the chief difficulty lay in the fact that no provision was made for one baptized in infancy to seek believer-baptism as an adult, even if his convictions should change. The refusal was based on the unrepeatability of baptism in the life of any person. Such repetition would, it was believed, deny the validity of the baptism of the infant. In effect, this refusal labels the practice of believer-baptism as an oddity, and it nullifies the liberty of the individual.

In the case of the proposal for Christian Churches to enter a union with the United Church of Christ, it is undeniable that the pressure is heavy on Disciples to "soft pedal" differences in baptismal thought and practice, lest the merger be made impossible. As a practical matter, however, unless the witness to believer-baptism is safeguarded, not all congregations will enter the merger, and if the merger were accomplished under such conditions, it would hardly endure. Eventually some sturdy soul would read his New Testament and would insist on taking seriously what it says about baptism.

If Christian Churches should enter any merger, doubtless the right of the local congregation to continue the practice of believer-baptism would be guaranteed. But the mobility of population would intensify the problem of "transfers." Large numbers of those baptized as infants within the United Church of Christ would, as they move to new communities, seek a relation to a believer-baptist congregation in the same group. The local congregation would find it difficult indeed to require baptism of those already acknowledged as members of their denomination, and even more difficult to maintain a witness to believer-baptism without exercising the right to require baptism. The forced closeness of relation within the merged group would only intensify the problem already existing, and as yet unsolved, of accepting "transfers" to membership in Christian Churches.

The combination of three factors in the present scene, together with the lack of a theological position that recognizes them while proposing a solution, constitutes the problem. The factors are first, the determination of Disciples of Christ to maintain their witness to believer-baptism as a matter of conviction; second, the equal conviction that we must move toward true

Christian unity; third, the recognition that there are Christians among other Christian groups who have not received baptism as believers. Christian Churches have drifted into inconsistencies in practice, largely because practice has not been based on clearly held principles. The "liberal," proposing to accept into local membership those who are members of any church, finds himself refusing to administer a baptism (i.e., infant christening) which he recognizes as baptism. If he accepts persons as members and later immerses them, at their choice, he creates classes within the congregation—a higher, the immersed, and a lower, the others. He forces upon other Christian Churches, who may not follow such a practice, the ethical problem either of refusing to honor the action of a sister congregation, or of violating their own convictions. The "conservative" faces inconsistencies also. If the "transfer" is baptized, does this mean he was no Christian? Or is the ceremony simply the imposing of a denominational peculiarity? What is the theological reason for the practice?

The attempt to move into a middle ground by the device of an "ecumenical fellowship roll," as proposed, e.g., by A. T. DeGroot in *The Christian* for January 29, 1961, is not free from practical difficulties and inconsistencies. The proposal would bring those from pedobaptist backgrounds into the *fellowship*—as distinct, presumably, from the *membership*—of the congregation, but would not require baptism. These would be registered as Presbyterians, etc., and upon their removal to another community, they would be commended as Presbyterians, etc. This plan has the merit of making the relation, under these conditions, local rather than denominational, and thus avoiding the difficulty of committing other congregations to such a procedure. DeGroot advances this plan on the basis that Christian Churches will maintain their witness to believer-baptism. In practice, it is very doubtful that many pedobaptists would desire to enter the "fellowship" if it were explained that they are now witnessing to believer-baptism. Silence as to this point, or minimizing it, seems to be the requirement for them to be enrolled. A further question will inevitably arise. If and when the congregation acquires a majority group whose commitment is not to believer-baptism, why should not these move to change the position of the congregation? The fact is, of course, that an individual can witness to the validity of an act—such as believer-baptism—not by words of assent, but only by himself performing the act. Otherwise, his words and his actions contradict one another.

It is not in the province of this paper to attempt a final solution of this problem, but it should be evident to all that it must be solved. In view of the confusion generated by the growth of denominationalism, it is possible that we may never eliminate all the inconsistencies, and may have to settle for some adjustment in practice that moves in the direction we desire to go. It would seem, however, that some explanation of the meaning of believer-baptism, as administered to those previously christened as infants, is an urgent requirement. A first step could well be the attempt to secure a definition of baptism to which all could agree. Proposals in regard to infant baptism such as those in the Church of North India–Pakistan, and those proposed by the Bishop of Oxford, referred to above, offer interesting possibilities for discussion. Meanwhile, Disciples of Christ have the clear obligation to think through their own position, freeing themselves of sectarian pride and exclusiveness as well as maintaining whatever witness in regard to baptism their understanding and their commitment to unity in truth would lay upon them.

As a final word, let us recall ourselves to the purification of our doctrine and practice of baptism by constant reference to the New Testament and what it discloses of the meaning of the rite. It is all too obvious that many ministers and more laymen of all denominations consider baptism as a joking matter. The tasteless jokes bandied about in civic club meetings, and in church gatherings, that refer to the minister of a Christian Church as "the deep-water brother" and the Methodist as "leader of the dry sox," as well as stories that depend for their point on embarrassing incidents in the baptistry, should be disposed of forever. It is to be hoped that Christian baptism may attain the status in popular thought and in ministerial regard which is already accorded to the Lord's Supper. Emphasis upon correct practice alone will not achieve this, but only a return to the deep discernment of the meaning of baptism as a real sacrament, an act in which God asserts again his mighty power for human redemption as portrayed in the symbolic and effectual rite which sets forth the death and resurrection of our Lord in our behalf.

NOTES

1. Alexander Campbell, *The Christian System,* sixth edition (Cincinnati: Standard Pub. Co., n.d.), pp. 148-149.
2. Benjamin Franklin, "Positive Divine Law," in *New Testament Christianity,* Vol. II (Columbus, Indiana: New Testament Christianity Book Fund, 1926), p. 148.
3. D. M. Baillie, *The Theology of the Sacraments* (New York: Charles Scribner's Sons, 1957), p. 42.
4. *Ibid.,* pp. 45-46.
5. *Ibid.,* p. 52.
6. *Ibid.,* p. 55.
7. *Ibid.,* p. 58.
8. William Robinson, "The View of Disciples or Churches of Christ," in *The Ministry and the Sacraments,* Roderic Dunkerly, editor (London: S C M Press, 1937), pp. 261-262.
9. O. Cullmann, *Baptism in the New Testament* (Chicago: Henry Regnery Co., 1950), pp. 9-22.
10. Neville Clark, "The Theology of Baptism," in *Christian Baptism,* A. Gilmore, editor (Philadelphia, The Judson Press, 1959), pp. 313f.
11. *Ibid.,* p. 316.
12. Eric Dean, "Baptism in the Denomination," in *Encounter,* Vol. 21, No. 3, Summer, 1960, p. 284.
13. Emil Brunner, *The Divine-Human Encounter* (Philadelphia: Westminster Press, 1943), pp. 178-179.
14. Arndt & Gingrich, *A Greek-English Lexicon of the New Testament* (Chicago: University of Chicago Press, 1957), p. 502.
15. Robert Dobbie, "The Validity of Sacramentalism," in *Encounter,* Vol. 21, No. 3, Summer, 1960, pp. 296f.
16. Stephen J. England, *The One Baptism* (St. Louis: The Bethany Press, 1960), pp. 90ff.
17. Neville Clark, *op. cit.,* p. 321.

9

Worship and the Lord's Supper

W. B. BLAKEMORE

THE first section of this presentation will be a brief analysis of the twentieth-century renaissance in Christian worship, followed by a second section which identifies the fundamental issue in Christian worship. The concluding section will elaborate some understandings in the light of the fundamental concern.

I

Accompanying the theological renaissance of the twentieth-century there has been a parallel liturgical or worship renaissance in both Roman Catholicism and Protestantism. The Roman and Protestant movements are, by the 1960's influencing each other markedly, but the concern of the first section of this essay is to trace significant trends in the renaissance as it developed in Protestantism, and especially among Disciples of Christ.[1]

Mid-American and Western American worship during the nineteenth century was necessarily frontier worship, simple in structure, crudely housed, and spare in adornment. With the passing of the frontier, two of civilization's amenities entered the churches: carpets and organs. Each became the center of controversy, and together they were the vanguard of a century of "enrichment of worship" which has not yet run its course. The term "enrichment of worship" has come to be despised in theological quarters because much of the enrichment was primarily an aesthetic or emotional, at worst a sentimental, response to new possibilities. Much of the enrichment lacked the check and balance of theological, biblical, and historical consciousness, and, often enough, it resulted in adornments and procedures that found no Christian commendation beyond the few who originally adopted them. Nonetheless, "enrichment" effected many real gains. Doxologies became more doxological (glorious). The *Gloria Patri* was called by that Latin name (even when it would have been considered Romanist to use the *Sursum Corda* by that name). In a brotherhood which was still so strongly Puritan in 1900 that so simple a symbol as the cross was never used, the cross began to appear, and with it a readiness to employ a wider range of symbols. Granted, there remain offensive crosses of light bulbs or neon tubes and Disciples of Christ have cluttered their communion tables with too many brass crosses. But many of them know the wisdom of keeping the communion table clear for communion purposes, as most Catholics and Episcopalians do, and placing crosses, candles, and flowers on retables back against the reredos—or, appropriately enough, on the baptistry sill. Enough Disciples nowadays know the difference between a dossal and a frontal, so that knowledge about these pleasant embellishments of worship can no longer be the basis of liturgical snobbery. Our traffic in orphreys and paraments is becoming subservient to our reasoned understandings of the origins, history, and dynamics of Christian worship.

A second important modification of American Protestant worship in this century came in the early 1920's with the psychological study of religion. The pioneer in the psychology of worship was Von Ogden Vogt, for many years minister of the First Unitarian Church in Chicago, Illinois. His books on *Art and Religion* and *Modern Worship* were comparative studies of the vast literature of Christian worship.[2] Dr. Vogt discerned in all worship a psychological structure. Beginning with a vision of God which inspires adoration or reverence, there follows a mood of confession of sin. That in turn is followed by renewed affirmation which leads on to instruction and dedication.

Virtually every denomination recognized that Dr. Vogt had brought to light the psychological sequence they sought in their own worship, and his analysis provided a critical clarification as they went about the task of creating and conducting worship services. Disciples of Christ participated strongly in this understanding through a series of almost forgotten Christian Life Conferences conducted by W. S. Lockhart during the 1920's.

Dr. Vogt's next-door neighbor in Chicago, E. S. Ames, a most effective leader of Christian worship, found significance in the Hegelian analysis of life sequence in terms of thesis-antithesis-synthesis. Dr. Ames used such triads as aspiration-doubt-redemption, and longing-hope-exaltation for the structure of services of worship.[3]

Another analysis based on comparative studies of worship was devised by Dr. G. Edwin Osborn. His extensive use of it as editor of *Christian Worship: A Service Book*[4] published in 1953, has almost made of it an "authorized" analysis—if Disciples can have an "authorized" worship. Dr. Osborn's key terms are: Reverence, Fellowship, Dedication, and Renewal. These psychological conditions he calls "acts," and builds worship services in terms of a sequence of such actions. It would be more precise to recognize these terms as identifying inward conditions which accompany worship—and to recognize that they do not necessarily follow any one sequence, nor are they present in the same degree in all worshipers during any one service.

A similar type of analysis, more clearly understood by its author, was presented by Dr. Joseph Sittler at the North American Conference on Faith and Order held at Oberlin, Ohio, in 1957.[5] He discovered that in the historic forms of Christian worship there is universally present a fivefold pattern: recollection, thanksgiving, participation, proclamation, expectation. Furthermore, Dr. Sittler asserted that these five elements persist in a sequence which gives "shape" to Christian worship: recollection, engendering thanksgiving, which in turn effects participation, and so forth, with expectation as the prevailing mood of Christian worship.

Such "psychological" analyses have their uses, and more of them can be expected from time to time. Perhaps as useful as any is a widely used analysis of prayer. Since a worship service is in one sense an elaborated common or public prayer, this analysis offers guidance and information for the conduct of worship: Adoration or Praise, Thanksgiving, Confession, Petition, Intercession, Ascription.[6] This sequence is as applicable to most short collects as it is to the great prayers of the synagogue service and to the pastoral prayers of Protestant churches.

In recent years there has been a sharpening of historical consciousness regarding Christian worship. To a number of denominations it has brought a correction of their own understanding of themselves. Disciples of Christ are among those denominations. The majority of Disciples, until recently, have continued to think that in worship they had "restored" the New Testament order of things. This is the way in which Alexander Campbell interpreted what he had done with regard to worship. He persuaded his followers that such a restoration was possible and they had achieved it. Nowadays, however, it is recognized that Disciples of Christ effected no such sharp discontinuity with the backgrounds out of which they arose. A long generation ago it was discovered that Alexander Campbell had been deeply influenced, and more than he understood, by the Haldanean movement in Scotland. Sandemanian influences were also very great upon early Disciples of Christ. Both the Haldanes and Sandeman thought they were in revolt against Calvinism, but a study of history indicates that here again is one of those instances where the sense of difference is greatest between those who are closest together.

When the services of Protestant worship are compared, it becomes obvious that there are three major traditions or "families" of such services. Two of these families, the Lutheran and the Anglican, are fairly close together, and both of them are closer in relationship to the Roman Catholic Mass than is the third family, which is the Calvinist, or Genevan, or Reformed family. Familiarity with the whole scope of Christian worship brings to light a close relationship between typical Disciple worship and the "Directories of Worship" prepared by John Knox at the time of the Scottish Reformation. Indeed, most "free church" worship owes a great deal to Zwingli, Calvin, and Knox as well as to the Bible, and it must be admitted by any honest student of the Bible that the "Reformed tradition" is in its distinctive ways as removed from apostolic practice as the Eastern, Roman, Lutheran, and Anglican traditions are removed in their distinctive ways. When Ulrich Zwingli on Maundy Thursday, 1525, in the city of Zurich, instituted the practice of distributing the communion elements to the worshipers seated in their pews, he felt he was restoring biblical custom. The method of distribution would without doubt have been as novel to the apostles as it was to the Zurichers.

A century ago, the discovery of divergence from apostolic practice would have sent Disciples of Christ scurrying to discover exactly what the apostles did in order to "restore" their practice. Today it is recognized that an absolute identity with apostolic practice is neither possible nor desired. Continuity with that practice there must be, and it is one of the major tasks of Christian thought to establish the character of continuity which must be maintained with the apostolic period.

The most general continuity with aposotlic worship is achieved for the majority of Christians by a practice which ensures that worship can never be understood apart from the Lord's Supper. Oddly enough, the Christian minority which indulges in practice which allows a divorce of the definition of worship and the Lord's Supper is the majority of Protestants. Disciples of Christ find themselves in the strange company of high Anglicans and Mormons, as well as the Catholic and Orthodox, in their insistence upon the weekly observance (at least weekly) of communion. And these can take for their champion, if they wish, none other than John Calvin. He pleaded the cause of the weekly observance of the Supper, and, if one is a Disciple of Christ, it is impossible to understand why all the other churches of the Reformed tradition have ignored his plea and forgone the joy of the frequent impress of God's seal of forgiveness and redemption.[7]

For Disciples of Christ, as for the majority of Christians, participation in the communion is the central and definitive act of worship. To grasp the meaning of the Lord's Supper is to grasp the meaning of worship. The understanding of worship and communion must be sought in the same concepts, and this the second section of this essay will seek to do.

Before these concepts are identified, however, a few words should be said about the structures of Christian worship. Christian worship is built up out of half a dozen major actions, each of which may be treated very simply or given a considerable elaboration. The acts are: Opening Praise, Scripture reading, Prayer, Offering, Communion, and Sermon. In Protestant worship these units of action may appear in virtually any order, though in most denominations communion, when it is held, follows the sermon. Among Disciples of Christ who observe communion weekly it precedes the sermon in two thirds of their churches. The units of action may vary in elaboration. For instance, in one situation the act of scripture reading may be no more than the reading without announcement of one passage of scripture. In another instance, the unit may include a hymn as preparation for the reading, several lessons instead of one, appropriate transitions from reading to reading (one of which may be anthiphonal, i.e, read responsively, or chanted), and responses after each reading. Quite typically in Protestant worship the scripture unit and the prayer unit are close to each other so that the scripture becomes a powerful preparation for the main prayer. Among Disciple churches the sermon unit typically includes an "invitation." In Roman Catholic usage the major units have all become so complex, and with such shreds and patches of historical materials clinging to them, that the presence of these units of major action is obscured, but they are there in the Mass, just as they are present in any Christian service. In Catholicism and Orthodoxy there is a tendency to suppress the sermon, while in most of Protestantism there is a tendency to suppress the communion. There are certain pressures which prevent the suppression of the offertory unit, though that has happened occasionally in history!

In the early days of Disciples of Christ, the key scriptural passage for their consideration of worship was Acts 2:42, "And, they devoted themselves to the apostles' teaching and fellowship, to the breaking of bread and the prayers." The early Disciples understood the term "fellowship" in this verse as the New Testament *koinonia* which, in Paul's usage and elsewhere, involved offerings. This simple text from Acts the early Disciples took as their guide. From time to time, there arose men who tried to prove that teaching, fellowship, communion, and prayer had to follow in some particular order if they were to be valid. But Alexander Campbell always replied that the order was inconsequential, that each congregation could order its worship as it wished, and that any order which contained all these elements was certainly an acceptable Christian worship. The descendants of Campbell have followed his advice, as a perusal of the myriad bulletins of the churches reveals. The variety of ways in which the building blocks of Christian worship may be put together has led Disciple ministers to overestimate the character of freedom in worship, because it has obscured the fact that all of them faithfully build their worship only out of those actions which are very traditionally the building blocks of Christian worship. In this respect, and in some others, Disciple practice is markedly traditional at points where allowable flexibility has led them to speak as if they were actually antitraditionalists. But here, as throughout their communion, there has been a controlling tradition—and that tradition is Jesus Christ. At their best, Disciples of Christ have known that in worship they meet their Lord, and it is that confrontation which illuminates the two major concepts by which they understand what occurs in the Lord's Supper and its accompanying worship.

II

Throughout the history of the church, there have been two terms of crucial significance for the understanding of the Lord's Supper: "remembrance" and "presence." Unfortunately, these two terms, instead of being understood in relation to each other, have come to be set over against each other. Worship theory tends to be divided between those on the one hand who interpret communion in terms of a "memorial" and "symbolic" character and those on the other hand who stress the "presence" and insist that it is "real." Where men should have known better, they have allowed the distinction between the "symbolic" and the "real" to create an invalid divorce between "remembrance" and "presence." Each of these terms will be explored in turn and a statement regarding their positive relationship will be made.

The term "memorial" is, in recent communion theory, most frequently identified with the name of Ulrich Zwingli, and many other Protestants along with Disciples acknowledge their debt to him. What is not recognized is that the increasing rationalism since the sixteenth century has led more and more to the interpretation of "memorial" in symbolic terms. "Remembrance" has come to be understood more and more only as an "act of memory." Less and less the churches have understood the force and power associated with the concepts of "remembrance" and "memorial" in biblical times, and it is only by a return to biblical study that the term "remembrance" in its biblical character can be recovered. The road of escape from "mere memorialism" is a return to the meaning of "memorial" found in both the Old and the New Testaments.

Worship and the Lord's Supper

A. Remembrance

One might suppose that on turning to the Old Testament the terms "memory," "commemorate," "memorial," and "remembrance" would be found most frequently in the historical books. On the contrary, they are found most frequently in the books which deal with ceremony: Numbers, Leviticus, Deuteronomy, and most notably the Psalms. This is a first hint of the high liturgical meanings of these terms in their biblical usage.

On reading the passages in which the relevant terms appear it is discovered that remembrance is as much a characteristic of God as of man. Indeed, the divine activity often seems to initiate in God's remembrance. It is written that, after the flood had lasted one hundred and fifty days, "God remembered Noah and all the beasts and all the cattle that were with him in the ark. And God made a wind blow over the earth, and the waters subsided." (Genesis 8:1) Or again, God sets a rainbow by which "I will remember my covenant . . . and the waters shall never again become a flood and destroy all flesh." (Genesis 9:15) Lot's escape from Sodom and Gomorrah came because God remembered Abraham and the promise he had made. (Genesis 19:29) Psalm 98 calls us to sing a new song unto the Lord because he remembered his loving-kindness and his faithfulness towards the house of Israel. Psalm 103 blesses the Lord

> "For he knows our frame;
> he remembereth that we are dust."

Amongst the causes for gratitude mentioned in Psalm 105 is God's eternal remembrance of his covenant. When God commissioned Jeremiah to speak to Jerusalem, the prologue to the message emphasized God's remembrance of Israel's early faithfulness.

It is equally important that there are some things God does not remember. Both Jeremiah 14:10 and Isaiah 64:5 reflect God's intention to remember not iniquity. Even more surprising is God's assertion in Isaiah 65:17 that in creating a new heaven and a new earth the former things shall not be remembered nor come to mind.

While we must recognize in these references to God's remembrance and forgetting their figurative character, we notice also that in every instance the divine remembrance is immediately related to divine action, either to bring about a result or to inhibit it. It is with God's remembrance as with "his Word." Just as God said, "Let there be light, and there was light," so he "remembered" Abraham and Lot was saved. The two activities were one. As A. G. Herbert states it, "his remembrance is one with his action in judgment and forgiveness."[9] He remembered Rachel and her womb opened for the conception of Joseph.

When we say that God remembers no more our iniquity, we mean that in God's providence the just desserts of our own acts have been swallowed up and frustrated. God's remembrance, then, is not simply a matter of pleasant or unpleasant memories. It is that characteristic of God which gives permanence and surety to his promises and provides for the annihilation of the ultimate consequences of sin.

The idea of God's remembrance is strongly reflected in the worship of the ancient Hebrews. The sacrifices made upon the altar were "memorials." This is particularly true of cereal sacrifices. When such sacrifices were brought to the temple, they were divided into two parts. One part was for the use of the priests who kept the temple. The more important ceremonial portion was burned upon the altar as a "memorial." (Leviticus 2:1-13; 5:12; 6:14) The bread of the sanctuary ordained in Leviticus 24, and for so long a central feature of the Hebrew tradition was a "memorial." It is as if when the temple worship was ordered, God had said, "This do in remembrance of me." And it is impossible to suppose that when Jesus took bread and broke it he was devoid of deep-laid associations with the tradition of memorial bread.

Probably the greatest number of biblical instances of "remember" and its cognate terms is to be found in the petitionary aspect of Hebrew prayer. Frequently the reference is to God's remembrance.

"Be mindful of they mercy O Lord,
Remember not the sins of my youth." (Psalm 25:6-7)

Psalm 89:47 calls on the Lord to remember what the measure of life is. Psalm 132:1 asks God to remember in David's favor all the hardship he endured. The imprecatory Psalm 109 calls on God to not remember an adversary because the adversary remembered not to show kindness. The association between ritual prayer and memory is very close in the words of Psalm 20:3,

"May he remember all your offerings
and regard with favor your burnt sacrifices!"

In some instances the petitions for remembrance are intercessions for others as in the beautiful lines of Psalm 74:

"Remember thy congregation, which thou hast gotten of old,
which thou hast redeemed to be the tribe of thy heritage!
Remember Mount Zion, where thou hast dwelt."

In many another instance the psalmist seeks a blessing not upon "me," but upon "us."

Certainly, the idea of arousing God's memory by the sweet savor of burnt sacrifice is to the modern mind a very primitive expression of religion, but the modern Christian has not seen fit to reject out of hand the habit in prayer, learned from the Psalms, of calling God to remembrance. This is not to presume that in reference to God we understand what the term means, but it does reflect a high respect for the faculties and functions of remembrance as we experience them in our own lives and as they have been long experienced. In this respect the Bible provides many instances, and these Old Testament references indicate a level of experience that demands that we appreciate a religious dimension to memory.

The remembrance of God always has some strong effect upon the spirit. Sometimes remembrance brings a sense of well-being:

My soul is feasted as with marrow and fat
and my mouth praises thee with joyful lips,
when I think of thee upon my bed,
and meditate on thee in the watches of the night.—Psalm 63:5-6

Or, again, there may be not only a sense of well-being, but also some moral strengthening of the soul:

When I think of thy ordinances from of old,
I take comfort O LORD.
I remember thy name in the night, O LORD,
and keep thy law.—Psalm 119:52, 55

When Nehemiah sought to encourage the restorers of Jerusalem in the face of hostile forces he said,

"Do not be afraid of them. Remember the Lord, who is great and terrible, and fight for your brethren, your sons, your daughters, your wives, and your homes." (Nehemiah 4:14)

The prayer recorded as from Jonah in the fish's belly (2:7) records that the Lord brought his life up from the pit.

When my soul fainted within me,
I remembered the LORD;
and my prayer came to thee,
into thy holy temple.

In other circumstances the remembrance of God is discomforting. In the midst of trouble and suffering the remembrance of the Lord and the good days of old only intensify the suffering. In Psalm 77, the remembrance of the Lord is disquieting, yet the sufferer remains confident that he should remember the Lord even though it hurts him to do so:

And I say, "It is my grief;
that the right hand of the Most High has changed."

I will call to mind the deeds of the Lord.

Or the Psalmist pours out his soul (Psalm 42) in the recollection of past experiences at the house of God, and of the throngs and the joy. But just because his soul by these remembrances is cast down, he will remember the Lord and wait upon him.

In connection with the commandments, the Old Testament throughout accords a very high place to memory.

Remember the words which Moses the servant of Jehovah commanded you. (Joshua 1:13)

Remember all the commandments and do them. (Numbers 15:39)

"You shall remember all the ways in which the Lord your God has led you. (Deuteronomy 8:2)

You shall remember that you were a slave in the land of Egypt (Deuteronomy 15:15). Many another Deuteronomic verse commands to remember.

Remember also your Creator in the days of your youth. (Ecclesiastes 12:1)

Seek the Lord and his strength, . . .

Remember the wonderful works that he has done (Psalm 105:4-5)

"You that have escaped from the sword,
go, stand not still!

Remember the Lord from afar,

and let Jerusalem come into your mind." (Jeremiah 51:50)

"Remember the law of my servant Moses." (Malachi 4:4)

In such statements, "remember" is not just a way of speech. It has ceremonial, communal, ethical and religious dimensions. Such remembrances as God calls for are to be full of commitment to him and his ways. It was therefore a terrible thing when the people of God did not remember him. Indeed, in the very early days of the Hebrew community, a shortness of memory too often characterized them. Despite the great leadership of Gideon, "As soon as Gideon died, the people of Israel turned again and played the harlot after the Baals, and made Baal-berith their God. And the people of Israel did not remember God" (Judges 8:33-34).

Through the prophet Isaiah (57:11) God told his people that their failure to remember him was all of a piece with their fear and the growth of deception in their midst. Ezekiel also indicates forgetfulness at the root of Israel's troubles (16:22, 43).

But the great inventory of Israel's failure to remember is found in the forty-eight verses of Psalm 106:

> We, and our fathers have sinned;
> we have committed iniquity, we have done wickedly.
> Our fathers, when they were in Egypt, did not consider thy wonderful works;
> they did not remember the abundance of thy steadfast love,
> but rebelled against the Most High at the Red Sea.

This long Psalm recounts many ways in which Israel forgot God:

> And the waters covered their adversaries; . . .
>
> Then they believed his words.
>
> . . . .
>
> But they soon forgot his works, . . .
> But they had a wanton craving in the wilderness. (11-14)

They forgot their Savior who had done great things in Egypt (21)

Yet the Psalm concludes:

> Nevertheless he regarded their distress,
> when he heard their cry:

He remembered for their sake his covenant,
and relented according to the abundance of his steadfast love. (44-45)

The remembrances and memorials of the Old Testament then must be understood as deeply religious, bound up with the ceremonies and rites of the temple, pregnant with demand for commitment, and strongly efficacious in the lives of men and of nations. These connotations of "remembrance" in its Old Testament usages we can hardly ignore as we approach the New Testament.

In the Letter of Jude, the author writes to put his readers in remembrance of the way God dealt with Israel, and to call them to remember the words of the apostles. In 2 Peter 1:12-13 the moralizing power of remembrance is recalled as the author declares his right as long as he lives to stir up his reader by putting him in remembrance. Similarly in 2 Timothy 1:3-6, by recalling to Timothy the faith that was in him, the author hopes to "rekindle the gift of God that is within you through the laying on of my hands." In another instance, we read that Paul sent Timothy to the Corinthians "to remind you of my ways" (1 Corinthians 4:17), and Paul hopes that they remember him in all ways and hold fast to the tradition. (1 Corinthians 11:2)

The idea of God's remembrance appears again in the New Testament. An angel of God tells Cornelius, "Your prayer has been heard and your alms have been remembered before God." (Acts 10:31) Paul tells the Corinthians (2 Corinthians 7:15) that God's affection is the more abundant toward them while he remembers their obedience: "His heart goes out all the more to you, as he recalls how you all obeyed him, and with what reverence and trembling you received him."[10]

When we understand the significance of divine memory, we appreciate anew a deeply prayerful quality in the petition of the thief on the cross: "Remember me when you come into your kingly power." (Luke 23:42)

Some of the New Testament instances of religious remembrance are in passages which probably contain material that was used liturgically in the early church. In the *Magnificat* (Luke 1:54) Mary declares that God "has helped his servant Israel, in remembrance of his mercy," and in the *Benedictus* (Luke 1:72) Zechariah praises the salvation wrought by God, "to perform the mercy promised to our fathers, and to remember his holy covenant." The Letter to the Hebrews twice quotes the promise of God through Jeremiah that in a new covenant "I will remember their sins no more." (Hebrews 8:12; 10:17)

The remaining instances of the New Testament occurrences of "remembrance" which are of interest to us are, of course, those related to the institution of the Lord's Supper, and particularly the two instances in which the words, "Do this in remembrance of me" occur: Paul's account in 1 Corinthians 11, and the account in Luke 22.

The fact that the words of remembrance do not occur in the accounts of the Last Supper given in Mark and Matthew raises some questions regarding their authenticity on the lips of Jesus. Whether or not Jesus actually said those exact words, the view of the communion as "remembrance" in the biblical sense of the term was present at a very early date, so early that we cannot doubt its institution by Jesus himself, nor that he was in some way instituting ritual remembrance of himself.

In the early Christian church, communion came to stand where memorial sacrifice had stood in the Jewish temple. But the early Christians did not, with respect to communion, adopt the term "memorial" *(mnemsynon),* but the term "remembrance" *(anamnesis).* "Memorial" would have implied that the worshiper made a sacrifice, whereas the early Christian understood that it was God who had made the sacrifice. The work of communion was not to stimulate God's remembrance by offering him a memorial. The work of communion was to awaken in the worshiper the remembrance of the Christ.

The Gospel of John demonstrates the relationship between the Last Supper and remembrance. Though it does not describe the Supper itself, the Gospel records the discourse in which Jesus took farewell. One stage of the farewell ends with these words, "These things I have spoken to you, while I am still with you. But the Counselor, the Holy Spirit, whom the Father will send in my name, he will teach you all things, and bring to your remembrance all that I said to you." (John 14:25-26) However else we understand this passage, we recognize that as Jesus' life drew to its close he was concerned to stress the importance of remembrance about him for his followers. Just as the Exodus should never have been forgotten as God's mighty act, so he should never be forgotten as God's Son. The Gospel of John therefore confirms the emphasis on remembrance recorded by Paul and Luke. The relationship of the Holy Spirit brings into view also the matter of "presence," and illuminates these words from Professor John Knox of Union Theological Seminary:

> . . . the early Christian community was a sharing in a common memory and a common Spirit. The church's self-consciousness might be analyzed into a consciousness of the Spirit and the remembering of an event. . . . It is true that Christ was present in the early church as the Spirit; that is, he was known as the living personal center of the church's life. But he was also remembered as a man and Master. The two facts—he was known still and he was remembered—constitute together the miracle of the Resurrection; and neither was more important than the other. . . . Whatever may be true of Christianity as it might have been, the memory of Jesus was an absolutely essential constitutive element in Christianity as it actually came to be.[11]

B. THE PRESENCE

In his paper for the Panel of Scholars on "The Place of Jesus Christ in the Lord's Supper," James Clague writes, "So long as bread and wine have somehow to change into something other, either in nature or in function, the presence of Jesus Christ is linked with subpersonal and magical phenomena."[12] In speaking thus, Professor Clague knows that the problem for the Protestant has always been that of preserving his faith that Jesus Christ is present at the Lord's Supper, and at the same time avoiding subpersonal and magical ways of explaining the fact. By the Middle Ages the dominant view in Eastern Orthodoxy and the dogma of Western Catholicism were that during the Eucharist or Mass the bread and wine were transubstantiated into the body and blood of Jesus Christ. East and West differed in their view regarding the moment in the service when the change occurred; the East associated the change with the words, "This do in remembrance of me," while the West associated the change with the words, "This is my body." For the medieval Christian this "substantial" presence of the body and blood of Jesus Christ was accepted as the method and warranty of his presence.

From the Protestant point of view, the most objectionable aspect of the medieval theory is not the "magical" taint in ideas of change of substance; it is the failure of this theory to account for the way in which the Christian knows his Lord to be present at the Lord's table. Medieval theory offers the presence of the real flesh and real blood of the Lord and declares this to warrant his "real" presence. But the presence of flesh and blood is not personal presence; as Professor Clague understands, that for which medieval theory can account is only subpersonal. What the Christian has always known over and above this inadequate medieval theory is that in Christian worship Christ the Lord is a living Presence, a living and personal Presence.

It must be admitted that frequently Protestants have allowed the sense of the presence of the Lord at his worship to become dull or obscure, and, indeed, the possibility of that decay was already sensed at the time of the Reformation. Both Luther and Zwingli were discontent with Roman dogma. Each wanted doctrine that would do greater justice to the "mystery." And it is only when we properly identify the location of the "mystery" in relation to communion that the shortcomings of the medieval theory become most clear.

The term "mystery" is, by the way, the New Testament term which points to the general character of baptism and the Lord's Supper. The New Testament knows neither the word "sacrament," nor the word "ordinance." It does know the word "mystery," and increasingly among Disciples of Christ this term is preferred to the term "sacrament" against which our forefathers rebelled, and is preferred to our forefather's term "ordinance" which has proved little improvement over the word "sacrament." In New Testament usage the term "mystery" applies to the whole event of the Supper.[13] Medieval doctrine robs the whole event of its character as mystery by appropriating the term to the "changed substance" on the altar. The magnificent mystery of the living Presence of the Lord Jesus Christ is perverted into a preoccupation with a single moment in the service in which a mysterious change takes place.

Struggling to find their way free from dependence upon "substance" theory, the early Reformers found themselves at an impasse when they sought to arrive at unity of doctrine regarding communion. At a Colloquy in Marburg, Germany, 1529, Luther and Zwingli tried to resolve their differences. The concerns of each man are easily identified. Zwingli's concern was to rid the interpretation of Christian worship of any magical connotations. The Zwinglian concern was not, however, with the doctrines of transubstantiation or consubstantiation. These theories attempted to explain how the bread and wine became the body and blood of Christ. But the Zwinglians no longer believed that the bread and wine were the body and blood. They were striving for a way of understanding how, by the Lord's Supper, they met their Lord. They accepted the bread and wine as figures or emblems of Christ's body and blood.

It is at this point that Luther's concern can be identified. He realized that there is always the danger of "spiritualizing" the Christ, of repeating the docetic mistake. If the bread and wine are taken symbolically, perhaps men will next take "the Body of Christ" symbolically, and next they will take "the Living Lord" symbolically. Luther sensed that in the assertion that Christ's body and blood are present on the altar, there was an anchor point for those truths conveyed by the whole stream of incarnational theory in Christianity. In his insistence upon a literal understanding of "This is my body," Luther was seeking to keep Christianity from drifting off into spiritism. Though with Zwingli he would say that the flesh profiteth nothing, Luther knew that the redemptive work of Christ had not been accomplished apart from flesh.

What must be made clear is that it is neither anything used in the communion service, nor anything there done that makes Jesus Christ present.[14] Jesus Christ the Lord is already the context within which the whole service of communion is performed. What bread and wine affect is the awakening of the worshiper's remembrance of the historic event through which God reconciled the world to himself. This indeed means that the living Christ cannot be thought of docetically because he is remembered in terms of his incarnation and his bodily life upon earth. And this is also "remembrance" in the full biblical sense.

The Eucharist is a sacrifice in so far as it is the *anamnesis* of Christ's own sacrifice. To translate this term as "remembrance," with the inevitable implication that this is the mental recollection of what is absent, is to do less than justice to the biblical categories of thought. "Remembrance" to the Hebrews involves the presence of past events through their effects; hence "recalling" is a preferrable term. But this "recalling" should involve not only the death on the Cross but the whole saving work of Christ and therefore his Resurrection and Ascension, and, since the liturgical act belongs to the time of the Church, to the time between the two Advents, it should also look to the coming again of Christ in glory.[15]

C. The Crucial Issue

The crucial issue is not yet identified. The crucial issue lies in the misunderstanding of the "mystery" by any notion that by any communion act or emblem Christ becomes present with us. The "mystery" is that we enter into the presence of the Lord and feast with him. The mystery is horribly perverted by any notion that by "remembrance" *(anamnesis)* or by the words *Hoc est enim corpus meum (episclesis)* Christ becomes really present. The role of remembrance is not that it brings the Lord into our presence, but that remembrance opens our eyes to him into whose presence we have already been brought by faith. Remembrance completes in us the work begun by faith.

III

Even so, we must not misunderstand the work of faith as a work that makes Christ present. All Christian theology must begin with the recognition of the omnipresence of God. Faith is not needed to make the Lord present; faith is our recognition of his presence. By faith we know that when two or three are gathered in his name, there is he in our midst. Furthermore, by faith we know where we are when we confront the Lord. We are in his presence and to be in his presence is to be in heaven.

Christian worship has always been full of intimations, nay of assertions, that worship—all worship—takes place in heaven.

> But the Lord is in his holy temple;
> let all the earth keep silence before him.
> —Habbakuk 2:20.

"Surely the Lord is in this place; . . . This is none other than the house of God, and this is the gate of heaven."
—Genesis 28:16-17.

> Make a joyful noise to the Lord, . . .
> Come into his presence with singing!
>
> . . . .
>
> Enter his gates with thanksgiving,
> and his courts with praise!—Psalm 100:1, 2, 4.

> The Lord has chastened me sorely,
> but he has not given me over to death.

Open to me the gates of righteousness,
that I may enter them
and give thanks to the LORD.
This is the gate of the LORD:
the righteous shall enter through it.—Psalm 118:18-20.

Let us then with confidence draw near to the throne of grace—
Hebrews 4:16.

It is indeed very necessary for twentieth-century man to straighten out his thoughts regarding paradise, hell, and last things. What will be written in the following sentences may to some seem too paradisaical, but it is the position to which the contemplation of space and time as we know them in the twentieth century has forced me. There was a time when heaven could be conceived in terms of a there and then—a yonder "there" and a future "then." But modern man no longer lives in a Ptolemaic space nor in an Ussherite time. Space is infinite and time eternal. What an earlier age meant to identify by such terms as heaven and hell can no longer be thought of in "then and there" terms.

Earlier in this century, when men began to realize this circumstance, they began to think of heaven in earthly terms. There are upon earth hellish experiences and heavenly ones, and men began to say that these here-and-now experiences are what we mean by heaven and hell. Such a way of speech is correct in so far as it begins to recognize that the only location within which anything may have its existence is in the ever-present here and the eternal now. But their way of speech was wrong when they defined heaven in earthly terms. It was wrong when they changed the last line of an old table grace:

Be present at our table Lord;
Be here and everywhere adored.
These mercies bless and grant that we,
May feast in paradise with thee.

to read

May feast in fellowship with thee.

To make such a change is really to give up the idea of paradise and to be content with earthly things. It is to indulge in that reductionism which binds us to earth, and ultimately reduces Jesus Christ from his divine stature to an earthly stature, as if he has his greatness because he exemplifies all that is best on earth instead of recognizing his power to redeem all that is worst and fallen on earth and reunite it with its Maker. What twentieth-century man has to realize is that within this same here and now in which he has his earthly existence, there is a heavenly existence and he may stand within its gates. The Lord's Supper and its accompanying worship on a Sunday morning is not a "foretaste" of things to come. It is the very feast of those who at heaven's gate receive the forgiveness of God.

It is not this or that particular thing in the Lord's Supper that makes Christ to be present. By participation in the Lord's Supper the worshiper is present with his Lord at whose table he sits —and by faith the worshiper knows it, which without faith he would not have known.

Christians in all ages have sensed that at worship by faith they stand in the courts of the Lord. Eastern Orthodoxy has, perhaps, preserved this sensitivity more adequately than any other part of the church, but there is every reason why twentieth-century man with his new understandings of the church should easily recognize what the oldest parts of the church have always known. "Heaven upon earth" is one of the favored Greek definitions of the Church.[16] To look into an icon is to peer into heaven.[17]

It is now that the moral meaning of communion can be understood. Communion does not celebrate what would be an erroneous idea, namely, that by doing good works we may become fit for heaven, that by participating in the sacrificial merits of Christ we may gain admission to grace. On the contrary, communion is that actual participation in heavenly and divine things that by its bestowal of grace makes us a little more fit for earth.

NOTES

1. The development of the liturgical renaissance in Roman Catholicism is presented in E. B. Koenker, *The Liturgical Renaissance in the Roman Catholic Church* (Chicago: University of Chicago Press, 1954).

2. Von Ogden Vogt, *Art and Religion* (Boston: Beacon Press, 1960). —, *Modern Worship* (New Haven: Yale University Press, 1927).

3. *The Calendar,* which is the worship bulletin of University Church of Disciples of Christ, Chicago, Illinois, is preserved in the archives of that church. Examples of the type of services cited can be found during the issues for the late 1930's.

4. The greatest value of this service book is its extensive use of biblical materials for worship purposes.

5. Joseph Sittler, "The Shape of the Church's Response in Worship," in *The Nature of the Unity We Seek.* Official Report of the North American Conference on Faith and Order, Oberlin, Ohio, 1957 (St. Louis: The Bethany Press, 1958), pp. 103-105.

6. The analysis has been widely used, but I have not found its original. I first came upon it, and immediately memorized it, over thirty years ago and before entering seminary, while browsing in the Public Library of St. Louis, Missouri. Further research might lead to the origins of this useful analysis.

7. W. B. Blakemore, "John Calvin and the Disciples of Christ," *The Christian Evangelist-Front Rank,* Vol. 97, No. 36, Sept. 6, 1959, pp. 1120ff.

8. Any number of actions which were candidates for liturgical tradition, even in apostolic times, have been rejected: e.g., foot washing, the kiss of peace, becoming drunk on communion wine, speaking in tongues, etc.

9. A. G. Herbert, "Memory" in Allan Richardson, *Theological Wordbook of the Bible* (London: SCM Press, 1950), pp. 142-143.

10. From *The Bible, an American Translation,* by Smith and Goodspeed. Used by permission of the University of Chicago Press.

11. John Knox, *The Early Church and the Coming Great Church* (New York: Abingdon Press, 1955), pp. 52f.

12. James G. Clague, "The Place of Jesus Christ in the Lord's Supper," in R. G. Wilburn (ed.), *The Reconstruction of Theology* (Vol. II of W. B. Blakemore, ed., *The Renewal of Church*) (St. Louis: The Bethany Press, 1963), p. 297.

13. Calvin emphasized the whole event rather than any particular part. See footnote 7 above.

14. There is a tendency among some Disciples (notably in the British Churches of Christ) to stress the "actions" in communion—the breaking of bread, the pouring out of wine, etc. Occasionally this point of view verges on giving to these actions the functions which medieval theory assigned to the emblems. Care regarding the conduct of the communion service has its place, but safeguard against overly precious attitudes is always in order.

15. G. Cope, J. G. Davies, and D. A. Taylor, *An Experimental Liturgy* (Richmond: John Knox Press, 1958), p. 21.

16. G. P. Fedetov, *The Russian Religious Mind* (New York: Harper and Bros., 1946, HTB 1960), p. 51. The special envoys of Prince Vladimir of Russia, c. A.D. 1100, said of worship in Santa Sophia, "We knew not whether we were in heaven or on earth."

17. See Ernst Benz, *The Eastern Orthodox Church* (New York: Doubleday and Co., 1963). Chapter I, "The Orthodox Icon" passim.

PART THREE

THE WORK OF THE CHURCH

10

A Theology of Evangelism

HUNTER BECKELHYMER

THE word "evangelism" comes from the Greek word *euangelion,* translated into English as either evangel or gospel. It means glad tidings, or good news. By Christian usage it refers to the good news of man's salvation through Jesus Christ. By popular extension and usage evangelism has come to mean any activity by which men are persuaded to accept that salvation, and by still more popular usage, any activity by which names are added to the church rolls. Probably the best known and most widely accepted definition of evangelism is that of the late William Temple: "Evangelism is so to present Chirst Jesus in the power of the Holy Spirit that men shall come to put their trust in God through Him, to accept Him as their Saviour, and serve Him as their King in the fellowship of His Church." Few Christians would make serious objection to that.

Philosophical Premises

Before one can seriously undertake the enterprise of evangelism, however, he must of necessity make certain assumptions about what he is doing—the chief of them being that he is dealing in realities. Good news is good news only if it is true. And if it is true, it is inherently of importance to all men. Alexander Campbell probably overstated his case when he said that "faith never can be more than the receiving of testimony as true." But he was surely right in insisting that faith begins with the "belief of testimony," or confidence in "testimony as true."[1] And thus, as Julian Hartt stated the same promise, "the great business of the church is to show forth the nature of the realm of which we are all participants, so that the law and the Lord thereof may be rightly obeyed."[2]

Lest it be thought that we are laboring the obvious, let us take note of the fact that the above stated position is by no means universally accepted even among Christians. We live in a day and culture that is shot through with relativism, both thoughtful and thoughtless. The writer was recently discussing this issue with a group of high school youngsters from his church, all from Christian families. All of them considered themselves Christian, and believed in the major tenets of their faith. They were, however, unwilling to go further than to say that the Christian faith was true *for them,* and were quite willing to concede that other faiths might be equally true for other adherents brought up differently. There was little sense among them of any objective order of reality with which it is incumbent upon all men to come to terms, or of the transcendent God who comes to "judge the world with righteousness, and the peoples with his truth" (Psalm 96:13). Other observers have documented a similar relativism all through American life, including the churches. The religious boom in this country is more of an amiable approval of religion in general, and a faith in faith, than it is a great searching for verities, and a faith in God through Jesus Christ.

We plead not for a return to premature and sectarian claims, based upon biblical literalism, that the truth is wholly and surely known. We plead, rather, for a sober recognition that its approximation to truth is the most important thing about a religious faith, and a belief in the possibility of discerning truth in ultimate matters as well as in immediate ones. "There cannot be any important sense in which God is *for me* unless there is some real and objective sense in which *God is,* irrespective of my belief or my lack of belief," writes Elton Trueblood.[3]

> All that is needed is the notion that the truth about God, like the truth about Julius Caesar, has in it a once-for-all quality, though finite men may be slow in understanding it. What we need to recognize is the ancient distinction between truth and opinion. . . . The truth *is,* even though it may be beyond us. . . . Though the truth is something which we cannot grasp with perfection, much of our glory lies in the fact that we can make approximations to it. To see through a glass darkly is better than not to see at all.[4]

Furthermore, all truth is one. All truth is God's truth. All truth is the self-expression of God. Some of truth is best discovered by some methods and other parts of truth are best discerned by other methods. The language by which truth is expressed in tangible and immediate things is different from the language by which truth is expressed in intangible and ultimate things. But there is no contradiction or conflict between portions of truth. Thus the Christian should welcome truth from whatever source, and should make no efforts to insulate or isolate his religious faith from any of the knowledge of mankind. He should never exhibit less than exacting standards of honesty in dealing with the evidences for or against his own most cherished beliefs. Nor should he begrudge to any non-Christian faith or secular faith whatever measure of truth it discerns. By its very nature, however, Christian faith deals with ultimate matters; it is a perspective upon, and interpretation of, the whole of reality. It sees in Jesus Christ the disclosure of God as he is and the real meaning of our human existence. It therefore holds that any body of truth without Jesus Christ is incomplete and that any perspective on the whole of life which is manifestly contrary to what he discloses is wrong. Ernest E. Best put it this way:

> The Christian faith has historically proclaimed a body of truth which rests upon special revelation. This particular truth, if really true, must necessarily be universally true. While it may correct and supersede other truths in the same category, excluding them from

the same degree of validity, by the same token it may establish the degree of validity those insights into truth do possess.[5]

Here, I believe, is firm ground for fruitful contact between Christian and non-Christian, between church and community, between Christian missionary and rival faiths. Here is ground for evangelism that is both humble and urgent, flexible and firm. The claims of Christian faith upon men are the claims of truth. No one has stated it better than Daniel Day Williams when he wrote:

> It is, literally, an infinite task to show that a theological perspective can solve the knotty problems of nature and law, ethics and politics, life and death, and bring them all within an interpretation which possesses an intelligible unity. Yet however difficult this task, and however far from realization it must be in our time and perhaps in every time, to try to fulfill this demand is the obligation which Christian thought must accept for itself. Christian truth is not a separate truth within the whole meaning of life. Christian teaching cannot be put into an intellectual hot house and there kept safe from the chilling blasts which blow in our human journey. If belief in the creative and the redemptive God makes sense at all, it must enable us to see more deeply and clearly into the whole of our experience, and to find what in the end of the day all honest thought must find there.[6]

Thus we preach the gospel not to contain Communism, not to combat juvenile delinquency, not to swell our church statistics nor yet to quiet peptic ulcers. We preach it because we believe it to be history's most important revelation upon life's most important matters. We preach it in order that stumbling and sinning men may rightly come to terms with the universe in which they live, and with the God who made it.

The Faith We Proclaim

In Christian evangelism we tell the world of what Julian Hartt has called "goings on of an utterly decisive character." What those "goings on" are has been very ably stated by G. E. Phillips, former professor of missions at the Selly Oak Colleges in England.

> Within the history of the world there is a certain stream of events, recorded in the story of the Jews, culminating in the life, death and resurrection of Jesus and the gift of His Spirit, thereafter flowing in ever larger volume within human history, which stream of events can only be understood in its totality as the Act of God communicating Himself to mankind, in a mode which supplements and corrects the communications which come through nature, conscience, or the sense of the infinite. So to tell of that series of events as to awaken faith that here is the final good news about God is to evangelize. At the heart of the telling is the setting forth of Jesus, Who is recognized by faith as the Incarnation of God, and Whose significance is seen most clearly in His death and resurrection.
>
> Evangelism is thus the communication of something objective, and is distinct from general uplift, service of humanity, the attempt to make a better world, or even the advocacy of the good life, though all these things may play a subordinate part in connection with it.
>
> The initiative having been taken by God, we simply report what He has done. No credit for it belongs to us; no sense of superiority is implied in the fact of our making this proclamation. We recognize that some adherents of other religions (or no professed religion at all) may be wiser and better than ourselves, but if they have not heard this news, we have something to pass on which they deeply need.[7]

Alexander Campbell had narrowed the essence of the Christian message still further when he wrote, that "THE BELIEF OF ONE FACT, *and that upon the best evidence in the world, is all that is requisite, as far as faith goes, to salvation. . . .* The one fact is expressed in a single proposition—*that Jesus the Nazarene is the Messiah.*"[8]

It is at this point that someone, perhaps most Christians, will be prepared to say that "Christian faith is not propositional." That is so. Perhaps it is better said that Christian faith is not *merely* propositional. Propositions there are, and Christian faith would be too amorphous to live without them. But in addition to them—or behind them all—is the tremendous personal appeal of Jesus himself, who is able to evoke love and loyalty and obedience in men today as he did in those who knew him in the flesh. He is able to draw men to himself. Theology grows out of this personal relationship which still comes into being between Christ and the believer today. Thus Christian theology is most vital when it is most fluid, bubbling from overflowing hearts and teeming brains, as it once did onto the pages of the New Testament. It is most unwise to freeze theology, and the Disciple tradition seems to me to be valid when it keeps propositional confession of faith to a single statement—not thereby to limit or impoverish it, but to keep the rest of it fluid and vital. Disciples preachers and laymen have yielded to none in devotional appreciation and love of the living Christ. Even Campbell himself asserted,

> the belief of what Christ says of himself terminates in trust or confidence in him: and as the Christian religion is a personal thing, both as respects *subject* and *object,* that faith in Christ which is essential to salvation is not the belief of any doctrine, testimony, or truth, abstractly, but belief *in* Christ; trust or confidence in him as a person, not a thing.[9]

Whether the proposition or the relationship comes first, both must be there. Nearly everyone will testify of the goodness and purity of Jesus, of his tenderness and love, of his mercy and forgiveness. What we confess in the proposition that Jesus is the Christ, the Son of the living God, is that God is therefore good and merciful, and that in Jesus' forgiveness of his crucifiers God's forgiveness is extended to you and me. In proclaiming Jesus to be divine we say more about divinity than we say about Jesus. It is this identification of the eternal God, maker of heaven and earth, with the compassionate, loving, suffering Christ that is Christianity's boldest and most daring assertion. Other doctrine is supportive or derivative. This much is propositional and essential: "God was in Christ reconciling the world unto himself."

The Nature of Conversion

John Bennett has said that a person's perspective on life is determined by which facts have hit him the hardest. We reason from the facts that we consider most significant, but which facts those are is determined largely by our experiences in life. It is here that the church has its responsibility, both to the community of men around it and to its own members. We strive by all honorable means to subject men to the impact of God in Christ. We "tithe, sing, and testify" to the end that men may become aware of the transcendent importance of what occurred in the life, death, and resurrection of Jesus of Nazareth, depending upon God to wing our words and to bring from them a harvest pleasing to him. This must be something of what Archbishop Temple meant when he spoke of presenting Christ Jesus in the power of the Holy Spirit.

All evangelism proceeds on the assumption that men are capable of responding to the love of God as seen in Christ Jesus when it is presented to them. The words "whoever," "if any man," and "everyone who" were frequently upon the lips of the Master. And they were followed by active, volitional verbs—"believes," "acknowledges," "humbles himself," "loses his life for my sake," "would come after me," and so on. He himself came "to seek and to save the lost" (Luke 19:10), and this because "it is not the will of my Father who is in heaven that one of these little ones should perish" (Matthew 18:14). It was as a speculative, and retrospective, theologian that Paul spun his tortuous arguments about predestination; as an evangelist he worked on the assumption that any man who heard his voice could respond positively to the gospel, and he became "all things to all men, that by all means [he] might save some" (1 Corinthians 9:22). Alexander Campbell handled very deftly the speculative issue about the part that God himself played in selecting those to be saved, by refusing to separate the work of the Holy Spirit from the working of the word to which all who hear may respond:

"Whatever the word does, the Spirit does; and whatever the Spirit does in the work of converting men, the word does."[10]

Who are the lost? And in what does their lostness consist? Essentially, they are men separated from, or alientated against the God of their salvation. The Bible, from the story of Adam through the prophets, Jesus, and Paul, pictures man's lost condition as being rebellion against God, characterized by idolatry of various kinds—putting something else in the place in their lives that belongs to God alone, or having other Gods before him. Worshiping other gods may be no more than deifying oneself, or striving to realize oneself without any reference to God.

Following Emile Cailliet, Robert Versteeg, in his book *The Gracious Calling of the Lord,* has identified the most prevalent idolatries as the worship of Mammon, Moloch, and Baal. Versteeg finds these three idolatries represented in the excuses given to the gracious host in Jesus' parable of the banquet (Luke 14:16ff.). "I have bought a field and must go out and see it," is the refusal of one who finds the meaning of life in possessions, and who lives for acquiring. This is the worship of Mammon. The man who replied, "I have bought five yoke of oxen, and I go to examine them," stands for the many worshipers of Moloch, the god of nationalism. "Moloch's cult possibly originated as a religion of nationalism, and we see it recrudescent in all nationalistic power lust. 'I have made a new bomb, and I go to test it.' " The man who gave his marriage as the reason for his refusal could well represent the devotees of Baal, the nature god, the fertility god. He is more than a god of sex, however.

> In its more sophisticated forms, Baalism embraces the most of scientism and materialism, systems which deceptively appear to demand of the adherent neither faith nor sacrifice and in which the how and why of life are determined and explained by reference to 'nature.'[11]

Luke records in chapter 15 three parables of Jesus in which the nature of lostness is represented in three more ways. The lost lamb is away from the shepherd and the fold, and thus is in grave peril. The lost coin is lost to its owner's purposes for it, and hiding in uselessness. The lost son, who belongs to the self-realization school of idolatory, has to learn for himself the hard way that there is no place like his Father's home, and no relationship comparable to that of a son in the family.

To man in his lostness, the Christian responsibility is to let the Master's words again be heard, as they were heard by so many in his lifetime and since: "Come, follow me."

> This—"follow me"—Mr. Versteeg continues, is the classic New Testament formula and very probably a verbatim report of the Master's own words, which must have been unforgetable to those to whom they were addressed. And this—"follow me"—spells out the nature of the relationship with God in Christ to which man is invited. These words tell us everything that is required of us; and these words require of us everything.[12]

First and foremost they require of us a decision. There is no possible way of entering the Christian life without making a decision to do so, or perhaps a series of decisions. One cannot slip into it or drift into it, however much pious habits and upbringing may have combined to make the decision easier and more natural. "It will be impossible for millions to respond to the Christian invitation until they have first rid themselves of the illusion that they already have."[13] We can prepare the way for the decision thoroughly, gradually, and gracefully, but evangelism has not occurred until the appeal has been made to the human will, and opportunity given for decision for or against discipleship. To the invitation, "Follow me," there can at any one time be only the answer of yes or no, although the full range of discipleship may not then be comprehended, and although the call may be repeated. "We let faith happen, or we prevent it from happening, according to a deep willingness or unwillingness within us," writes Sam Shoemaker, who then continues:

> The longer I think about conversion the more convinced I am that it consists of decision plus growth. We do not convert ourselves: the Grace of God is the primary factor. But we can hold out on the

> Grace of God, or we can welcome Him in. Our willingness to surrender as much of ourselves as we can to as much of Christ as we understand may be our first step in the experiment of faith. This beginning of self-surrender is our part in our own conversion, and helps to bring us into the stream.[14]

Shoemaker means the stream of the Holy Spirit, but this also seems the appropriate time for entry into the stream of baptism.

Alexander Campbell said that the entire change effected in man by the whole Christian system could be named as four things: a change of views (or being enlightened), a change of affections (being reconciled to God), a change of life (repentance unto life), and a change of state (being born again—passing from death to life).[15] It might be noted here that only one of these changes is likely to be an abrupt, either-or matter. And that is a change in state. This is the matter which, unfortunately, if naturally, has received the most attention from evangelists and laymen alike—whether or not one is saved or damned, a matter which in the last analysis is known only by the Lord himself. It is around this matter that legalistic requirements are debated, and sectarian differences magnified. Let us note that the other three changes not only can be, but in most instances inevitably are, gradual changes. They are processes. Thus, as D. T. Niles pointed out in his Beecher Lectures, the proper question for Christians to ask themselves and each other and the world, is not "Are you saved?" but rather "Are you *being* saved?" The most important thing we can do for others is to help them get the process of salvation under way, and to help it continue. To this matter we now turn.

The Fact of Growth

Our day and age does not lack for testimony from writers in many fields of learning that men are lost, confused, bewildered, and damned. The rediscovery of the fact of sin by the literary world is one of the signs of our times. Probably never before has the pervasiveness of evil in all human motives and enterprises, particularly the genteel ones, been so thoroughly explored, so elaborately documented, and so exquisitely savored, by both Christian and non-Christian writers. Modern man seems rather to enjoy wallowing in his sense of guilt.

Nor do we lack in our day for ponderous utterance of theological orthodoxies. There seems to be the feeling among some modern Christian writers that a sort of liturgical recital of certain New Testament phrases will somehow exorcise the sin which has so metastasized throughout the human system. For instance, this from an eminent professor (who is helpful at other points): "Salvation comes to my house when I hear the Lord saying: 'Behold, I have overcome the world.' "

The real question is, however, whether some victory over sin and evil actually occurs in human lives that have undertaken to respond to Jesus' gracious invitation, "Follow me." "Either some break with sin in fact as well as in principle is possible or else the whole of Christian experience is a delusion," writes Daniel Williams. "That break takes place in human experience, in history, in the process of life."[16] The nature of that victory over sin and evil is "growth in grace"—the possibility, through God's help and in the fellowship of the church, of the transformation of character and of maturing in Christian living. These changes could be listed and documented in several ways. Those of Alexander Campbell, which we have already mentioned, will serve as well as any.

One transformation that ought to, can, and often does, occur in men who have decided to embark upon the Christian way is a change of views, a change in opinions, a new interpretation of the meaning of life. Perhaps what is really new is a new viewpoint, a new perspective upon the whole of life. Jesus has been called, by himself or his first followers, "the light of the world." He illuminates the whole scene before us; he lightens corners of existence otherwise dark. He enables us, in a limited way of course, to see ourselves, our neighbors, and our world as they appear to the eyes of God—and hence as they really are. Christian faith involves a *Weltanschauung.* Now such transformation of a man's views can take place gradually. It begins when we surrender as much of ourselves as we can to as much of Christ as we understand, which very act of commitment shifts our viewpoint. By commitment we are carried deeper into the understanding of life. " 'My teaching is not mine,' " said Jesus, " 'but his who sent me; if any man's *will* is to do his will, he shall *know* whether the teaching is from God or whether I am speaking on my own authority' " (John 7:16-17).

A second change that occurs is a change of affections—being reconciled toward God, beginning to love him rather than regarding him with hostility, fear, or indifference. The first and great commandment is that we love God with all our heart, soul, mind, and strength. This we begin to do when God becomes real to us in Christ—or I might say, *as* Christ. "We love, because he first loved us" (1 John 4:19). We have all seen men develop a new devotion in the service of God, and a new degree of participation in the workings of God on earth. The second commandment like unto the first in importance is that we love our neighbors as ourselves. This, too, is a grace that develops gradually. I have never seen this change occur in a man overnight, save in Ebenezer Scrooge, but I have seen men grow toward it slowly, episodically, but unmistakably through the years, under the influence of Christian fellowship, teaching, and worship, and the Holy Spirit. "Beloved, if God so loved us, we also ought to love one another. . . . If we love one another, God abides in us and his love is perfected in us" (1 John 4:11-12).

A third change is a change of life, which is more or less implicit in the other two changes. Under Peter's preaching, the hearers were cut to the heart, and cried out, "What must we do?" Peter's reply was clear: "Repent and be baptized every one of you in the name of Jesus Christ for the forgiveness of your sins; and you shall receive the gift of the Holy Spirit" (Acts 2:37-38). It is not out of line to observe that repentance too is only begun at first, that it must be frequently renewed throughout a lifetime, that remission of sins is not the same as final triumph over all temptation, and that the Holy Spirit is frequently resisted in the lives that have received him. A man's habits, values, attitudes, and character can and do change under Christian influences. Man is led "to the place where he is able to accept Christ's measure because he has accepted his love."[17]

> The beginning and maturing of the life of love is a fact. Let the possibility of perfection take its proper place as an ideal which lies always beyond existence. . . . But let us not insist upon the achievement of perfection in the Christian life any more than we insist upon it in the works of our hands or our minds.[18]

It is our hope that these other changes add up to, or culminate in a change of "state," salvation, being born again, passing from death to life. I have little taste for attempting to say who is saved and who is damned, who is among the elect and who is not, who is going to hell and who to heaven, and which ceremonies are essential and how they are to be performed. Many of Paul's anguished writings were wrestling with the theoretically impossible but actually manifest phenomenon that saved Christians were still behaving like damned heathen. This phenomenon has caused great consternation ever since. The mischief is caused, in my judgment, by the notion that a person is at some moment either among the saved or the damned, whereas becoming a Christian is a lifetime job—at least. "Salvation is going on; it is in process. . . . Therefore, the Christian does not say that he is saved. He says that he is under the promise of salvation. But he is enabled to say also that he is caught up in the initiatory phases of salvation. He lives in the Now of salvation."[19]

Let us leave the matter of a person's state, or his standing with God at any given moment to God himself, perhaps saying as Father Mapple said to his congregation of New Bedford whalers in Melville's *Moby Dick;* "And eternal delight will be his, who coming to lay him down, can say with his final breath, 'O Father, chiefly known to me by Thy rod, mortal or immortal, here

I die. I have striven to be Thine, more than to be this world's or mine own. Yet this is nothing; I leave eternity to Thee.' "

The Work of the Church

We cannot discuss the nature of evangelism without considering the role of the church in which evangelism began, and through which it has continued and is continuing. It has been a matter of common observation since the time of the apostle Paul that to be in the church is not necessarily to be a Christian. (Some have insisted that the converse is also true—that to be a Christian is not necessarily to be in the church. Usually this position is maintained by those who are neither Christians in any serious sense, nor church members.) Nevertheless, there ought to be, and is, some positive and integral connection between the Christian life and church membership. Adding names to the church roll, and evangelism, are at least similar enough to have become confused in the minds and utterance of Christian people. What is the connection between church membership and conversion to the Christian life and hope?

Without going into the problem of ecclesiology in any historical or systematic sense let it be noted that the church is the fellowship, the community, in which conversion is most likely to occur. Julian Hartt was right in saying:

> In good conscience we people of the church cannot tell others that the radical ills of human life are healed by joining our ranks, or that the ultimate perils of the world are thereby avoided or mollified. But we can say, and we must say, that to join a church may provoke a hunger for a higher righteousness. It may create an awareness of the demand for a world-transcending loyalty, and it may open the eyes for the first time upon the possibilities of communion with God in Christ.[20]

The church, whatever its essential and ideal nature (and I deny no high concept of the church by not discussing it here), is at least a fellowship of people among whom Jesus is systematically remembered and the presence of God repeatedly requested.

It is an organization which deliberately teaches the story of Jesus and avowedly professes to be his followers. It is a community which exists to hear the word of God and to tell of it, to seek the will of God and to do it. Imperfect as it is, it is the organism which the spirit of Christ sometimes inhabits, and in and through which God sometimes works. In such a fellowship, one is more likely to become a Christian than he is outside of it. In it he is more likely to be saved. In it he is more likely to die to sin, and to rise to walk in newness of life (cf. Romans 6:4). In it spiritual nurture and growth in grace are more likely to occur. In it a person, experiencing to some degree the forgiveness of God and the love of his fellows, may learn to extend that love and forgiveness to others. "The church is not to be thought of . . . as the place where people are miraculously shorn of their sins. It is the place where, by the miracle of Christ's love, people learn to take deepening responsibility for other sinners."[21] Kyle Haselden writes,

> . . . To convert the unconverted remains our primary ministerial function, but this certainly does not mean that our primary duty is to turn non-Christians into the kind of Christians most Christians are. The mission of the church now has its widest frontier within the boundaries of the Christian community. The mission *of* the church has become a mission *to* the church. "The problem," said Kierkegaard, "is being in a certain sense a Christian, to become a Christian."[22]

While it is true that the church contains many unconverted or half-converted people, it also contains many men and women whose bearing and deeds and strength testify that they know God, and that Christ lives in them. "If you are merely pointing backwards to a Christ that lived two thousand years ago," says D. T. Niles, "you are pointing in the wrong direction. . . . Christ is present tense. You must be able to say 'Look there,' pointing to a community or an individual: 'there He is.' . . . To put it another way, we are witnesses of God primarily by being part of the evidence ourselves."[23] There is evidence that God can use even such congregations as we are in bringing men through them to him.

The implications of this seem to be that the church doors should swing wide. When Jesus said that the gate was narrow, he was talking about the entrance to the way to life—not about the church door. Perhaps the evangelistic function of the church could be diagrammed as a funnel between the wide world and the narrow gate. Once a man is within the redemptive fellowship of the church, the task of converting him has only begun. He is not necessarily among the saved, but he is among those who, by God's grace, are being saved.

"The church in the administration of baptism is evangelizing in an effective and dramatic manner," reports a study committee of the World Convention of Churches of Christ. "The observance of the Lord's Supper makes the salvation-occurence a present reality in that it 'proclaims the Lord's death until he comes.' "[24] But so is it evangelizing when it operates Sunday schools and vacation church schools, missions to migrant laborers, chaplaincies in industry and hospitals and armies, conferences and retreats in which the gospel's relevance is explored and stated in greater depth and breadth. It is evangelizing when, in the words of Theodore Gill, it asks "the world questions about the shadowed context of its brilliant competence."[25] It is evangelizing even when it seeks to bring the secularist inside the church doors, and onto its membership roll. "Whatever is concerned with bringing men to God or to faith in God is evangelism. Wherever the end result of bringing persons to God through Jesus Christ is sought, these efforts are true evangelism."[26]

NOTES

1. *The Christian System*, p. 114.
2. Julian N. Hartt, *Toward a Theology of Evangelism* (Nashville: Abingdon Press, 1955), p. 75.
3. D. Elton Trueblood, *Philosophy of Religion* (New York: Harper & Row, Publishers, Inc., 1957), p. 34.
4. *Ibid.*, pp. 42 and 46.
5. Ernest E. Best, "Facing Other Faiths," *The Christian Century*, January 11, 1961, p. 40.

6. Daniel D. Williams, *God's Grace and Man's Hope* (New York: Harpers, 1949), p. 62.
7. G. E. Phillips, *Evangelism for the World Today,* edited by John R. Mott (New York: Harpers, 1938), p. 83.
8. Campbell, *op. cit.,* p. 122.
9. *Ibid.,* p. 53.
10. *Ibid.,* p. 64.
11. Robert John Versteeg, *The Gracious Calling of the Lord* (Nashville: Abingdon Press, 1960), Chapter VII, passim.
12. *Ibid.,* p. 43.
13. *Ibid.,* p. 75.
14. Sam Shoemaker, *With the Holy Spirit and With Fire* (New York: Harper, 1960), p. 69, p. 40.
15. Campbell, *op. cit.,* p. 60.
16. Williams, *op. cit.,* p. 38.
17. Versteeg, *op. cit.,* p. 104.
18. Williams, *op. cit.,* p. 181.
19. Hartt, *op. cit.,* p. 77.
20. *Ibid.,* p. 66.
21. *Ibid.,* p. 86.
22. Kyle Haselden (editorial), From *The Pulpit,* January, 1961, p. 3.
23. D. T. Niles, "Evangelism in a World of Rapid Change" *The Pulpit,* August, 1960, pp. 7-9.
24. Unpublished study document on The Theology of Evangelism for Edinburgh Assembly of the World Convention of Churches of Christ in 1960, p. 16.
25. Quoted by Sherwood Eliot Wirt in "The Young Turks of Evangelism," Christianity Today, May 23, 1960, p. 692.
26. World Convention of Churches of Christ document, p. 16.

11

God and the Day's Work

Considerations for a theology of vocation

STEPHEN J. ENGLAND

ONE of the urgent challenges facing the Christian church today is that of providing a theology of vocation that is theoretically valid and practically relevant. The sense of emptiness and meaninglessness pervading the lives of so many members of our technological society has had serious consequences in the realm of vocation. In this critical situation the Christian church has the opportunity of bearing witness to the reality of the lordship of Christ over all of life.[1]

This sharp statement sets before us a topic of deepening concern among contemporary Christians. The increasing interest in the place of the layman in the life of the church and of all Western society has produced an enormous literature, in the Ecumenical Movement and in other areas, emphasizing the lordship of Christ in the life of the individual. The present study will touch upon only one aspect of the problem: the lordship of Christ in the daily work of the Christian.

I Dimensions of the Problem

The lives of countless lay churchmen are beset more or less seriously with the sense of the ultimate meaninglessness of the work done to provide material support. Necessary as the job may be in the utilitarian sense, many workers see no connection between the work and purpose in living, nor does the task seem to have any relation to the providence of God, beyond economic support. One phase of the problem, and a troublesome one, is the relation between work and worship—whether God knows, or cares, what one must do to earn a living.

As Robert Calhoun points out[2] the modern attitude has developed out of a primitive society in which work and worship were closely, though uncritically, linked. The work necessary to support life was conditioned by a view of nature and the supernatural, a view which held that no work could be productive unless demonic forces were appeased. In some areas of the so-designated Christian world today, the same appeasement is practiced in the blessing of field and seed, of flock and herd, of fishing boats and nets. The atheistic Russian Communists have had a field day as they delightedly demonstrate that the benediction of the priests is considerably less important than scientifically designed fertilizers and modern methods of tillage. In the primitive scene, worship was practiced for frankly utilitarian purposes. The practice of praying for rain survives in America, not only among the primitive Indians of the Southwest, but also in supposedly Christian congregations, whose prayer for a break in the drought rejects the assertion of Jesus that God makes his rain to fall on evil and on good without partiality. No one could guess how many sincere Christians attend church regularly with the unspoken feeling that this practice will somehow insure against financial catastrophes.

Such beliefs of the pious, that God will intervene in the productivity and profit of daily work, have suffered deflation as the increase of man's control over nature has convinced him that he is the real power behind production. As a result, "religion" has become the occupation, as well as the business, of a clerical caste, and is increasingly irrelevant to busy and productive people. This development has operated to the detriment of both work and worship. While the economic returns of the layman's work are more and more necessary to the programs of the church, the layman's religion is felt to be less and less relevant to what he is doing for a living, and the occupation of Sunday, which is traditionally religion, has too little significant relation to what happens during the rest of the week.

The domination of the scientific world view, that has so decisively displaced religion as effective in the control of natural forces, has been accompanied by the rise of the huge mass-production industries. In Medieval Europe the great artists, operating individually, no doubt felt truly creative as they produced the paintings, sculpture, buildings, and music which they bequeathed to subsequent generations. Even at that time, of course, the great mass of the people were peasantry, whose bowed backs and calloused hands (without benefit of the sense of creativity) produced the foodstuffs that supported the population—including the creative artists—by labor that had precious little of the creative about it. We live now in the atmosphere of democracy, which asserts that everyone is as good as anyone and that the day laborer therefore has as much inherent right to feel creative as does Arthur Miller, Irving Berlin, or Frank Lloyd Wright. In practice, however, the laborer will probably spend his day on the production line of a factory, performing over and over some simple operation that occupies his mind little or not at all. He may come to feel that he is a part of the machine, and that his work has no ultimate meaning beyond that of the whirring wheels. When he finds himself displaced by automation, the feeling may well deepen. The "mechanical man" can do everything that his human prototype can, and can do it faster, better, and more cheaply. God's relation to the day's work, and to people who spend their lives in doing it or who are made idle by advancing mechanization, becomes more and more remote.

One attempt to inject Christian faith and ultimate meaning into the life of the man, if not into his work, is the frank assertion of the dichotomy between work and worship. The job is engaged in to provide the necessities of life, plus more or less of the luxuries. Worship is engaged in to provide purpose for living and an ultimate goal. Work occupies six days (or five or four, depending on what the union can bargain for); worship, part of one. Work provides for this life; worship for the next. Work supports the body; worship the soul. Work is secular; worship is sacred. The logical outcome of this dichotomy is little if at all concerned with the worker's work, rather with his worship when he takes time out from work.

If accepted seriously, this dichotomy is fatal to the life of faith. Fortunately it has not been followed to its logical conclusion of monasticism by many. Martin Luther led the way in rejecting the monastic ideal, together with his monkish vow, asserting that the monastic life (which is the separation of the sacred from the secular *par excellence*) is the one vocation that has no claim whatever on the character of a Christian, since in it a man tries to be truly Christian at the expense of his neighbors and in separation from them. The modern man, for whom the theoretical attractions of the monastic life are usually negated by the more potent attractions of "the more abundant life" that is "the American way," may yet feel the deep frustrations of his own view, which severs the center of his daily occupation from his Christian faith. As his interest and involvement in his work increase, he is the harder put to it to relate his work to his profession of religious faith. The severance can too easily lead to a thoroughgoing secularism that concentrates the entire man upon his work, and measures success by the material rewards.

As a sort of sop to religion, one may hold an uncritical eschatology, based on biblical literalism, that expects the world, in which the job is supreme and which the job helps to build, to end in the destruction of that world in a fiery tornado; the rewards held so high in the worker's world to be supplanted by draped robes and a harp; and the worker to be promoted from hard, productive labor to twanging the harp while sitting idly on Cloud Nine. It would be difficult to imagine an eschatology better calculated to destroy any ultimate significance of the worker's daily task.

More recently, the need to inject ultimate significance into the job has taken the form of the attempt to involve God in each man's choice of a lifework, or "vocation." The basic concept is that God "calls" each person to some particular type of work, for which his special abilities fit him. The vocational aptitude test, as the "scientific" means of revealing hidden abilities, may come to be looked on as a means of divine revelation. The psychological tester may be cast in the role of the priest who presides over an oracle, whose pronouncements are heeded with pathetic docility by multitudes of eager youth. According to the concept of "vocation," the purpose of life is self-fulfillment. Life may become rich and full, and God will be pleased, if one discovers the kind of work God intends him to do, and develops his God-given "talents" to the fullest degree. God may want him to invent or build automobiles, or to sell them; to compose music or to lead a band or a dance orchestra; to sell life insurance or repair automobiles or a TV set. The logical conclusion of this view would seem to require something akin to ordination as the religious setting apart of each person to his lifework. This, however, has been reserved for the clerical caste. Among the Christian Churches (Disciples of Christ), which have been historically anticlerical, the rising emphasis on ordination of ministers has frequently been based on such a concept of the "divine call" to this specific "vocation."

This concept, based on the extension of the characteristically Protestant idea that God deals with each man individually in his salvation, faces difficulties that seem insuperable. It emphasizes a very rugged individualism that drives each person to press ruthlessly ahead in his own development, leaving small room for God and little place for consideration of one's fellows. The damage to both piety and ethics is well expressed by Calhoun:

> The doctrine of earthly vocation is through and through equivocal and unworthy of honest, intelligent folk. At best it is an attempt to serve God and Mammon; at worst, a mask for egotism and exploitation.[3]

It baptizes the material goal, bows before the vocational aptitude test as God's oracle, and exalts the criterion of "success" as proof of God's "call" to the task. It gives little or no help to the great mass of workers. The creative artist, the "go-getter" in business, and the research scientist may (if religiously inclined) feel that God has "called" him to the work; but who could believe that God has "called" him to collect garbage, sweep the shop, or perform any of the undistinguished and menial tasks essential to the functioning of a community? It is equally difficult for the assembly-line worker to believe that God has "called" him to the monotonous task that demands so little of his mind, yet is so necessary for the way of life and the welfare of huge populations and is required if the "creative" caste is to receive the material rewards that prove the reality of its "call."

The theory of divine vocation is historically unrealistic. It assumes, for example, that God never gave any man the "talent" of a highly skilled neurosurgeon or an aerodynamic engineer until the twentieth century, when general scientific advance made the exercise of such "talents" a possibility. It pronounces the disapproval of God upon the one whose family situation or social status in a racial minority effectively prevents the discovery or development of any "talent." Inherent in the theory is a subtle and deadly spiritual danger. Its emphasis on self-fulfillment as the purpose of life may easily exclude God and his redemptive purpose; while the temptation to complacent self-righteousness on the part of one who has vocationally "fulfilled" his life may be all but irresistible.

A further aspect of the problem of Christian vocation is the meaning of work itself in the life of the worker. The judgment of society at this point is ambiguous. Productive work is a status symbol of considerable importance so that one who does no work is regarded as inferior or a failure—unless he has no economic need to work, in which case his situation is considered ideal. Work is believed to be necessary, but the purpose of work is to attain the goal of freedom from work. The daily task is therefore in some sense a penalty put upon living. The same evaluation has been given scriptural sanction on the basis of Genesis 3:17-19. In our society, the minor recess, such as the extended "coffee break," is highly prized. The shortened work week is demanded, not only to stretch out declining employment, but also to give more freedom from work; while longer and longer paid vacations are vigorously sought. Presumably complete retirement from all work should be the earthly equivalent of the worker's heaven.

The facts belie the assumption. As the work week is shortened, "moonlighting" becomes more common, and the reason is not solely economic. The increasing ill health, the frustration, the disillusionment, and the predictable early death of many retired workers point up practical aspects of the problem of the meaning of work in the worker's life. Psychologists tell us that every person lives by his sense of being needed so that, when the work is taken away, the reason for living may go with it. The Christian would classify this as a spiritual problem. When one's life ceases to be meaningful and purposeful, the reason for living is gone.

The solution of this problem does not consist in prolonged employment for the aged. This is only palliative, for in the end unemployment—or retirement, which is the same thing—must be faced. The real solution lies in a Christian view that sets the day's work in proper perspective to the life of the worker, and provides for that life some center other than performance of the daily task.

The ethically sensitive worker faces another kind of problem when he sees the products of his work turned out as cheaply and shoddily as possible to be sold at a price far above its value. Still more disturbing is the plight of the scientist whose knowledge and skill have unlocked the secrets of atomic fission when he sees it used to destroy the population of a city in a single blast and to threaten the destruction of all civilization. Is the Christian ethically obligated to refuse to engage in work if the products are used to defraud or destroy? Too often the problem is avoided by letting the employer or the government decide on the use to be made of the product. But this shifting of responsibility seldom answers the questions arising in the mind of the serious Christian who seeks to know the relation of his work to his faith. A theology of Christian vocation in which the lordship of Jesus Christ is the determining factor is the urgent need.

II Jesus and Work

It has been generally and properly held that the central affirmation of the Christian faith is found in John 1:14: "The Word became flesh and dwelt among us." So H. H. Farmer asserts "unless a man is prepared to make the affirmation in some sense or other . . . any claim he may make to be a specifically Christian believer . . . is . . . extremely dubious."[4] Farmer interprets the incarnation "to mean that Christ in his divine-earthly life was veritably a man in the wholeness of man's being as an embodied and historic person."[5] Those who are prepared to make such an affirmation for themselves will hold that the life of Jesus, no less than, although not apart from, his death and resurrection, is relevant to Christian faith. They will also hold that his manner of life as a man is more than an ethical example to the Christian. The incarnational ethic makes the life of the man Jesus relevant to the daily life as well as to the faith of his twentieth-century follower. We turn, therefore, to the record of his life, to his teachings concerning work, and to inferences that may justly be drawn from his life and his teachings concerning the Christian in his daily tasks.

Jesus shared neither the world-rejecting attitude of John the Baptist (Luke 7:34) nor the world-hating fears of the apocalyptists who looked for and longed for a fiery catastrophe as the consummation of history. His ministry—which was his daily life—was in and to the world. This attitude must characterize the lives of those who acknowledge him as Lord.

The record does not show that Jesus did any work for a livelihood, whether manual labor, buying and selling, practice of a "creative" art, research for increase of knowledge, serving as a functionary of government, or engaging in theological or philosophical speculation like some Hebrew Socrates. Those who seek this kind of example in Jesus must make the best of disappointment. We have no information concerning any work he may have engaged in prior to the day when the preaching of John the Baptist called him from obscurity into public life, although it is reasonable to assume that he did something for his support. To the American mind it seems more honorable to hold that he labored to support himself and the family left dependent by the supposed early death of Joseph, than to imagine him a recluse or an indigent preacher who relied on the alms of the pious, but it is possible that he was among the unemployed all his life. The assumption that he was a carpenter, apprenticed to Joseph, is widely accepted, but has no firm support in our records. Origen (*Contra Celsum* vi. 36) asserted that he knew of no statement in the Scripture that made such a claim. To eliminate Mark 6:3 as a text for Labor Sunday sermons, together with the sentimental picture of the young Jesus as one whose calloused palms and aching muscles made him akin to the modern laborer, is likely to excite little acclaim from the preachers. But that picture of Jesus is unsupported by the Gospels, the only source of information, and the silence of the records reflects the obvious fact that their authors were unconcerned about the question whether Jesus ever held a job.

Whatever the nature of his work before his baptism at the hands of John, the record is clear on one point: he left it, and never referred to it in his teaching. The work was not his "vocation." During his public career, he subsisted without visible means of support, thus providing the perfect example for the denunciations of the modern Communist who regards the clergy as parasites on society. It is possible that Jesus was supported by being a guest in the home of friends (Luke 10:38-42), or of patrons (Luke 7:36ff.), or of others (Luke 14:1-24). He was reported to have accepted the contributions of pious women

(Luke 8:1-3), and perhaps of others. But of "work" there is no hint in the record.

He "called" certain men to be his followers; some of these were later designated "apostles." Those whom he chose as followers were called away from "work": Peter and Andrew, and Zebedee's sons from their fishing boats (Mark 1:16-20), and Levi from the tax-collector's desk (Mark 2:14). We may suppose that the others left productive employment to be in his company. When they became his followers or disciples, their *work* was no longer their *vocation*. The silence of the record allows us to suppose that these, like their Master, engaged in no gainful employment during his ministry.

In that ministry he did not denounce any kind of work, nor did he praise any. Many of the parables are based on reference to various kinds of work, chiefly the tilling of the soil or fishing, but there is no pronouncement on work as such. An obviously dishonest manager is commended (Luke 16:8f.), not for the kind of work he did, but because of his wise foresight in the use of his opportunity. Those who rejected the Great Invitation because of their involvements in business or matrimony (Luke 14:18-20) were not rebuked for the kind of work they did, or because they were engaged in it, but because they used it as an excuse for refusal to accept the invitation to the king's feast. That is, man's true "vocation" is not his gainful employment but the invitation of God to accept his rule.

Yet while Jesus called some away from work to follow him, there were others who did not forsake all employment and still received his blessing for their service. He who shares a cup of cold water (Mark 9:41) or the hospitality of his house (Luke 10:5f.) will share in the blessings of the coming kingdom. Almsgiving is praised (Matthew 6:2f.; Luke 12:33) and those who provide for relief of the destitute are to win the inheritance of the kingdom (Matthew 25:31ff.). These material helps can be provided only by those whose labor has made their accumulation possible, but in the preaching and teaching of Jesus man's "vocation" is not to the work itself. That to which Jesus' teaching calls man is obedience to the will of God, to witness, and to service. Those who hear and respond to this call will meet their Lord in the persons of the needy with whom he identifies himself. The work which enables the disciple to respond to need has real importance in his fulfillment of his true vocation.

Some of Jesus' teachings have been modernized by interpretation that makes them the support of a theory of work as vocation. An agraphon says, "Hew the wood and thou shalt find me; cleave the stone and there am I." This saying, if genuine, can scarcely mean that the humble woodcutter or stonemason will find his Lord by the faithful plying of his trade. It is rather that he may find his Lord in the midst of his daily tasks, whatever they may be. The parable of the talents (Matthew 25:14-30) has been widely quoted as Jesus' recognition of the inequalities of individual abilities, which God has given, and his assertion that each man fulfills his God's will for his life by developing his talents to their fullest. While it is evident that Jesus' parable put the word "talent" into the modern vocabularly, it may be doubted whether, in the figure of the ancient sum of money, he prefigured the modern concept. In any case, it is impossible to believe that Jesus, who called on his followers to deny self (Mark 8:34), would approve self-fulfillment as the goal of life and therefore God's "vocation" for every man.

The statement attributed to Jesus (John 5:17) that he worked because God is still working is an accurate reflection of his thought whether the saying is authentic or not. The context is a healing on the Sabbath, denounced by Jesus' opponents because this "work" was Sabbath violation. Jesus' claim does not mean that he believed that God had called him to the vocation of healer. This is made clear in the story of the temptations (Matthew 4:1-11; Luke 4:1-12). These disclose the terrible pull of ambition upon the young Jesus, based upon his recognition of his ability to heal and thus relieve material need, and of his capacity to rule. His decision was that he could not engage in a ministry of healing, since his "vocation" was in another area (Mark 1:34).

His decision is illuminating to us. The faith of the Christian asserts that the mighty powers of Jesus were granted him at his baptism, not to be exercised for their own sake, nor developed as self-expression, nor employed for material gain. His "vocation" was to witness by his healings to the presence of the kingdom of God (Matthew 12:28), as well as to witness by his words the eschatological coming of the kingdom. In a secondary sense, the healings also served to relieve the needy (whose destitution must have touched his sympathy) and as real testimony to God's gracious favor (Matthew 11:2-5; Luke 7:18-22) disclosed in the ministry of Jesus.

His response to the insidious and powerful temptation to seize the rule over men at the price of yielding to evil must be seen in a similar light. He was governed by deeper convictions than the certainty that he had the capacity to rule, or even that God had destined him to rule. The kingdom is God's, not man's; and it will come by God's giving it to man, not by man's vain attempt to set it up (Luke 12:32).

As the truly human bearer of God's redemptive self-revelation, Jesus' "vocation" was to proclaim God's gracious purpose in giving the kingdom, and to witness to its presence and power in his own time. The goal of his own life, as a truly human person, was not self-realization by self-expression, and still less the accumulation of the material rewards of work. It was self-realization by serving others and by self-giving in their behalf (Mark 10:45). Whatever the particular work might be, in which he was engaged at any moment, his "vocation" was to obedience to God, to witness, and to service. It is in this understanding that he becomes the shining example for all those who acknowledge him as Lord and Christ in their lives.

III Considerations in a Theology of Christian Vocation

A theology of Christian vocation begins, not with the daily task, but with the lordship of Christ. The Christian is one who has made the most ancient of all confessions, "Jesus Christ is Lord" (Romans 10:10; Philippians 2:11). His lordship, established by his resurrection from the dead (Romans 1:4), is over the Church, over human society, and over the life of each individual Christian.

Man's "vocation" as a Christian is not primarily the call of God to any task or type of daily work, but first of all to accept forgiveness, to witness to God's mercy (1 Peter 2:9f.), and to make real in his life the lordship of Christ. It is the call to love God with the entire being, and one's neighbor as oneself (Mark 12:30).

In the ongoing of his redemptive purpose, God established the church as the community of faith and fellowship. Because he loved the world (John 3:16), God placed the church in the world for ministry to it. Each Christian, including both the unordained and the ordained, is called of God to be in the church and in the world. Just as the church is to be in but not of the world (John 17:16), so is the Christian, for it is only by his being in the world that he can fulfill the call of God to love and serve his neighbor. The call of God comes to each person at the moment of baptism when he acknowledges the lordship of Christ in his own life. The Christian, therefore, cannot say, "I am a Christian and incidentally an engineer (or a physician or a preacher)," nor, "I am an engineer, and incidentally a Christian." He will say, "I am both a Christian and an engineer, and it is by means of my occupation that I fulfill my true vocation and ministry in witness to God and in serving my neighbor."

In his choice of a lifework, the Christian will find peace and assurance in his acceptance of God's providential ordering that has placed his life at a particular time in history and in a given structure of society by which his choice of daily work is largely determined, and in which God gives him the neighbors whom he is to love and to serve. In this society, he will willingly do what is needed. He may be able to serve most effectively if he engages in work for which he has special natural aptitudes. Tests that help to discover these aptitudes are neither to be despised nor to be regarded as the indisputable evidence of some divine "call" to a given work, and this applies to the work of the ordained ministry no less than to other occupations. By his increased effectiveness in the daily task, the Christian may both witness to God's gracious gifts to him, and also serve his neighbor the better. Yet satisfaction in doing the work well must not lead to the denial of the lordship of Christ, who taught his followers, "Let your light so shine before men, that they may see your good works and give glory to your Father who is in heaven" (Matthew 5:16). The temptation to every skilled craftsman, especially in the creative arts, is toward self-pride, self-glorification, and self-idolatry which, in practice, exclude God from the center of life.

In choosing among the many occupations open to men, the Christian will face ethical decisions which he will make in the conviction that he must act responsibly as under the just demands of God whose will is righteousness as well as love. He cannot engage in any occupation if the work, or the sale of its product, depends on the debasing or manipulation of human personality or the impoverishing of persons or depriving them of the means of supporting life adequately. No more can he engage in the production of that which depends for its acceptance on the harming of persons in mind or morals. The requirement to love one's neighbor, underscored by the example of the Lord who came to love and to serve (Mark 10:45), must find expression in the daily work of the Christian.

The ethical quality of many types of daily work is ambiguous, due to the infinite complexity of modern society, and its heavy demands on the time and activities of workers. For example, an economy based on pastoral or agricultural pursuits found it easy to designate every seventh day for rest and worship. In our society, transportation and communications must function on a seven-day, twenty-four-hour basis if the economy is to be maintained. Christians, no less than unbelievers, expect to purchase on Monday foodstuffs made available by the labors of those who distributed them on Sunday. The problems of witness to faith and of love and service to neighbors are not to be solved by some easy and radical formula. A choice even more difficult ethically is forced upon the Christian citizen by the demands of government. Peace and order in society call for courts, police, prisons, and armed forces by means of which offenders may be forcibly restrained. The Christian must decide whether service in some of these capacities is inconsistent with his acknowledgment of the lordship of Christ, and with loving service to his neighbor. The choice is complicated by the apparent inconsistency of his accepting the services of others for his protection if he refuses to engage in them.

Modern scientific developments have made ethical decisions especially difficult. The Christian who is skilled in atomic science and who sees his knowledge used to devise a bomb that destroys a city and threatens the world with apocalyptic destruction may ask in agony of spirit whether he should refuse to engage in research to be used in this way. No pat answer can be given. If the scientist, as a Christian, believes that every advance in human knowledge increases his comprehension of the greatness and goodness of God, he can scarcely refuse to do his part in such an advance. He who believes that the God and Father of our Lord Jesus Christ turned the unutterable horror of the crucifixion toward human redemption will not doubt that despite human willfulness and sinfulness, God can and will turn every increase of knowledge toward the blessing of humanity.

The difficulty of ethical decisions in such cases results from the fact that society, composed of finite persons, is inescapably sinful. Each person (including the Christian) shares in this corporate sinfulness. The decision of the Christian as to his lifework will inevitably be a compromise between the ideal good and the possible. Whatever his agony of spirit, the Christian can neither withdraw from the world which is the scene of his witness and service, nor can he fatalistically and complacently accept the *status quo*. His sense of the lordship of Christ requires him to protest against every wrongful use of knowledge and skill, every impairment of the true welfare of every person, but he may not withdraw from society as if to seek his own salvation at the expense of and in separation from his fellows.

When the Christian has made choice of an occupation, he faces further questions. In what way shall he do his work as a Christian? For what reason does he engage in it? What is the meaning of his work for his own life?

Because he acknowledges the lordship of Christ over all his life, the Christian must obey the admonition (Ephesians 4:25) to put away falsehood and speak truth with his neighbor. This applies to the work of his hands no less than to his words. The product must be honest. Work done must be full measure, with good will, as to the Lord (Ephesians 6:7). Such truthfulness witnesses to the righteousness of God who called him, and is the honest serving of his neighbor.

The ultimate meaning which one's work has for his own life depends in part on the reasons he engages in it. It has been claimed by the proponents of "free enterprise" that the profit motive is necessary to insure the increase of knowledge and adequate production of goods for the support and enrichment of life. Comparison with communized societies is cited as proof, and criticism of the profit motive is regarded with suspicion as subversive. The comparison is in fact between two social orders which are based upon the identical assumptions that the acqusition of things is the measure of the abundant life. Christian faith rejects the assumption. It remains to be demonstrated what would be the result in society if every worker labored under the lordship of Christ, governed by his dedication to witness to the glory of God and to serve his fellow man in the spirit of Jesus Christ.

Whatever the daily task of the Christian, he must avoid preoccupation with the material, with acquistion of wealth, with fame and popular acclaim as his goal. He will remember that "a man's life does not consist in the abundance of the things he possesses" (Luke 12:15), a difficult assignment indeed. Acknowledgment of the lordship of Christ requires his followers to witness to this truth in the midst of a sensate culture, ridden and riddled with the desire for "security," frantic to get, to "get ahead," and to experience whatever the holding of things can bring.

The meaning of one's work may be illumined by vision of its significance in meeting real needs of people. The deadening monotony of mass production, for example, will be relieved, for the worker sees the enormously increased population of the earth whose teeming multitudes require food, clothing, medicines, books, and other materials in unending profusion if life is to be supported and enriched. Such production is possible only by mass effort; no task is menial or deadening if the worker sees its purpose in the serving of those with whom the Lord of the church identified himself (Matthew 25:40).

The ultimate meaning of the Christian's life will not, however, be determined by the work he does in the world. The emptiness that attacks the retired worker, whose work was the center of his existence, attests only that he has tried to live out of his own resources and has inevitably failed. Self-fulfillment, for the Christian, is not by self-development or by engrossment in the task. One's life is to be truly saved by taking self out of the center and by putting the Lord Christ in that place. The meaning of both the daily task and life itself lies in witness to Christ's lordship, and in loving and serving one's neighbor under that lordship.

He who confesses Christ as Lord will find his work, whatever it may be, fulfilled in the community of faith and illumined by the community of worship. Daniel Day Williams has phrased it:

> The divine call to us men, and our response to it, means that we are responsible for doing here and now, in the situation in which we stand, whatever will serve the work of God who is seeking to bring all life to its fulfilment in that universal community of love which is the real good of every creature.[6]

NOTES

1. McCullough, Thomas E., "The Theology of Christian Vocation," in *Religious Education,* Jan.-Feb. 1961; p. 26.
2. Calhoun, Robert L.: *God and the Common Life* (Hamden, Conn.: The Shoe String Press, 1935), chapter one.
3. *Ibid.,* p. 28.
4. Farmer, H. H., "The Bible, Its Significance and Authority" in *The Interpreter's Bible* (Nashville: Abingdon Press, 1952), p. 5.
5. *Ibid.,* p. 12.
6. Williams, Daniel Day, *God's Grace and Man's Hope* (New York: Harper & Row, Publishers, Inc., 1949), p. 148.

12

The New Opportunities for Religious Education

WILLARD M. WICKIZER

THE subject assigned me was "The Opportunity of the Church in American Culture." I would like to limit the field a little and address myself to the theme "The Opportunity of Christian Education in Contemporary American Culture." I take the liberty of changing somewhat the focus of my address for several reasons. For one thing, much has been written and said during the past few years concerning the implications of changing American life for the church. As professors and researchers I am sure you are acquainted with this literature. Parenthetically I might say that three or four years ago I read a paper to the Division of Home Missions of the National Council of Churches on this very theme. If I had wanted to take the easy way out, I would have read this paper to you. But there are some new things that I feel need desperately to be said to Christian education at this particular time.

Perhaps it might be well to delineate the background from which I speak. I hold a Master of Religious Education degree from the old school of Religious Education and Social Service of Boston University. I attended this school in its heyday. I served for several years as a regional director of religious education for Disciples of Christ, then as minister of education on the staff of a large congregation, then as pastor of a church of more than nine hundred members in a college community, then as a denominational home mission executive for twenty years, and now as executive chairman of a division that embraces home missions, Christian education, and social welfare. I no longer claim professional status in the field of religious education but I have never been completely unrelated to that area of the church's life.

I A New Theological Orientation

Christian education needs a new theological orientation. Historically men have been divided into two camps in regard to human nature; one group holding that it is basically evil and corrupt, while the other group has held that is it normally pure and good. In the fifth century Augustine introduced into Christian theology the idea of hereditary guilt, holding that in Adam's sin there had entered into the whole human stream a continuing pollution from which the individual could be freed only by an act of divine grace. Said he, "The infant who is lost is punished because he belongs to the mass of perdition and as a child of Adam is justly condemned." And Calvin, adopting and developing the views of Augustine, declared, "They bring condemnation with them from their mother's womb—they are odious and abominable unto God."

The theory of salvation held by Augustine and Calvin and all who have followed in their train has been that just as sin entered human nature through the transgression of one man, so salvation comes to the race through one man—Jesus Christ. This theology has been developed very largely out of certain words of the Apostle Paul:

"Therefore as sin came into the world through one man and death through sin, and so death spread to all men because all men sinned. . . . Adam . . . was a type of the one who was to come.

"But the free gift is not like the trespass. For if many died through one man's trespass, much more have the grace of God and the free gift in the grace of that one man Jesus Christ abounded for many." (Romans 5:12-15), and "For as by a man came death, by a man has come also the resurrection of the dead. For as in Adam all die, so also in Christ shall all be made alive." (1 Corinthians 15:21-22)

In more recent years the figure of Adam has loomed less large than was once the case for there has been a rather widespread discrediting of the idea that the human race has a single recognizable ancestor. But even among many of those who have given up the idea of Adam as the father of the race, the name of Adam has continued to stand as a symbol for man's fleshly or animal inheritance which, if left alone, will damn and doom him. Indeed, so strong and overpowering is this evil inheritance thought to be that for man to attempt to save himself is like endeavoring to pull himself out of a cistern with his own boot straps. Only as Christ, it is held, in some mysterious way mediates the grace of God can the human race free itself from the shackles of sin.

In the early part of the eighteenth century there was born in France one Jean Jacques Rousseau, a man whose philosophy was destined to have profound significance for society, for education, and for religion. Rousseau held that the natural or primitive state of man is preferable to the artificial one of civilization, and that human nature, unmolested and untampered with, is good. In society Rousseau's teachings produced a "back to nature" movement. In education it focused attention on child training. In religion it gave John Wesley insight to declare that children are "members of the kingdom."

In 1859 Charles Darwin wrote his *Origin of the Species,* and in 1871 his *Descent of Man.* The research of Darwin and the teaching of Thomas Huxley firmly established in the scientific world the idea of biological evolution. With this came a changed conception of man's origin and the forces and factors that have made him what he is. The human race did not start with the miraculous creation of Adam and Eve, but came out of long evolutionary development. There being no Adam to be the father of the race, there was no one who could once and for all have polluted the stream of human life by his sinfulness. Human nature, it was held, may not be essentially good, as Rousseau claimed, but neither is it essentially bad, as Augustine and Calvin claimed. It is, in all probability, nonmoral, with capacities within it for achieving a moral state.

In America, in 1847, Horace Bushnell wrote his famous book *Christian Nurture,* in which he contended that "the child is to grow up a Christian, and never know himself as being otherwise." Later in the century John Fiske made popular the idea of the guaranteed ascent of man. Said he in *The Destiny of Man:* "The future is lighted for us with the radiant colors of hope. Strife and sorrow shall disappear. Peace and love shall reign supreme. The dream of poets, the lesson of priest and prophet, the inspiration of the great musician, is confirmed in the light of modern knowledge."

Out of such a thought world as this the modern movement of religious education has developed. In writing some years ago of this movement George Herbert Betts, in his book *The New Program of Religious Education,* said:

"The advocates of religious education insist that the religious nuture and training of children and youth is a greater and more fundamental thing than reclaiming through evangelistic effort of adults, or than the promotion of philanthropic enterprises, or than the waging of social reforms. . . . So they demand that the church adopt a new program with religious education in capital letters at the head of the list of its enterprises, conceiving this as the foundation of all other church activities and programs.

"Pursuant to this policy the religious educationists undertake to apply the scientific principles of general education to the teaching of religion. They insist that religion can be taught just as other things can be taught."

The theme text of religious education has not been taken from the Gospels, nor from the writing of the Apostle Paul, but from the Old Testament, from Proverbs:

> "Train up a child in the way he should go,
> and when he is old he will not depart from it."
> —Proverbs 22:6

But this concept is being seriously challenged today by most thoughtful theologians, who suggest that religious education needs to re-examine its theological base. Says Walter Horton in his book, *A Psychological Approach to Theology:*

> Calvinistic pessimism about human nature is quite unwarranted; but Romantic optimism is just as misleading. Human nature is not inherently bad, but it is inherently ambiguous. It does not automatically push toward the goal of the good life; it is caught between the contrary pulls of what Freud calls the "pleasure-principle" and the "reality-principle": the one embodying the native inertia of the organism, the other embodying its native urge toward self-completion; the one leading inward, regressively and contractively, toward a life of cheap and easy satisfactions, on an animal plane of existence, or in a dream-world of wish-fulfillment, while the other leads outward, progressively and expansively, toward a life that is devoted to great and growing ends and in touch with ever-widening circles of reality. . . . On the whole we may conclude that if the facts of psychology tend to discredit the undue pessimism of traditional theology and the undue optimism of contemporary "self-expressionists," they tend to justify the attitude which the Founder of Christianity took toward human nature—an attitude which combined the most serious concern over man's actual plight with the most audacious faith in his hidden possibilities. Jesus seems to have perceived that human nature is, as Professor Wieman puts it, "both God-bent and hell-bent, and for the same reason; and in the face of that tragic paradox he dared to address to weak and willful men what have been called the bravest words ever spoken: 'Be ye therefore perfect, even as your Father which is in heaven is perfect.' "

Religious education needs to lose some of its bland optimism concerning human nature and achieve a more realistic view of what man is and the forces and factors that play upon him. It is not true, as George Herbert Betts claimed, that "religion can be taught just as other things can be taught." You do not make Christians in the same way you make engineers, or musicians, or linguists, or political scientists. The Christian educator has a much more difficult task than the secular educator. Children are not simply started in the right direction with the assurance that they will never turn aside. Man is not saved; he is always in the process of being saved. The development of Christian personality has its more formal aspects but much more than this is involved. Religious education therefore needs to give up its too sanguine claims as to the efficacy of present educative processes, its underestimation of the perversity of human nature, and its rather blithe and somewhat shallow spirit.

Above all, religious education needs to realize that all education is futile unless it is accompanied by an adequate dynamic and that there is no such thing as an adequate dynamic residual in man but only in God. Halford E. Luccock illustrates this point in a narrative which he recites:

> A speaker was launched on a hortatory flight in which he quoted with great fervor Kipling's poem *If*. All the "ifs" were recited, concluding that if you can do all these things "You'll be a man, my son". When he had finished a man in the audience asked this profound question: "What if you can't?"
>
> That, continues Professor Luccock "is the hardest question ethical exhortation has had to face all through history. What if you can't? Christianity has faced and answered that question. Its answer has been the demonstration of lives brought into energizing contact with power greater than their own, the power of God." (*Christianity and the Individual,* pp. 133-134.)

This certainly is a facet of Christian life and experience with which religious education needs to be more concerned—the dynamic of spiritual growth and change.

II A Fuller Recognition of the Place of Personality in the Educative Process

The second point ties in logically with what has just been said. Religious education has tended to have an obsession with methodology. One gets the idea that it is better to do the wrong thing the right way than to do the right thing the wrong way. Over the years religious educators have unquestioningly tied themselves to secular psychology and pedagogy. But there has usually been a time lag. They have "picked up" the latest thing in psychology or pedagogy about the time secular educators were moving on to new and different ideas. Not only so, but religious educators have tended to be faddists. Three of four years ago "buzz groups" were all the rage. Any considerable number of people could not be brought together without being divided into small groups to "buzz" the question under consideration. Now "group dynamics" is all the rage. We are told that people can learn only in groups of ten or less and that the procedures must be unstructured. No doubt there is some educational merit in what is currently being called "group dynamics" but this is certainly not the whole of the educative process. People, particularly those who are mature or who are intellectually sophisticated, can learn in groups of more than ten and there is still a vital role in the educative process for the expert. Groups that just sit and talk, without adequate background and without expert leadership, may only be sharing their ignorance.

Religious education, in its obsession for method, has tended to overlook the significance of contagious and dynamic personality in the process of Christian education. As a lad of twelve I came under the influence of a Sunday church school teacher by the name of Bossard. He was a humble man. He was a clerk in the post office and I am sure he never had more than a high school education. The only teaching training courses he ever had were of the Herbert Moninger variety. Yet this man loved boys and he gave himself to them. He organized our class into a Boy Scout troop—the first troop to be organized in the state of Oklahoma—and on Saturdays he would go on long hikes with us. Out of this group came two missionaries, a minister, a superintendent of a city school system, a college professor, and a number of Christian businessmen. Not a single boy has gone astray. Of course, this man was not solely responsible for the way these boys in his class turned out, but I think every one of us would witness to the fact that we owe him a very deep debt. What did this man have? Not education. Not training in pedagogy. Not even a very profound knowledge of the Bible. He had a contagious Christian personality and through it he influenced the lives of all of the boys who came in contact with him.

The greatest teacher I ever had was Walter Scott Athearn. He was certainly not the most scholarly but as we sat in his class, we could hardly wait for the session to end so that we could get out and do something about the thing he was talking about. There was a contagion about the man that was epidemic. He did not teach as many teachers do, handing out subject matter with the attitude that his students could take it or not just as they pleased. He sought to win converts to the things in which he believed and to commit his pupils to the cause he himself espoused.

I am not seeking to belittle methodology in education but I do insist that there is more than one way of accomplishing the same end and that what works for one teacher may not work equally well for another. Even more I am insisting that no pedagogical method has much value unless it is mediated through a warm, vibrant, dynamic personality. Jesus has been called the "Great Teacher." One might suppose therefore that one could study the Four Gospels and write a textbook on religious pedagogy, but such is not the case. As one studies the life of Jesus, one is forced to conclude that Jesus' methods were very simple and straightforward. It was the power of his personality, the dynamic character of his life, his radiant goodness that made him a great teacher. We need leadership training and methods courses but these alone will not make great teachers. We need to recruit for the church's teaching staff the really great souls of the church.

III The Challenge of a Rapidly Growing Population

For some strange reason religious educators in recent decades have frowned on promotional methods. They have said, "We are not interested in numbers; we are interested in quality." The result has been that they have built better buildings, written better curricular materials, conducted better leadership training schools, but have reached fewer students.

There is an interesting and revealing graph in the December, 1960, issue of the *International Journal of Religious Education.* It traces population growth, church membership, total church school enrollment and church school enrollment of denominations affiliated with the Division of Christian Education of the National Council of Churches from 1906 to 1958. Church membership during the period increased on a percentage basis faster than population. But church school enrollment in the old-line denominations barely kept pace with the percentage of population growth, if indeed it equaled it.

During the 1940's population in the United States increased by some 19,000,000 people. In the 1950's it increased by almost 28,000,000. The total number of teachers and pupils now enrolled in all church schools barely equals the population increase of the past decade. We hear a great deal about the stress being placed on our public school system by increased attendance but we do not hear a great deal about any stress being placed on our religious education system because of a rapidly growing number of students. This is understandable, for church schools are not growing rapidly.

Religious educators need to understand that quality will not of itself produce quantity. Manufacturers understand this, for they know that no matter how fine their product they still must advertise if they hope to sell any great amount. The leaders of the educational program of the church must understand that they have a promotional task to perform as well as a teaching task. Unless people are reached and involved, they cannot be taught. We should quit looking at promotion as being something beneath the dignity of the religious educator and demand that these leaders within the church develop and utilize methods and procedures that are designed to bring an ever-larger number of persons into active involvement with the educational program of the church.

In pioneer days in America, church school missionaries went up and down the frontier organizing little groups of people into church schools. These missionaries did not wait for expensive church buildings to be erected. They assembled their schools in homes, in dance halls, in public school buildings. Out of these small church schools grew some of our great churches of today. I am not suggesting that the program of the church school missionary of pioneer times should be re-established in our day, for conditions are vastly different, but I am suggesting that the missionary spirit of these people should characterize the modern religious education worker to a far larger degree than is currently true. We need a great crusade that frankly and avowedly has as its purpose the doubling of church school enrollment.

IV The Challenge of Cultural Diversity

The charge has been made, and with considerable data to support it, that the Protestant enterprise in America is largely middle class in its appeal and involvement. Certainly this is true of the Christian education program of the church. The basic curriculum is written and produced by middle-class people in the idiom of the middle class. It requires considerable education and sophistication to teach it. The leadership training program is even more sophisticated.

The religious educator has made much of graded curricular materials, but always when he speaks of graded materials he is talking of age-grading—nursery, kindergarten, primary, junior, et cetera. What he fails utterly to take into account is that there are cultural differences in the American population that demand a graded approach just as surely as there are age groups. For more than twenty years I have served as a national home missions executive. My work has brought me into contact with Negroes, Southern Appalachian Mountain whites, Mexicans in the Southwest, Puerto Ricans in New York, the underprivileged in the inner city of our great metropolitan areas, the agricultural migrants all across the land. From time to time I have endeavored to involve religious educators in a ministry to these people, but without exception, after a brief contact they have thrown up their hands and admitted that they did not know what to do with such folks. They were and are completely oriented to a middle-class society.

What those involved in Christian education must come to appreciate is that if we are to reach and interest and help people, we must begin with them where they are and we must scale our educational program for them to their present level of educational and cultural development. We must speak and write in their idiom, use illustrations that are within their range of experience, deal with life situations that they feel are their situations. I realize that it is nice for lesson writers and publishers to produce a single curriculum for everybody but this just cannot be done.

Let me illustrate by a recent occurrence. A new situation has developed in connection with our Armed Forces. The military is increasingly made up of married personnel, and families are following the men in service. Some of our largest church schools are now to be found on our military establishments. The chiefs of chaplains came to the religious education leaders of the church a few years ago and said that they desperately needed curriculum materials but that they did not think the military should produce such a curriculum. This was a task that should be performed by the church. At first religious educators and publishers showed little interest and in the end all they did was to assemble a curriculum for the military by taking the existing primary materials produced by one publisher, the junior lessons produced by another publisher, the intermediate materials produced by a third publisher, et cetera. No one asked the question, "Are the curriculum materials being used by the civilian church suitable for military personnel and their families?"

Today we must look to the foreign mission enterprise for curriculum materials for Spanish-speaking congregations in the United States. Migrant ministry workers must write and mimeograph their own materials for agricultural migrants. Independent publishers write and produce most of the lesson materials used by Negro congregations and by the small white congregations that dot the Southern Appalachian Mountain region. Does this not call for an appraisal of the responsibility that religious education has for such cultural groups? I think it does. Our population is too culturally diverse to force it into a single educational mold. Religious education needs to become "missionary," not only in the sense that it seeks to reach more people but in the sense that it should endeavor to reach people of varying educational and cultural levels.

V A Renewal of the Sense of Profession

In the tens and the twenties religious educators had a strong sense of profession. Religious education was to be for them a life vocation and there were a number of graduate schools where they could get specialized training for their profession that was on a par with the training being offered by our seminaries for men who wished to enter the pastoral ministry. Today many of our professional religious educators are young women with only a college education and with little specialization, or they are young men who have pursued a regular B.D. course, with a few courses in religious education, who are willing to serve as ministers of education for a few years until they take a pastorate of their own. There are few schools today offering enough in the field of religious education to really train people professionally in this area. For the most part religious education is taught only as a department or chair in a theological seminary and the orientation is toward the pastoral ministry.

Religious education suffered much in the great depression of the early thirties. Churches that had employed directors of religious education let them go for economic reasons. Weekday religious education became almost nonexistent. State and national denominational educational staffs were greatly curtailed. Graduate schools of religious education folded up both because of financial reasons and because young people concluded that there was no future for them as professional religious educators. Religious education has not yet recovered from what the depression of the thirties did to it.

If the church is to have a really significant program of Christian education, it must have professionally trained people leading it, just as our public schools must have professionally trained secular educators. The church must provide the educational facilities where such a corps of workers can be trained and must be willing to adequately support it. From 1926 to 1930 I directed the educational program in one of the largest Disciples' churches in America. My salary was half of that received by the minister of the church. As I looked around, I discovered that no local church director was getting more than half the salary being received by the minister he was associated with and that many were getting much less. I decided that the salary ceiling of the profession was too low and so I did what many another religious educator has done, I took a pastorate. If the church expects to have a professionally trained and competent leadership in the field of religious education, it must support it on a basis equal to the support it gives for equal training and competence in other fields of church leadership.

I am not here down-grading the role of the lay person in religious education. I do not think that it will ever be true that the religious education program of the church is staffed entirely by full-time professionals as are our public schools, but I do believe that at the center of the church's educational enterprise there needs to be a hard core of well-trained professional workers who are dedicated to their educational ministry as a lifetime vocation. Our seminaries should continue to have departments or chairs of religious education, for many ministers will have to develop and direct their own program of Christian education during all or part of their ministry, but we are in need of more graduate schools whose function it is to train professionals in the field of religious education; and, once trained, the church must give its professional educators a status and a salary commensurate with their training, skill, and responsibility.

VI A More Complete Integration of the Religious Education Program with the Total Program of the Church

The church school movement began as a lay movement almost outside of the church. As time passed, it was tolerated by the church but it was permitted, to a very great extent, to run its own affairs and to finance its own program. Denominational boards of Christian education were established quite apart from the other boards of the church. In the National Council of Churches Christian education was placed in one division while all of the other aspects of the church's program are to be found in other divisions, with little liaison between divisions. Both denominationally and interdenominationally, stewardship and stewardship education, social action and social education, missionary education, membership development, worship and the devotional life are programs that have little or no organic relationship to the program being carried on by the Christian education forces.

Is it not time that the church welds together its total program into an integrated whole? Why should it be compartmentalized as it now is? Christian educators insist that they are doing a comprehensive job of religious education but leaders in the other areas of church life do not agree. They feel that the religious education program is so broad and general in its impact that there is a need for specialized and more intensive programs of education in the areas of church life for which they are responsible. Not only so, but religious education talks about leadership education although it is not seeking to train a leadership for the total church but only for its own educational task. Each program area of the church endeavors to train its own leadership. The evangelistic forces train a leadership for evangelism. The stewardship forces train a stewardship leadership. The social action forces train a leadership for the social welfare program of the church. And so it goes. Is this compartmentalization of leadership education necessary and desirable? I do not think that it is.

Christian educators are in part responsible for the present situation for they have a rather snobbish attitude toward those who work in other program areas. They are the ones who possess the educational know-how. They are the ones who know what ought to be taught. They are the ones to whom the total educational task should be entrusted. All others are novices and meddlers in the educational field. Leaders in the other program areas are also in part to blame. They are suspicious of religious educators, for they feel that they are more concerned with method than they are with content. They are aloof in their attitude toward religious education, for they fear that if religious educators get their hands on the program in which they are vitally concerned, they will water it down to the place where it has no real thrust.

Both groups have considerable truth on their side, but the situation is not one that cannot be resolved. Religious educators should realize that they are not the possessors of all wisdom and the leaders of other program areas should realize that the Christian education forces have much to contribute if they will but join forces with them. The church needs to make a total, coordinated, balanced educational impact and it needs to develop a comprehensive program of leadership development that will supply it with all of the varied leadership that it needs to support its life and activity.

VII A Need to Spread the Base of Christian Education

Christian education needs to broaden its base of operation and discover new means by which Christian education can be carried forward. It is too completely wedded to the Sunday morning church school, the Sunday evening youth group, and the summer daily vacation Bible school. These are all good, but they are not enough.

With the coming of the forty-hour work week and the long week end, families have more time to travel more places and at greater distances. They can no longer be counted on to show up regularly at 9:30 on Sunday morning for church school. Nor can young people be counted on to show up at the meeting of the youth group on Sunday evening because there is no place else for them to go for fellowship and recreation. Many churches have found it futile to offer classes in their vacation church schools beyond the junior years, for junor high and high school young people are off to camp or have summer jobs. Adult departments of the Sunday church school have long been declining in attendance for a number of reasons.

It becomes apparent, therefore, if people are to be reached in increasing numbers by the educational program of the church, they will have to be reached in new ways and at new times. For children and youth the weekday church school on released or after-school time offers a real opportunity. We heard much of such a program in the tens and twenties, but, taking the country as a whole, we do not hear much of weekday religious education today. Why not? The adult education movement, in connection with our public school system, is growing rapidly.

Is it impossible to develop a weeknight adult education program in connection with the church? The summer camp movement has become very popular, not only for children and youth but for adults as well. Most of these summer camps are from five to ten days in duration. Is the idea of summer schools of three to six weeks' duration fantastic?

VIII The Need to Become More Experimental

Christian education needs to become more experimental and more scientific in its experimentation. There is too much of a tendency for Christian educators to feel that they already have the answers and to look critically at anyone who breaks with traditional ways to try new approaches and new programs. There is also a tendency, contradictory as it may seem, for Christian educators to grab up something new before it has really been proved.

We need controlled experimentation in the field of Christian education and we need scientific evaluation and we need to give experiments time to prove their validity or their worthlessness. Often curricula are built and educational projects are launched that are founded only on theory. Then new theorists arise and the whole thing has to be done over again. Theory should always be tested in the crucible of experience and new curricula, new projects, new procedures should not be launched until they have been tested by practical experimentation. This seems almost axiomatic in such a scientific age as this, but as far as Christian education is concerned, it needs to be said. We pick up ideas from secular education and appropriate them without ever asking whether they are valid for Christian education. An "expert" speaks—usually a college or university professor who is considered an authority—and we swallow what he says "hook, line, and sinker."

I cannot refrain from illustrating this point by a little incident that happened a few years ago. Children's workers were strongly opposed to the use of flannelgraphs, largely, I think, because a certain independent publisher first merchandised them. At a meeting of children's workers in Philadelphia a university professor—an assumed expert—was speaking and he made a case for the use of flannelgraphs, saying that inasmuch as the child built up the picture on the flannelboard, he was having a creative experience. One of our children's workers turned to the person sitting next to her and said, "Oh! I am so glad to hear that. I have long wanted to use a flannelgraph." Authority had spoken, so it was all right to go ahead!

Currently most communions are experiencing considerable criticism from the field regarding their graded lesson materials. Religious educators are, however, inclined to stand pat, insisting that they know educational theory, that they know how to build curricula, and that the material is all right. They can't help it if people are just too dumb to use it! But the field—the ultimate consumer—might have had something worthwhile to say on the matter of curriculum if it had been experimented with under typical conditions before it was put into print. Also, if curriculum materials were adequately field-tested before they were put into final form they might not have to be revised so frequently.

IX The Need for Greater Lay Involvement

Religious education started out as a lay movement in the church. The professional religious educator is a "Johnnie-come-lately." But within the space of a few short decades the professional has pushed the lay workers so far into the background that these lay people have come to say in increasing numbers, "Let's just leave it to the experts."

This pushing of the lay person into the background by the professionals has been due in part to the fact that the professionals in order to build up their professional status have represented Christian education to be something very complex and highly technical and beyond the understanding of the average man. Workers who taught church school classes or served as church school superintendents for years and got real joy out of their service became timid and fearful, wondering what blunder they would make because of their ignorance. Finally, they just dropped out of the picture, feeling that someone more learned and more able than they were should carry on.

I have already said that I felt the church needed a hard core of professional educators at the heart of its educational program —men and women who are highly trained and experienced; but these professional educators, if they are to lead, must not build such a gap between themselves and their lay workers as to make these workers feel inferior and futile. Indeed, the thing that the professional should seek to do is to involve the lay worker in such a way as to make him feel increasingly important in the educational program of his church. As I have watched local directors of religious education at work, I would say that it is at this point they most frequently fail. They lack the capacity to involve people, to make them feel that what they are doing is really significant, to create loyalty, to build *esprit de corps.*

Everywhere we hear the cry, "We need more teachers! We need better trained teachers! We need youth sponsors! We need church school superintendents, departmental principals, secretaries! Where can we find them?" Yet all around us, in every local church, are hundreds and thousands of adults. They are no more busy, no dumber, no less concerned than the adults of the church have been in past generations; in fact, they have more free time, they are more highly educated, and they love and respect the church as much as their fathers and grandfathers did. Why cannot we recruit them for educational leadership? The failure is ours, of those of us who are the professionals. We lack the skills and the dynamic of involving people. It is high time we built a bridge across the chasm that yawns between the professional Christian educator and the layman and laywoman in the church and lead these lay people once again to feel that the educational program of their church is something in which they can be creatively and helpfully involved.

X Opportunity for Religious Education

What opportunity does our day offer for religious education? I believe it to be unlimited. There are more people to be reached and involved than ever before. The church has almost unlimited financial resources to support a program of religious education if it becomes convinced that the program is worthwhile. Church people have more disposable time that they can give to religious education if they are challenged to expend it in that direction. There are more well-educated people in the church than ever before. But above all, there are more voices being raised today from more different quarters as to the absolute importance of moral and religious education than has ever before been true. The climate is right for a great advance in the field of Christian education.

Great days are ahead for Christian education if religious educators will divest themselves of their obsession for method and give more attention to content; if they will become promoters and really seek to reach people; if they will but manifest a "missionary" passion that witnesses to a real concern for the needs of people; if they become truly scientific, and not just pseudoscientific in their approach to spiritual growth and development; if they are willing to begin with people where they are and not endeavor to force everybody into the same educational mold.

13

The Emerging Image of the Church College

ORVILLE W. WAKE

THE question of what constitutes a proper relationship between the church and the educational enterprise is one of the most urgent problems of our time. It is urgent both for the church and for the society which the church would redeem.

It is now obvious to almost everyone that the influence of the church in higher education is rapidly diminishing. Once the church that mothered the great universities of Europe regarded them and their scholars as a prized possession. Today there are theological faculties in many of these centers but any sense of common enterprise between the church and the universities is most obscure if it exists at all.

In America the first colleges were brought into being by people of profound religious motivation. The task of providing higher education for the youth of America was a prime aim of the church until shortly after 1900. Since that time the task has gradually been committed into the hands of the state. Today there are many able churchmen who wonder why the church should be concerned, for the state has made excellent provisions for meeting educational needs.

For many years now the educators of the church have been fighting a rearguard action as the church steadily retreats from the modern educational scene. As the retreat goes on in this and other areas of church activity, the fear is frequently expressed that the spiritual foundations of life are eroding away. There is a subtle and continuing suspicion in the church that the alleged erosion is aided if not actually caused by the rapid advances being made in other fields of knowledge, particularly the sciences. If man is being set adrift because his spiritual moorings are being eroded away as a result of the advancement of knowledge, he is surely lost, for the explosion of knowledge is just now beginning.

It is said that the principal cause of soil erosion is the removal of live roots from the soil. They not only hold the soil together but produce the material for revitalizing it. If the analogy holds, the best way for the church to protect and strengthen the spiritual foundations is to put down the life-giving roots of true scholarship in the fertile soil of the twentieth century.

The purpose of this paper is to examine the conception of the relationship between the church and higher education which has existed in the past, and to suggest a modification which might make the church college more effective in the twentieth century. The thesis will be advanced that there is an antithetical relationship between faith and learning, as these terms are commonly understood, which has resulted in some estrangement between the church and the community of scholars. Following a presentation of the way in which the relationship between faith and learning was understood by educators in the colonial period, there will be a presentation of the change, occurring in the nineteenth century, which made the church college into an evangelizing agency for the church. There will be a discussion of some of the inadequacies of the nineteenth-century image, and the possibility of a new image will be raised. It will be contended that the term "faith" can be understood as a state of being, that "learning" can be regarded as a state of becoming, and further, that these two conditions are necessary to each other in the life of the mind. Finally, the church college as the scene of the adequate encounter between faith and learning is described and put forward as the image towards which the church-related college should strive.

One further word of introduction needs to be said. We should recognize from the beginning that in the last analysis we are dealing with two genuine mysteries—the church and education. Christians have tried to understand the mystery of the church from the beginning of the Christian era and we have been greatly benefited by the effort. The church has been described as the mystical body of Christ. The visible and invisible qualities of the church have been discussed. In the here and now of sociological thought, it has been described as a gathered and scattered community. In all cases its basic nature remains a mystery because it is an agency to further the unsearchable, inscrutable love of God.

In spite of centuries of effort to understand the essential nature of man and the changes that occur in his thought, feeling, and action, his soul or the totality of his changing being, he is still a mystery. The question "Why does he have any thought at all?" is still without explanation. When we contemplate man with all of his accumulated knowledge and the processes by which he adds to it, we are still standing before one of the great mysteries of God's creation.

Saying this at the outset could have a depressing effect upon our thought. Some might feel that it is futile to embark on an intellectual enterprise that can end in no certain knowledge. However, this chapter is directed to people who are of sufficient Christian understanding to regard the ever-present mystery of the Infinite as an open invitation to understanding rather than as a deterrent to thought.

At some undetermined time in the long distant past an event occurred upon the Greek peninsula which is a part of the mystery of man to this very day. It was here that the mind of man first began to exercise itself in freedom without a haunting sense of guilt for doing so. Primitive peoples everywhere have, of course, used their minds before and since, but here for the first time the mind was conceived to be an instrument for the discovery of truth. The basis for a self-conscious intellectual life had been discovered.

For the Greek the matter of existing in the world had a light-hearted quality which was not characteristic of any earlier civilizations. He built and protected his cities not because he was authorized to by a spirit beyond the earthly realm, but because he wanted to. He developed codes of conduct and a political system which involved the submission to law, sharing one's wealth, and above all sharing one's thought for the common good. The common good involved providing safety and the physical requirements to free men for the exercise and enjoyment of their minds and spirits.

There was a peculiar mixture of self-confidence and humility in this new type of man. He believed in his ability to get at the truth but not to become the whole truth. What he did not know served to stimulate his learning but did not create in him any great sense of discouragement or guilt. In the face of the unknown he turned to speculation for long-term solutions and to oracles for help in getting out of the more immediate dilemmas of life.

A sense of the intertwining nature of the finite and the infinite was present in the lives of the Greeks but they reacted to it with less fear than people of the East. Their gods had many of the failings of mortals and seemed to them to have many problems common to humans. For them the problems of good and evil were not much closer to a solution in heaven than they were on earth. At any rate the philosophers of Greece attacked the problem with a view to producing solutions rather than receiving them from another realm.

With some such attitudes as these, this miraculously free man stood upon the face of the earth to enjoy his finite existence and make the most of it in thought and action. The belief that all phenomena are fit subjects for man's thought, and will yield, at least in a measure, to his understanding, is one of the foundational attitudes on which the whole Western community of learning has developed. To understand the nature of modern education we must understand the Greek's attitude toward himself and his world.

Another mysterious event took place in Ur of the Chaldees in the long-distant past which has done much to shape life from that day until this. Abraham heard the voice of God commanding him to go out into a land which would be given to him and his descendants. The voice was heard from time to time by the descendants of Abraham, and their effort to understand it forms a graphic saga of finite man in quest of the ultimate reality.

To the early Hebrew, hearing the voice of God was always a terrifying experience. Wherever it was heard—in the burning bush, in the pillar of cloud, or in the quietness of the temple—when that which was other than man spoke directly to man, man trembled. His own finitude was emphasized in every such encounter. Man, though a creature of this Mighty One, was in a sense a trespasser in God's world, chiefly because he could not or would not restrain his own errant will. He insisted on tasting the fruits of this world and he could not refrain from making judgments of his own, and time after time he was chastized by this all-seeing, all-knowing, all-powerful being who constantly watched the waywardness of man. The law was not created by man; it was given by God. The soil yielded not because it was cultivated by man but as a gift of the One who was beyond man and the world in which he dwelt and yet wholly in control of it.

The journey from Ur to the land of promise, to and from the exiles, to Sinai and again to Jerusalem, was not designed to make man confident of his own abilities to understand the mysteries of his existence through inquiry or speculative thinking. Understanding was the reward of submission and not inquiry. The proper approach to truth was petition, not thought.

It is true that the psalmist could marvel at the creation, but he called his fellow man to reverence before it and the power of the creator, rather than to an understanding of it. The priestly class, with keenness of mind, accumulated and conserved the revelations given to the Hebrews and codified religious practice and the law, but they never analyzed or speculated. Truth was not to be discovered; it was to be given.

For the Christian all that happened before Bethlehem was but prologue, for in Christ is found a new interpretation of that which is ultimate. In the events which occurred between Bethlehem and Golgotha man was permitted to see that the spirit in whom the universe reposes is not vengeful, but one of love that yearns for the perfection of man as the crowning achievement of creation. A new dignity was now possible for man as a person capable of cooperation with God. His body, mind, and possessions achieved a new sanctity because they could be freely used to promote the glory of this more completely revealed Father in heaven. Man still suffered for his self-centeredness, his willfulness, and for his ignorance of the will of God, but he had truly become something a little lower than the angels and, at least potentially, the younger brother of Christ and a son of God. Man was now advised to love God with all of his mind as well as his heart and soul, and the stage was set for the struggle between these two great ideas of the proper approach to truth—the cultivation of the mind as an inquiring instrument, or through revelation which results from faith.

The encounter of Greek and Hebrew thought began to occur before the advent of Christ. The conquering Greeks under Alexander did their best to hellenize Palestine, but the Hebrews again demonstrated their remarkable ability to live in a culture imposed upon them without being absorbed by it. Classical Judaism lacked both the desire and the thought forms to confront the Greeks; its strategy was to survive them as they had other captors. In Christianity, as it was expounded by Paul, the full power of the ancient tradition was focused upon the Greeks, and the conversation between Jerusalem and Athens, which is the root of our problem of the relation between faith as represented by the church and learning as represented by our colleges and universities, began.

Paul had all of the qualities needed for the task. He not only knew the Hebrew tradition; intellectually he was the embodiment of it. The fact of his conversion gave him a new content which probably was more nearly communicable to the Greek mind, but he was a Hebrew. As was the case with all religious Jews before him, there was no question in Paul's mind as to where truth resided; it was in God, and God had made his most complete revelation of truth in Christ. True to his tradition he conceived that the way to truth was through submission to God in faith.

However, at one point Paul was quite different from all other representatives of his tradition. When the prophets heard the word of God, they proclaimed it. They chastized kings and subjects alike on behalf of the most high. Paul heard the voice of God in Jesus Christ and he too proclaimed it with the same fervor as his forebears, but at other times he reasoned with those to whom he took the message. He even admonished his followers to be able to give reasons for their faith. It was this willingness to consider, to bring the power of the mind to play upon the religious question that brought the Greek and Hebrew traditions into sufficiently close proximity for a genuine encounter.

To me, the frontal attack which Paul made upon the stronghold of Greek thinkers on Mars Hill epitomizes much of the struggle between faith and learning that has gone on since the encounter between these cultures began. Paul put forth the insight which had been revealed to him with the full force of his powerful mind. The logic and style of the presentation were Greek, but there was nothing speculative about the content. Here was a committed man preaching for a verdict. He was imparting a truth revealed to him; not engaging in analytical thought with the Greeks to see whether they might discover some new thought. Paul had been through years of wondering, of seeking and suffering, but the revelation of Christ had brought this to an end. The master formulation of thought had been made and the facts of existence had fallen into place. This was not a matter for speculation; it was the whole cloth of reality requiring acceptance more than analysis. But when the presentation was over, no evangelistic fervor was evident in the scholars. Instead, the scholars said in effect, "This is very interesting. We would like to hear more about it." In that moment Paul must have known the disappointment that every man of faith has when his thought is presented to the inquiring community.

The power-centered colossus of Rome stood astride the minds of Western men for almost four hundred years before it came to its inevitable end. In this period the Greek men of learning were used as cultural embellishments for the homes of wealthy Romans. The men of faith managed to exist in less preferred places. In the desperate attempt to maintain the power of Rome, the struggle between faith and learning so recently joined between Athens and Jerusalem must have seemed insignificant indeed. But when empires die, they do so because they have either lost their purpose or achieved one that is too small. When purpose and meaning are dying, faith and reason are the physicians needed to resuscitate the culture or to bring a new one to birth. So it was that as Rome expired, the proper physicians were present, and out of the debris of Rome there arose a new theocratic culture which was a Christian flower on a Hebrew stem.

The compelling message of the love of God in Christ captured the minds of a people who had seen the folly of man's effort to take charge of the universe. The Roman training in obedience may have also played a part in preparing the Western mind to accept a given or revealed reality as the ultimate truth rather than one that is derived from his experience by learning. At any rate faith played the leading role in formulating the foundations for the culture of the Middle Ages, and learning was a willing helper.

Gradually it became apparent that some means would be needed to authenticate the body of Christian thought that was accumulating. Some decisions had to be made regarding the authenticity of apostolic writings. Further, if the faith were not to be vulgarized by the misinterpretation of worldly men who had to do some thinking to prepare for the act of believing, authoritative interpretations had to be made. For reasons like these, the hierarchy of the church of the Middle Ages came into being, and scholastic philosophy flourished.

As the system developed, learning increasingly found herself restricted by the demands of faith. There was still much intellectual activity and some of it was brilliant, but it went on in a closed system. Inquiry was not free to pursue the truth wherever it led; instead, the purpose of inquiry was to further authenticate the revealed truth canonized by the proper authorities. Under these conditions learning became restive as she always does when confined. Scholars dislike adjusting to conditions not dictated by reason and they despise recanting even when they are forced to do it in the name of the Most High.

The noise of the new battle between faith and reason was first faintly heard when Abelard, an early teacher at the University of Paris, defended the thesis that faith could be achieved by reason. This reversal of standard procedure, plus the fact that he wrote some rather ardent letters to a maiden named Heloise, got him defrocked. But it was in Italy that learning first began to recapture its freedom. Circa A.D. 1200 remarkable concepts of the shape of the earth and strange new ideas of the workings of nature began to appear, and artists began to depart from old themes with an abandon that alarmed the church. A little more than two hundred years later this same mood came over the schoolmen of central Europe, and shortly the whole matter came to issue in the Protestant Reformation.

Of course the basic issue of the Protestant Reformation was not cast in terms of the conflict between faith and reason, but the fundamental doctrine of the priesthood of all believers involves, at least tacitly, the notion that each individual person is free to stand before his God without the restricting influence of an intermediary. Freedom to approach the ultimate having been gained, how could freedom to approach the problems of earthly existence be denied? The prelude to the Enlightenment of the 17th and 18th centuries was now being played.

For those affected by it, the Enlightenment represented a triumph of learning over faith. Fashionable salons of Europe were meeting places for scholars who loosed their minds and imaginations on problems of every kind. Encyclopedic scholarship was the vogue, and in society at large the church, as the protector of the faith, was in low esteem in many quarters.

It was in this period that educational institutions began to be established in America, and they too have been the scene of the struggle between faith and learning. The early American colleges reflected in their charters an interesting duality of purpose. The desire to propagate the Christian faith was one clear objective, and instruction in scientific and literary disciplines was mentioned with equal prominence. Passages from the charters of a few of the colonial colleges will illustrate the point. The charter of Harvard in 1650 indicated that one of its prime purposes was "the advancement of all good literature, arts, and sciences" in the education of English and Indian youth in this country in "knowledge and godliness." The charter of William and Mary College in 1693 made it clear that those in charge envisioned that great institution as a place where "youth may be piously educated in good letters and manners and that the Christian faith may be propagated amongst the western Indians to the glory of Almighty God." In 1769 Dartmouth College was granted a charter "for the education and instruction of youth of the Indian tribes in this land in reading, writing, and all parts of learning which appear necessary and expedient for civilizing and Christianizing children of pagans." Knowledge and godliness, piety and learning, letters and faith—this refrain constantly recurred in the description of higher education when America was being born. Apparently the image of the college at that time was constructed on the twin axes of faith and learning. It is possible that the new political, social, and economic thought forms which were to characterize a new nation emerged from this tension.

The interrelationship of church and state in the arrangements for higher education in the colonial period was never quite clear, and was disrupted by the American Revolution. In the postrevolutionary period secular and republican views were pronounced, and the idea of an established church passed into limbo. This had profound influence on the development of arrangements for higher education. At first there was a brief struggle between the state and private interests for the control of existing colleges; however, all of them were able to maintain their privileges as private institutions. Dartmouth had the greatest difficulty, and it took a decision of the United States Supreme Court to prevent its conversion into a state university. It was decided in the famous Dartmouth College Case of 1819 that the action of the New Hampshire legislature in altering the original charter of the college was a violation of the constitutional provision forbidding a state legislature "to pass any law impairing the obligation of contracts." The decision was of the greatest significance in determining the character of higher education in the United States, for it gave the churches comprising the free denominational system which developed after the American Revolution opportunities to form their own institutions without interference from the state.

A second and probably more important development preliminary to the formation of large numbers of church-related colleges was the rise of influential missionary or evangelizing agencies of Protestant churches which took place in the years around 1800. The Congregationalists developed local and state missionary societies in 1798 and 1807. This led to the formation of national organizations like the American Board of Commissioners for Foreign Missions in 1810, the American Society for the Education of Pious Youth for the Gospel Ministry in 1815, and the American Home Missionary Society in 1826. These organizations became interdenominational and created an environment favorable to the development of the church-related college.

This development occurred at a strategic time, for the great Western migration was about to begin. Between 1800 and 1840 the number of states west of the Allegheny Mountains increased from two to eleven, and the population from 386,413 to 6,302,915. About fifty per cent of this increase occurred in the western states and territories.

Early in the nineteenth century the Protestant churches generally saw the opportunity to have an impact on the future course of American life through the establishment of colleges which would evangelize the frontiers through education. A new culture was about to be born and the church was convinced that its form would be determined in part by the colleges and universities it brought into being. The thought that "Christian education was the hope of the world" moved with force in Protestant circles in the middle of the nineteenth century. The powerful potential of higher education as an evangelizing agency was obvious to everyone; the image of the college was clear: it was a place where learning was resolved into or made the servant of faith, and the old dichotomy between faith and learning disappeared.

In the nineteenth century evangelization through education was not too difficult. The church through its long history had more or less domesticated the liberal arts, and in spite of an occasional renegade scholar, learning was generally regarded as the handmaiden of faith. But in the latter part of the nineteenth century learning overplayed her role and complicated the situation. Biblical criticism arose to terrify many of the faithful. The possibility of having to find something with which to replace an easy literalism proved to be too much for some into whose hands the faith was committed. The new scientific way of learning about the physical world was applied to man himself and some of the things that turned up astounded men of learning and shocked conventional Christians. The close bond between knowledge and faith which had existed in the early 1800's weakened after 1870 and broke around 1900. This, however, was not generally realized by the congregations of Protestantism until the close of World War I. But ever since the break occurred, the church college has been increasingly uncertain about its own basic nature. As long as learning was clearly the handmaiden of faith, instruction in any discipline was obviously a way to promote the cause of Christianity, but when the arts and sciences insisted upon asking questions in their own way and suggesting answers that could not be believed by the believers, what then?

This problem has been too difficult for us and we have avoided it in several ways. Many excellent colleges have concluded that the task of scholarship is inimical to that of faith and have let their relationship to the church lapse. Fine scholars on the faculties of these institutions have honestly felt that there was no vital relationship between their scholarship and the faith of the supporting church and that it was something of a sham for the college to claim a relation to the church. At the same time the church has become increasingly bewildered by the behavior of its wayward child, the church college. The intellectual advances of the late nineteenth and early twentieth century had threatened the faith of the church and it appeared to her that her children were collaborating with the enemy. All of this led to the deep cynicism about the church college which characterized the period between World Wars I and II. It appeared to many educators and churchmen that simple honesty required divorcement of the church and the college because learning could not or would not continue to be the handmaiden of faith.

Of course the opposite reaction took place in some quarters and this accounts for the development of the more fundamentalist Bible colleges. In this case the conflict was recognized, but faith in her great strength overpowered learning and made her a slave. Here the church came to regard free scholarship as an enemy and went on the defensive to do battle with every scholar who would do more than rearrange the data out of which the faith had evolved. The strength and extent of the Bible college movement are evidence that even the most conservative churches feel that faith and learning cannot be separated, for they bind scholarship to faith in a master-slave relationship.

A second way of dealing with the apparent estrangement of

faith and learning involved the use of theology. The advances being made in biblical scholarship and theology are giving new impetus to the growing edge of Christian thought. This has caused some to feel that the church college could revitalize itself by re-examining the curriculum, teaching procedures, the activity program, and the relationships of all persons comprising the college community in terms of the theological presuppositions on which the institution is built. A few years ago the Danforth Foundation sponsored a series of conferences to aid college teachers in discovering the relationship of their own disciplines to religion. Books and articles on the sciences and religion are being produced in great numbers. "Religion in the Fine Arts" is a popular theme today. Doubtless, life in the college as well as life in the church needs deeper theological foundations. Certainly, a profound sense of Christian vocation which should characterize the graduates of church colleges requires a more widespread and thoughtful use of theology. That many disciplines of the liberal arts can be deepened and enriched by theological thought has been demonstrated many times. After saying all of this it must be admitted, however, that learning can never be "theologized" into captivity by faith.

The theologian as a man of faith is always something of a mystery to the philosopher or the scholar of the arts or sciences. Regardless of how scholarly the theologian or man of faith may be, he lives and moves inside the framework of his faith. His task is to bring knowledge into a tenable relationship to that which he considers to be ultimate. On the other hand, the philosopher stands outside his field of inquiry. His concepts are objectified in the sense that he deals with them outside his personal values, aspirations, or concepts of what is ultimate. In fact, the philosopher likes to "universalize" his insights, and to do so he tries desperately to make them independent of his own personal experience. To put this in different terms, when the theologian undertakes to "theologize" learning, or when the philosopher tries to "philosophize" faith, the result is not likely to satisfy both parties. It is because of this difference in approach of the theologian and other scholars that the dilemma between faith and learning cannot be reconciled by the use of theology.

A third way in which we tend to avoid coming to grips with the fact that a church college may have a function to perform in the twentieth century distinctively different from that which it performed in the nineteenth century is indicated by the manner in which Christian higher education is presented to churches, prospective teachers, and students. The usual description given of a church college is something like this: It is a small institution where members of the administration and faculty seek to know students as individuals. It is a place where the Christian understanding of life is fostered by a curriculum which requires a certain amount of formal work in the field of religion and compulsory attendance upon certain services of worship. It is an institution that employs teachers who profess Christian purposes and ideals, and it encourages a free, democratic life which undertakes to give to each member of the college community the greatest possible sense of "belonging" and personal worth. These qualities are undoubtedly most desirable from every point of view. Few people will contend that mass education is better than individualized education. No one will assert that an atmosphere in which students and professors accept each other and know each other well is undesirable. Certainly no Christian will contend that it is undesirable for people to receive formal instruction in the Christian religion and attend worship services, though some would question the desirability of making these experiences mandatory. There are many fine educational institutions not related to the church which have all of these desirable qualities—smallness, friendliness, Christian professors, courses in religion, and worship services. This approach to defining our fundamental task as church college is another example of a weak effort to hold on to the conception that the church college is primarily an evangelizing agency of the church.

By holding on to this blurred conception of the relation of the church to this college we have tended to confuse our churches and to further many misconceptions of the church college. Prospective teachers have been somewhat wary for fear that the church college would require something other than honest, high-type scholarship. Even after some years of work in a church college some productive teaching scholars, through lack of understanding of the relationships of faith and learning, feel that there is something slightly subversive about honest inquiry. More discouraging still, the image of the church college which we have held before the public has frequently been misinterpreted in such a way that these colleges have too often been regarded as sentimental institutions providing havens for the inept. Those who are familiar with the accomplishments of the graduates of our better church colleges today and with the contribution these colleges have made to life and thought in the past are, however, under no such misapprehension.

What has been said to this point should be sufficient to demonstrate that historically a fundamental dichotomy exists between faith and learning. This ancient problem which arose as a result of the encounter of Hebrew faith and Greek thought lies at the center of our efforts to devise a proper relationship between the church and its educational agencies. In summary the dichotomy is this: The teaching scholar sharpens the critical powers of students but Christian faith affirms an answer. The church has a gospel committed to it which must be preached in its colleges, but at the same time colleges cannot escape their responsibility to help students acquire the art of critical thinking. Is there a way in which these antithetical phenomena can be brought into a fruitful relationship in the church college in the twentieth century? The remainder of this paper is devoted to finding an answer to this question.

If in the years ahead the church college is to have an influence comparable to that which it has had in the past, educators of the church must search for a new definition of the church college and help a new image to emerge, for the image which we have clung to so tenaciously is now expiring and the diminution of the influence of the church in higher education is ample evidence. What is now needed in higher education sponsored by the church is the full and free admission that the college is principally a setting which the church makes possible in order that the processes of scholarship, of learning, and of inquiry can confront and be confronted by the demands of Christian faith or the ultimate aspirations of Christians. To meet this need we must, I believe, again acknowledge the dual function of the church college and make it explicit in the minds of students, teachers, and the friends of this kind of education.

If we could come to regard faith and learning as two distinct, antithetical, but related conditions of the individual and give up the effort to resolve one into the other, we might be on our way to a fruitful conception of the church college which could save it from becoming an anachronism in the twentieth century. In fact, if the fully developed image of the church college as the scene of the encounter between faith and learning could grasp both the church and the college, we might possibly make the greatest contribution needed in the twentieth century, which is to bring the vast knowledge of our time into a creative relationship with the ultimate ends of life.

In addition to the historical evidence broadly sketched in the first part of this chapter to support the idea that faith and learning, while being necessary to each other, are fundamentally antithetical, there are certain theoretical grounds which also support this conclusion. To understand them we must inquire more deeply into the nature of faith and the nature of learning. Of course an exhaustive treatment of either of these subjects would require volumes. Here we must be content to summarize a few of the more important ideas. Let us begin by considering what is usually meant by the term "faith."

There are two quite different senses in which the term "faith" is used by Christians. On the one hand they regard faith as the act of accepting as true something which is not supported by evidence, or is supported by evidence that is doubtful. One frequently hears a statement like this: "I know this and I take that on faith." The person means that there are certain phenomena which have sufficient evidence to satisfy him intellectually, and that there are other phenomena which have not been adequately explained but which nevertheless he finds it necessary to accept in order to make sense out of his existence. Another way of saying this is that faith is the profession to believe, however absurd the proposition may seem. If faith is that and nothing more, it amounts to simple credulity.

There is nothing wrong with simple credulity, for should man in existence refuse to think or act without definitive proof or intellectually convincing evidence, he would soon be as inactive as a stone. The fact that man has cognitive power, that is, ability to distinguish phenomena, and that he seems to be unable to refrain from using it requires him to distinguish between that which can be accepted as true for the purposes of thought and action and that which cannot be so accepted. This is a part of the reason for genuine anguish in the mind of the scholar. As a finite being who must exist in an infinite universe, he is required to relate himself to things that are cognitively unknown as though they were known in order to know anything at all. In short, without the ability to be credulous, meaningful existence would be impossible. Because religion is an effort to approach the ultimate, which is necessarily enshrouded in mystery because it *is* ultimate, faith always involves credulity. The important point is that it also encompasses much more.

In a sense the existence of a great body of Christian literature actually contributes to our tendency to reduce faith to simple credulity. The Christian message is communicated by both word and deed. Words are necessary because any form of experience, Christian or otherwise, is in part cognitive. The great body of Christian literature which has been developed by prophets, saints, historians, philosophers, theologians, poets, and ecclesiastical authorities is designed primarily to present admonitions, propositions, and records of experience out of which the one to whom the message is communicated can form the cognitive basis for taking the first step toward Christ. In a sense these pronouncements, of whatever kind, stand between man and his God, pointing to the God beyond. To arrive at a state of being at one with this God, which is in the most profound sense the state of faith, the individual must necessarily make distinctions as to what is for him tenable and what is not. The great creeds, for example, are submitted to Christians as the intellectual foundations of the Christian community. In various ways churches that place great reliance upon these creeds conduct educational programs designed to lead potential or immature Christians to intellectual assent to the propositions set forth, again as a first step toward entering the Christian community.

The point being made is that when the individual presents his whole being to God, as he does in the act of faith, he presents his mind also, and that in undertaking to do so, intellectual activity is inevitable but it is not the whole of faith.

Faith can also be conceived of as a state of being in which the individual is identified, at least to some extent, with that which he regards to be ultimate. A person in a state of faith is gripped by that power which he has come to regard as ultimate because all the meanings of life are dependent upon it. In a perfect state of faith he is gripped in such a way as to be at one with this power. Thus it is quite possible for a person to be in a state of faith and at the same time retain much of the freedom of his mind. He can be gripped by his ultimate hopes and aspirations in such a way as to require him to do things for which there is no adequate intellectual explanation. In the case of Abraham's response to the call of God, Abraham's action was irrational by any intellectual standards. He was called to go to a land he knew not where, to produce a son when, as Paul says, "his body was already as good as dead," and to sacrifice this son for no earthly reason. Far from being merely an act of giving intellectual assent, faith is a matter of the total organization of the personality. In other words, faith is not what one professes; it is what one is.

When faith is described in terms of "giving intellectual assent to," as in the first case above, it is usually thought that doubt is an antonym for faith. A person either has faith or he doubts. When faith is considered to be the total organization of the personality, doubt becomes a creative agent in the emergence of faith. As Abraham climbed the mount with his son, he must have doubted the wisdom of this act. As Paul rejected vast parts of his previous experience to follow the vision of Christ, he must have had questions about the wisdom of his course. Even in the case of Christ, the anguish in the wilderness at the time of temptation, and again in the garden when he prayed that the cup might pass from him, can be thought of as expression of doubt arising in one who was completely identified with God. Again the very presence of doubt may be an expression of faith. The fact that man cannot withdraw his mental powers from a consideration of the mysteries involved in seeking the ultimate indicates that he is already gripped by its power. It was no accident that Paul persecuted the Christians before he led them.

If faith is conceived in this second sense, there is adequate room for the most profound scholarship. If, however, its meaning is restricted to simple credulity, as it unfortunately has been for many, scholarship is truly a threat to faith and should not be tolerated. Before any thoroughgoing understanding of a more productive relationship between the church and education can be achieved, faith will have to be understood in some such terms as a state of being grasped by that which is holy.

Let us turn our attention to the nature of learning. At an earlier time the act of learning was believed to be a rather simple process of adding information to the mind. Unfortunately much educational practice today proceeds as though this were the case. The theory of the mind as an entity set apart from the rest of the person's being encouraged this belief. To think of a mind as a piece of paper on which impressions were made by data transmitted through the sense organs was far too easy an explanation. Behavior frequently appeared which could not be traced directly to any of the so-called impressions, and furthermore, continuous application of certain stimuli to the sense organs frequently produced a variety of results and sometimes no results at all.

Thought gradually turned from the matter of training the mind to the question of how to change behavior. This new emphasis led to defining learning as changing behavior. When a child begins to respond to a stimulus to which he has not previously responded, or when he responds in a new way, he has learned. In this approach it was clearly shown that feeling, physiological factors including maturation, the organization of previous experience, and the physical conditions surrounding the learning situation were all involved in the matter of learning. Developments in this direction have advanced to the point that the act of learning is considered to involve the total individual. The following definition of learning would be satisfactory to many present-day students: Learning is an event in which a new datum or a new configuration of data becomes a part of the total personality of the individual, changing his behavior in some respect.

Along with this development a new emphasis is necessarily being placed on experience. To experience a thing means to react to it and be reacted upon by it so that behavior and personality, which is the totality of behavior, are changed. Thus it is through experience, emotional and intellectual, that personality becomes what it is within the biological limits determined by heredity.

Psychologists speak of personality as being structured, meaning that different individuals react in characteristic ways due to the way their experience is organized. They also speak of syndromes which are several related patterns of behavior in an individual. It appears then that through experience and biological predetermination personality gets organized into constellations of attitudes and ideas which in the integrated person are related to each other dynamically. This is to say that change in one aspect of the personality produced tension which produces reactions, however slight, in other behavioral systems of the personality. It appears further that the act of learning is the event in which an experienced datum enters the behavioral systems comprising the personality, producing modifications in them. Learning is like a drop of water falling into a pool which produces a large ripple where it drops and which diminishes as it moves across the pool. This is the sense in which learning is dynamic.

It is obvious that all learning does not take place in the placid manner just described. When a new datum seems contrary to or incompatible with the organization of ideas and values already established in the personality, a great disturbance is set up in the person. As he struggles to assimilate this new and different element of experience, many systems of the personality may undergo far-reaching changes. The conversion experience of some people is violent because of the more or less sudden reorganization of value systems. If the new datum cannot be integrated into the personality, the individual may resort to a number of psychological tricks to handle the situation. He may repress it by pretending that the event never occurred, or he may give the new and incompatible experience a separate place in his mental life but fail to relate it to the rest of his experience, and thus begin the splitting of the personality.

There are many other implications of this learning theory, but with this rough outline we should now relate this to the description of faith given earlier. Faith was spoken of as a state of being—as the totality of personality. Learning has been described as the event in which the totality of the personality is modified. The first and most obvious observation is that these two situations are of different but related orders. Faith is a state of being while learning is an event or act in which a state of being is modified. In the second place, in terms of these concepts, neither faith nor learning is comprehensible without the other.

Learning as an act presupposes a personality in which the act can occur, and faith as an organization of personality around God presupposes learning. There are other observations that could be made, but this is sufficient.

Let us turn our attention to some of the implications for higher education. Granted that something like what has been described above happens when faith and learning confront each other in the experience of the individual, what is its significance for the college as a community? In an institution which boldly admits that it is principally a setting for a continuing forum involving both faith and learning, faith is made relevant and learning saved from irresponsible erudition. The bond which unites all members of such a community is the acknowledgment of the tension and the determination to use it to further both learning and faith. In such a college, learning is not to be regarded by faith as its technical servant, and neither is faith the captive of learning. They are adversaries, and the college recognizes this and plans its life in such a way as to promote the confrontation.

It should be clear from what has been said that the tension between faith and learning would be manifested in the community at several different levels. First there is the tension within the individual person briefly referred to above. Second, the tension exists between scholars in different disciplines. Third, the disciplines represented in the curriculum impinge on each other and particularly upon religious scholarship. There would also be considerable tension between the college and the church to which it owes allegiance.

I shall say no more about the tensions within the individual. Let me comment briefly about the others. In such a college as the one being suggested, the function of the administration and the policy-making board of trustees would be to establish the ground rules for the dialogue. Together they would assume the difficult task of assuring that honesty and order prevail. It would constantly seek ways to make it clear that the college is not so much a Roman arena where gladiators fight to the death as it is an Athenian grove where thinkers nourish each other into life.

With regard to the tensions between the disciplines comprising the curriculum, the whole faculty would be concerned to see that in each area the content would have sufficient breadth and depth to arouse students to the ultimate concerns which have brought the discipline into being and won for it a place in higher education. The entire faculty would be alert to the necessity of each member's organizing his work in such a way as to bring the student to a knowledge of these ultimate concerns underlying or embodied in the discipline.

Most educators of the church and many laymen are somewhat familiar with the tensions that arise from time to time between colleges and the church to which they are related. Since the church is essentially a community of faith while the college is a community of both scholarship and faith, this tension is inevitable. In the past the church has spoken to chasten the college when it seemed to the church that the college has not dealt justly with the faith. Likewise the college has spoken to the church to encourage the church to deeper understanding and to make its faith relevant to the prevailing thought world. Up to the present time these conversations have been painful for both parties, and it will probably always be so. However, if the church could come to understand the polarity between faith and learning which must exist in the church college, the tension between the church and the college would cease to be regarded as tragic. Instead, the pain resulting from this tension could be understood as pangs of the continuous rebirth of faith.

Some such development as the one described here is now taking place. It might be said that many fine church-related colleges in America are in reality built around this polarity of faith and learning, though few of them have made it explicit in their own communities or in the constituencies which they serve. The resurgence of religion at Harvard under President Pusey, particularly the vigorous proclamation of the gospel in the Harvard Chapel, is a most significant demonstration of the creative use of the tension between faith and learning in the academic community. Alexander Miller prepared a working paper for the Quadrennial Conference of Church-related Colleges held at Drake and later elaborated on this paper in his volume *Faith and Learning.* This work makes the image of the church college suggested here quite explicit. An official statement on *The Church and Higher Education,* approved by the 173rd General Assembly of the United Presbyterian Church in the United States of America, implies much of what has been said here.

The image of the church college described here will require a much deeper understanding on the part of the clergy and the laity than is now in evidence. It may be true that the process of winning souls in the academic community is too complicated to be understood by those who must support it. On the other hand, it might also be true that the typical churchman would not only understand but would become enthusiastic about a college which would frankly state and take seriously this polarity between faith and learning. In spite of the difficulties involved, the church and its educators have the possibility of lifting from just below the threshold of present educational and religious thought a new image of the church college which could lead both the college and the church to the spiritual frontiers of the twentieth century.

CONCLUSION

14

The Unity We Seek

Ralph G. Wilburn

PRESUPPOSITION: we begin with the assumption that the Christological motif is the key to an understanding of the essential nature of the church. Why are we justified in beginning with this presupposition? Because the unique thing about the Christian community is that the substance of its life is derived from the redemptive impulse of Jesus as the Christ.

The church is not an institution. It is the "people among the people" which has heard and committed itself to the call of God in Christ, and which is conscious of the abiding presence of his Holy Spirit in its midst, to judge, redeem, and reconcile men to God and to one another. The church is a fellowship of persons "in Christ," the ethos of which is found in the *agape* motif.

From the above-stated presupposition it follows that the basic character and qualities of the Christian community are determined by the Christ-event from which it was born and by which it grows and is sustained, in history.

The unity of the church is therefore a "given" unity, in the sense that it is a unity of God's making. In the words of the Evanston assembly of the World Council, "Only at the Cross of Christ, where men know themselves as forgiven sinners, can they be made one. . . . And those who know the Christ is risen should have the courage to expect new power to break through every human barrier."[1]

During the past quarter century, the ultraliberal view of the church as a mere voluntary religious association or a mere human contrivance growing out of the natural need for fellowship, has steadily lost ground, mainly as the result of developments in theology and in the realm of biblical studies. In the shift toward greater evangelical definiteness in liberal theology, the church has been rediscovered, as the community of *God's* creation.

It follows from this "given" character of the church that its unity cannot be correctly understood *merely* as growing up from below, as a summation of sociological adjustments, though these are of course involved. If the unity of the church were merely something which religious men meet and decide upon, we would be at liberty to choose what class or race or cultural group should be included, and what excluded. But church unity is not so determined. The church is the body of Christ; it is a gift "coming down from above." As the Orthodox writer, Jean Meyendorff, correctly says, "The unity of the Church . . . is not merely a unity between men; it is created and granted by God . . . we are only brothers of one another because we are sons of God; we are only members of one another because our Head is Christ. To the question 'What holds the Church together?' there can be only one answer: the unity of all its members *with God*."[2]

This redemptive act of God establishes the unity of the church as a power of reconciliation, breaking down the barriers, so that "there is neither Jew nor Greek, there is neither slave nor free, there is neither male nor female; for you are all one in Christ Jesus" (Galatians 3:28).

To express this Christocentric principle more concretely, we may say that only the power of *agape,* which works mightily through Christ, can break the vicious circle of man's self-love and enable him to determine his being in community by attitudes and qualities which embody Christlike love, "which binds everything together in perfect harmony" (Colossians 3:14).

To this extent we can agree with our Orthodox brethren when they contend that true unity is "essentially sacramental" in nature. For by this, as Meyendorff says, they mean that "the reality of the sacrament and of the liturgy consists . . . in giving the Christian assembly—gathered in the name of Jesus Christ—a value which is *greater* than that of a mere collection of individuals. . . . It is he [Christ] who transforms their human unity into a divine unity."[3]

Fallacious Types of Unity

On the basis of this Christological premise, we proceed to do two things in this essay. First, we shall point out the fallacies of three basic types of unity, to which the church, in wide areas of its life, has adhered—types which persist to this very day, impeding the movement toward a more adequate manifestation of the unity which God has given us. Second, we shall delineate seven fundamental principles, which should serve as guideposts as we feel our way toward the greater unity to which God is calling us.

THE AUTHORITARIAN TYPE OF UNITY

By the authoritarian type of unity, I mean the *kind* of community in which the basic bond which unites the group is, in fact and confession, something other than, or in addition to, the lordship of Christ.

This external authority other than Christ, which serves as an absolute bond of unity, may find its locus in a variety of things. It may take the form of centralized church government, which clamps down on individuals and congregations, unduly restricting their freedom, as in Roman Catholicism. It may center in a creed, giving assent to which is made a requirement for church membership, as in both Catholic and Protestant Orthodoxy. Or again, it may find expression in a uniform liturgy, which is regarded as the only valid form of worship.

Whatever the variation on the theme, the genius of this authoritarian type lies in the belief that a *specific external form* (polity, creed, Bible doctrines, liturgical order) is essential to the *being* of the church. It therefore sets about to establish the cherished form *as part of the very esse* of the church, and therefore also the *very bond* of her unity.

Throughout the centuries, Roman Catholicism, the State Churches of Protestantism, and the denominations also have clung to this notion that unity means uniformity. Karl Adam, Roman Catholic theologian of the University of Tübingen, expresses this dogmatic uniformity clearly. Speaking of the *plenitudo potestatis* of the Pope, Adam writes:

> As the authorized preacher of the truth, the church will never cease to give her authoritative witness to it *and to oblige all consciences* to accept it. . . . The Church does not supplicate or discuss terms with conscience; she makes a direct demand upon it, and *requires* that it surrender itself to the Word of God *as proclaimed by her*. . . . When the Church speaks to conscience, there can be no *subjectivism . . . no doubt or scepticism.*[4]

Let the Roman position serve as a constant reminder of how easy it is for the church-centered approach to unity to lead to an idolatrous clericalism, which distorts the truth of church unity into an excuse for institutional pride and presumptuous self-adoration.[5]

It may be seriously doubted, however, whether *Protestantism* is yet wholly free from this idea of unity as uniformity. To what extent, I wonder, is it true that Protestants, as well as Roman Catholics, would like for the Great Church to be a kind of *enlarged model* of their own denomination? To what extent do Protestants who insist upon "union on the truth" *really* mean "the truth as our denomination sees it"? Lutherans would like a united church, but in accordance with the teachings of the Augsburg Confession. Episcopalians want unity, but on the basis of the historic episcopate, and perhaps also apostolic succession. Disciples want unity, but they would like it so that everyone submits to immersion and to "the ancient order of things" as Disciples understand it.

One of the main blockages to greater unity is this persistent lingering of doctrinal and ecclesiastical absolutism. For those who are aware of the intellectual development of the past one hundred years, the absolutist rationalism of the Enlightenment has given way to a new awareness of how profoundly all human thinking is enmeshed in, and determined by, the processes of history. All thinking is colored by one's point of view, which point of view is shaped by the time and space and condition of the individual enmeshed in a particular context.

If all Christians could appropriate these modern insights and recognize the historically relative, and subjectively determined, character of *all* Christian understanding and response to the call of God in Christ, we might be able to get the authoritarian fly out of the ecumenical ointment. We still believe that Thomas Campbell was correct when he said: "Resume that precious, that dear-bought liberty, wherewith Christ has made his people free; *a liberty from subjection to any authority but his own in matters of religion.*"[6]

These, then, are the major fallacies in the authoritarian type of unity:

(1) It is hung on traditional absolutism, and has not yet faced up to the new understanding of human life and thought implied by the historically relative character of human existence. It needs to recognize, as Schleiermacher puts it, that no definition of doctrine or ecclesiology "even when arrived at with the most perfect community of feeling, can be regarded as irreformable and valid for all time."[7]

(2) It tends to idolatrize Christ, because it fails to distinguish clearly between the living Word of God, which *is* Christ, and man's response to this revelation. This failure leads it to *bind* Christ *inseparably* to some particular expression of his significance, thereby imparting to this form of expression absolutistic qualities, which belong solely to Christ. The result is an idolatrous

attachment to relative religious forms.

(3) It not only fails to promote one of the inalienable rights which Christ bestows upon us, the right of liberty, but it actually tends to stifle this liberty by clamping down upon it from without. This reveals its lack of Christian love and its spirit of sectarian exclusiveness, which shows how far removed this authoritarian type of unity is from the heart of the gospel. Even God himself refuses to violate the freedom of man which he created. God gives himself to us in the only way that he can, so as to elicit our response *in freedom,* namely, in the suffering of the cross. In this gospel light of the *modus operandi* of God, how terribly wrong Christians are to think that they possess some sacerdotal right to give expression to this gospel, in an authoritarian way, which contradicts the character of the working of God, by clamping down from without and attempting to deal with dissent by methods of coercion!

(4) Those who hold the authoritarian type are operating with a distorted view of revelation, as something objective, something fixed and frozen, and find little room in their theology for the *continuous* work of the Holy Spirit, who in prophetic souls may disclose needed self-criticism and new insights for further correction and growth. As Walter Marshall Horton says, "Honest dissent is the church's sensitive antennae, through which the Holy Spirit helps us to 'keep abreast of truth' as we face 'new occasions' in each new generation."[8]

The Reductionist Unity of Rationalism

A second major type of unity is also inadequate. I call this the reductionist type. This pathway to unity represents the latitudinarian spirit of modern rationalism. It says: *Reduce* the basis of common agreement to the least common denominator. Agreement on these few essential points of doctrine is all the unity that we want or need.

Leibnitz was one of the early exponents of this approach. Standing on the watchtower of the new seventeenth-century rationalism, Leibnitz, in his discussions on unity with Bossuet, Roman Catholic bishop of Meaux, summoned all Christians to boil down the essentials to a basic residuum and regard all other theological differences as insignificant.

Liberal Protestantism, determined by Enlightenment rationalism, has made much of this Leibnitzian approach to the problem of unity, in terms of a reduction of confessional requirements for unity.

Now there is both truth and error in this reductionist approach. *If it is correct* to construe the *theological import* of this plea as an affirmation that the *basic content* of the faith has power to unite Christian people, then the plea is true. The very fact that the World Council of Churches became possible on the basis of churches' agreement that "Jesus Christ is God and Saviour" would seem to validate the reductionist approach. And of course it did establish the right of liberty.

History has shown, however, that modern rationalism did not *always* move in the Christological direction. The spirit at work in this modern surge of liberty sometimes cultivated an attitude of theological indifference. Adolf Harnack made explicit what was implicit in this reductionist method when he contended that the message of Jesus was "simpler than the churches would like to think. . . . The Gospel, as Jesus proclaimed it, has to do with the Father only *and not with the Son*."[9] The reductionist road seems thus to end in the rationalistic plea for nothing more than belief in the fatherhood of God and the brotherhood of man, as the ground of unity. And the humanists go one step further; they trim away the idea of God, for after all this is a *theological* belief; they want a unity based solely on the belief in human brotherhood, with no theological foundation.

Now we freely grant that it is legitimate for social clubs and community gatherings to hold together by the vague feeling that "the more we get together, the happier we'll be." And it is equally consistent for those of the Hindu religion to follow the call to this vague type of unity, for the central principle of Hinduism is that all religions and philosophies, equally, represent broken lights of the Ultimate *(Brahman)*. Hence for some twenty-seven centuries India has been the home of this boundless kind of religious tolerance and theological indifference.

But now, is Christian unity really *nothing* but the humanism of *Hinduism?* If so, perhaps we should cease witnessing to the gospel and propagate the doctrine of the *Upanishads*. Is it not stretching things a bit to say that Christians can dip their hands in that from which the gospel silently turns away?

This unity of indifference shows itself to be lacking in evangelical depth and in the quality of imperativeness. It is weak theologically. It does not possess an adequate vision of that supreme and all-commanding revelation-reality, dedication to which alone can bring the fulfillment of Christian humanism. Furthermore, one cannot blithely ignore the fact that in the New Testament there is recognition of such a thing as a *misuse* of the name of Christ.

This, then, is the first thing wrong with reductionist unity: it contains a tendency *away from the gospel,* toward the unity of theological indifference. The result is that the central bond of community here comes finally to be something other than the Spirit of Christ; it comes to be universal reason, the natural social impulse, mere fellow-feeling, or something similar.

But there is also a second error in reductionist unity. Although the formation of the World Council demonstrates the validity of *one aspect* of the reductionist plea, other aspects of it have been shown to be inadequate and unrealistic. The *actual growth* of unity in ecumenical Christianity has shown that the amount of Christian conviction and practice which we share in common is amazingly large. In this sense, the advocates of the reductionist type have lost the battle; their plea has been outmoded by historical fact. The fundamentals have, of course, supplied a basis for cooperation and discussion; but *in themselves* they are not sufficient to supply us with the *fullness of faith and life,* which belongs to real growth in unity.

We must therefore overcome the negative attitude toward theology, which was generated by reductionist rationalism. The fullness of unity will not be achieved by theological indecisiveness. There *is* a function which theological statements can perform, other than being used legalistically as instruments of division. They are necessary for the growth of really significant unity, in the sense that they represent movement in the right direction. The way to unity is not doctrinal uniformity; but it *is* the way of coming increasingly closer to the center of the gospel of God, through theological clarity and understanding.[10]

THE ETHEREAL UNITY OF PIETISM

Yet a third major historic concept of unity must also be labeled "inadequate." This is the pietistic view, which says that a spiritual unity in Christ is all the unity that we need, and that true unity does not require any historic continuity or concrete embodiment in ecclesiastical structures. Exponents of this view contend that the only linkage required for true unity is through the Risen Christ. This linkage with Christ, through the Spirit, automatically, so to speak, binds us with our Christian brethren in all other ages and places; and this "oneness in Spirit" is regarded as exhausting the meaning of Christian unity.

Seventeenth-century pietism (which lives on to this very day) may perhaps be cited as a classic example of this concept of unity. Pietism insisted that Christianity is primarily an individual experience and life, and that all who are truly saved, whatever sect or name, are really "one in Christ." The Dutch poet, Jeremias de Dekker, a friend of Rembrandt, expressed it aptly when he said:

> Do you believe that your Church gives salvation
> Condemning mine as heresy and sect?
> God has his friends in each denomination
> From every one Christ chooses his elect.

Pietism has made a valuable contribution to the church's thinking about unity. Its major emphasis contains an element of truth: the inward spiritual center of the church's life does transcend any and all forms through which it is expressed and manifested. We *are* one "in Christ," in spite of the diversity of outward forms of expression.

The way in which pietism construed the significance of sharing in, and fulfilling, this inner Spirit, however, is far from adequate. Its view of Spirit is much too ethereal and abstract. The unity which it advocates is, so to speak, suspended in the rarified atmosphere of the "wholly" spiritual. And it just will not do to say that this is all the unity that we need. Why? Because the church is not merely a spiritual entity; it is a concrete, empirical community, in history. All praise and honor to Zinzendorf when he exclaimed, "We will not let ourselves be imprisoned within any sect." He was much too one-sided, however, when he added, "we have only to do with the hearts of men . . . and our basic purpose is to realize the high priestly prayer: that all may be one."[11] A mere invisible or spiritual unity, which fails to manifest and express itself in visible outward ways, inevitably reduces to a vague sentimentalism that cannot properly be called either "spiritual" or "unity."

Because the unity of the church is to be realized on earth, it becomes imperative that the objective, historical character of its life be structured in ways which realize and manifest the inner oneness of its life in Christ.

These three approaches to the realization of the church's unity have been tried in Christian history and found wanting: (1) an authoritarian uniformity, which idolatrizes Christ, (2) a rationalistic reductionism, which veers from the Christological center of the gospel, and (3) a pietistic spiritualism, which tends toward an ethereal suspension of the body of Christ and fails to deal adequately with the fact that the church is also a concrete historical quantity.

No small part of our difficulty lies in the fact that, although, from our present vantage point, we can see inadequacies of the ways to unity that have been attempted, no Christian individual or group is wise enough to envisage clearly the form of unity toward which God is leading us. Yet even this limitation is part of the thrill of blazing new trails in the historical realization of the kingdom. As Leonard Hodgson reminds us, "We have to look ahead, discover as well as we can the best form of the goal we are aiming at, and make our plans accordingly. But it is in working them out, as the situations are changed through the steps that we take, that the nature of the goal is revealed to us more clearly."[12]

The latter section of this paper is by no means meant to be a full description of an ecclesiastical form which will promote and sustain the qualities and relations of ideal unity. More modestly, it is an attempt to delineate seven basic principles which we feel to be of formative significance in developing a concept of a form of unity which will adequately express the Christological motif.

REAL BUT NOT ADEQUATELY REALIZED

(1) We should not fail to recognize the *actual unity* which already exists. In this regard, the Roman Catholic, Canon Thils, has sadly misunderstood the attitude toward unity which prevails in ecumenical circles. Thils has made a thorough study of the ecumenical movement; but his theological prejudices have caused him difficulty in grasping the true import of it. He writes,

> The majority of the Christian groups who make up the World Council of Churches maintain a conception of the church according to which: (a) the true church of Christ does not now exist in its real essence (quoad substantiam) in any historical communion; and (b) since this is the case and since the essential unity of this visible historical church does not actually exist at the present time, the divided churches must proceed to become the Una Sancta, through the gift of God and by means of their unanimous action.[13]

This is an unfortunate misinterpretation of the basic concept of unity which obtains in ecumenical circles. We do *not* hold that "the visible historical communion of the true church does not actually exist." Canon Thils fails to get the real point. He cannot understand the difference between saying "that the essential unity of the church *does not exist*" and affirming "that it is *not yet adequately manifested* in the organization structure of the life of the churches."

To be sure, we gladly confess what our Roman Catholic brethren are still incapable of confessing, namely, that *no one* of the various confessional or denominational groups *alone* represents the true church. But the undergirding concept of unity which obtains in ecumenical Christianity is that in a basic sense the unity of Christ's church is an organic part of the very givenness of the church, as the creation of God; and this means that in a basic sense this unity already exists, for the church cannot be without the unity which it creates. The greater unity which we seek is the fulfillment, and more adequate realization and manifestation, of the unity which we already have, insofar as we are "in Christ."

Catholic in Substance, Protestant in Principle

(2) An adequately Christological unity must be catholic in substance but Protestant in principle.

By the word "catholic," in this context, we mean the substance of Christian history and tradition, in its universal sweep through the centuries, including the witness of Scripture, the mind and message of the historic church, the great confessional statements of the faith, church order, the sacraments, and the devotional life. To borrow a line from Lesslie Newbigin, the unity we seek must somehow be "recognizably linked to the whole Christian fellowship in all ages and places."[14] The unity of Christ's church is a truly catholic unity, embracing and reflecting the totality of the body of Christ.

Why now must this catholic scope characterize the church's

unity? First of all, because Christianity is a historic continuum, and it becomes blunted and distorted whenever it attempts to cut itself off from its historic roots. God has willed to actualize the revelation of himself in Christ by means of these historical media of Scripture and the witnessing historic community. Tradition is therefore an integral part of the togetherness of the ongoing Christian community.

A unity which is lacking in this catholic substance of the church's life thereby shows that it is based upon a distorted Christology and a questionable doctrine of the Holy Spirit, for the assumption would then be that one could share fully in the Holy Spirit, in a fragmented isolation which loses a sense of organic oneness with the wholeness of the church. This loses the historic sweep of the church, which binds us all together in the living stream of its life, reaching back to the original revelation in Jesus as Christ.

Protestants must banish the anticatholic illusion of restorationism, which misled many to ignore the bulk of tradition entirely and attempt to derive their life exclusively from Scripture. We cannot and ought not think that we owe nothing to the past. We cannot and ought not act as if there were no Christian history. It is an illusion to think that we can begin *de novo*. The unhistorical outlook of restorationism must be transcended by greater historical realism. The unity of the church can be what it ought to be only if Protestants and Catholics and the Orthodox overcome their fragmentation of the body of Christ, and learn to embody the wholeness of the church.

Protestants must also recover the catholic idea that the church is an integral part of God's redemptive work in the world, and that in a real sense the church is a bearer of God's grace. The church is a historic community by means of which, normally, God carries forward his redemptive work. As Emil Brunner puts it, "The New Testament *Ecclesia* . . . is divine revelation and salvation in action."[15]

Yet at the same time, the church's unity must be Protestant in principle. What do we mean by this? We mean that Christ the Lord is infinitely greater than our finite response to him. Christ remains what he is: the transcendent Lord of his body the church. He is not only Lord *in* the church; he remains, at all times, Lord *over* it.

The Protestant principle is the principle of prophetic judgment against all forms of human pride, all forms of ecclesiastical and doctrinal absolutism, all forms of human self-sufficiency. Protestant Christianity says that Christ the Lord is the dynamic source of all spiritual fulfillment in the church, but that this creative source cannot be *identified* with any form of its fulfillment.

The lordship of God in Christ is realized concretely in and through the historic church; this is the truth of catholicism. Yet never perfectly, never adequately, but always in a way in which the empirical church itself, together with the entire world, stands under the judgment of his transcendent Word—this is the truth of Protestantism. As Daniel Day Williams says, "A radical application of the Protestant principle does not mean *abolition* of form and tradition but a *continual openness* to reformation in the light of fresh encounter with God's Word and Spirit."[16]

The main problem for Protestantism, therefore, as it develops a more catholic consciousness in its understanding the church, is to do so in a way in which it retains the essential truth of the Protestant principle. The Bible, the holy book of the whole church, and the *kerygma* particularly, must be given a central place in the catholic substance of the church's unity; yet in a way so as to avoid any biblicism or kerygmatism. A critical understanding and use of the Bible is imperative if it is to serve the cause of unity, which finds its living center not *in* the Bible, but through the Bible, in the living truth of the gospel.

Similarly, in the current liturgical and sacramental development of the Protestant churches, the problem will be to keep this valid catholic development in Protestantism under the freedom of the Spirit of the Protestant principle. Unlike traditional catholicism, the sacraments must not be allowed to become ends in themselves, for this moves away from faith toward the *ex opere operato* concept of grace. On the contrary, it is Jesus Christ who is *represented* in the corporate sacramental action of the church. His grace must be received personally, by the faith of the participant.

This Protestant emphasis on subjectivity, however, can and should be correlated with a greater awareness of the corporate character of the church's wholeness. The faith which the individual Christian holds, he holds in mutual relationship and interdependence with that of all other Christians. The corporate, sacramental act of the church thus reinforces the individual's faith with the corporate faith of the universal church. Indeed, church liturgy is a celebration of this universal faith, which binds us all together in the one body of Christ, despite the formal diversity of the sacramental rites of the various Christian groups.

BIBLICAL BUT NOT BIBLICISTIC

(3) Ideal Christian unity is grounded in God's self-revelation through Jesus. The apostolic witness to this Christ-event therefore remains formally normative in the structuring of church unity.

The Christian community is grounded in the special light and power that came, and is continually coming, into the world through God's self-revelation in Jesus Christ. And since the original moment of this revelation, upon which the continuous aspect depends, includes not only the life, death, and resurrection of Jesus, but also the reception of the meaning of this event, in faith, the apostolic witness occupies a place of special significance in the life and thought of the church. Christology means that the church is "apostolic," in this sense of the term.

No one can deny this unique dignity of the apostolic witness if he pauses long enough to note that it is in fact the gospel message (the *kerygma*) which has remained the formal center of the church's life down through the centuries. The historical figure of Jesus, as such, disappeared from the scene of history. If therefore this historical figure is to remain in any sense central in the shaping of the life of the church, the early witness to his life and death remains a vital and unique part of the church's foundation.

It is true, of course, that the locus of the church's life and unity in the ongoing present is found in the ever-present working of the Spirit. But when the spirit which enlivens and animates the group fails to glorify Jesus as the Christ,[17] fails to vivify and cherish the hallowed memory of Jesus, but leads instead in some other direction, Christians may rightly question whether the spirit of such a community is in truth the Holy Spirit; for there are many community spirits abroad in the world.

One does not disparage the good which may be present in other community spirits, such as American democracy, Russian communism, Renaissance humanism, the Bahai religious faith, etc. But if we are to take the Christological character of church unity seriously, if the church is to be a redemptive power, overcoming the divisive barriers erected and perpetuated by many of these other community spirits, indeed often by Christianity itself, if the church is to be a significant force in the present human situation for the creation of brotherhood and Christlikeness of life, then theology must distinguish the Holy Spirit from all other spirits. And this, it can do only if it retains a secure anchorage in the transcendent word disclosed in the historic Jesus. But to retain such an anchorage, the apostolic witness must be regarded as a primary and indispensable guide and inspiration, as we seek to understand precisely what a Christ-centered life-unity really means.

There is a sense, therefore, in which the church can never again produce the canon. More than any other writings, those of the New Testament serve as a means whereby God lays his saving hand upon us, and a means whereby there is generated in our hearts the picture of Jesus as Christ, our inspired and inspiring norm. Through this apostolic witness we, too, are drawn into the life-giving correlation of the events of the redemptive community, and we experience the transforming power of the Christ who lives and reigns through the Spirit, in his body the church.

It is this unique connection of the New Testament writings (not through some illusory notion of their infallibility) with the eschatological history of the Christ-community which gives them their normative significance and formative power in shaping the character of the church's unity.

INNER AND OUTER DIMENSIONS DISTINGUISHABLE BUT NOT SEPARABLE

(4) If the church is a historical fellowship, but a fellowship of *faith* in Jesus Christ, bound together and empowered by the continuing presence of the Holy Spirit, a community which shares in the eternal life of God, there are two dimensions to its life, and therefore to its unity: the inner and outer dimensions, or the transcendental and the historical. An adequate concept of unity must keep in view the distinction between these two dimensions, as well as their organic interrelatedness.

Part of our ecumenical task is to promote a fuller realization of the inner dimension of unity, which has to do with the life that all Christians share in common: the gift of grace, the cultivation of life "in the Spirit," growth in Christlikeness, in short, sharing fully in the life of God, as he gives himself to us in the covenant community. The New Testament refers to this oneness as the *koinonia* (fellowship) of Jesus Christ,[18] or the *koinonia* of the Holy Spirit.[19]

The church, however, is not merely a spiritual entity; it is not a Platonic idea. The church is a concrete, empirical community *in history*. It is a real part of the life of the world. And this means that it has a destiny to be realized under the forms of finitude. At this point, the outer institutional aspect of the church's life comes into view. Here we are confronted with a wealth of diversity; doctrinal, ecclesiastical, liturgical diversity.

Since there is only one church, it is imperative that the internal unity be reflected and realized by external structures which do justice to it more adequately than is the case at the present time. True, the Christian community is bound to an authority which transcends the relative forms that express it. But so long as these outer forms and theologies about them are such that they prevent those who have been received into the body of Christ from sharing fully in work and worship, they are violating, and indeed separating themselves from, the *real inner unity* of the church, the bond of which is Christlike love. To the extent that this is true, the church must confess her failure to *be* the church, as God intends it. And to the extent that the church, in the outer forms of her being, allows herself to be determined by racial, national, social, and ideological barriers, which alienate men from one another and block the growth of creative love, to this extent she must confess her failure to *be* the community where the Spirit of Christ reigns. The churches can scarcely help fulfill Christ's ministry of reconcilation so long as their own life manifests the Spirit of unreconciled partisanship.

The large number of re-formations in the outer structure of the church's life which have been carried through in the course of the ecumenical movement, and those now in process, all represent praiseworthy efforts to fulfill, in some measure, the imperative of unity. The large number of church mergers in the past half century, the many forms of union which have come into being to carry out more effectively the social and missionary imperatives of the gospel, and the more recent conciliar developments as a fruitful form of unity, most notably the World Council of Churches—for all these we can thank God and take courage, for they represent enormous strides in the effort to make the outer forms of Christianity more adequate to its inner Spirit.

Unity Inclusive of Diversity

(5) Closely correlated with the interrelationships between the inner and outer dimensions of ideal unity stands another aspect: it is a unity which comprehends diversity.

Christological unity is "organic," at least in the sense that it is the unity of a living, historical community, and not the unity of a fixed mathematical form. The unity of a community of persons involves the richly complex, prehensive ways in which each person is related to the life of the whole, ways in which the values and meanings of the whole are "taken" by the individual and "brought home" to his own soul, so as to become significant for his own authentic existence. This shaping of creative personality, in the matrix of community life, necessarily involves the existential uniqueness of authentic individuality. And the structuring of historically diversified group individualities involves a similar kind of uniqueness. That Christian unity is organic in this sense means that it is unity in tension, a tension which embraces the formal diversity of unique individualities and groups.

Unity without this diversity of individuality leads to a rigid formalism (dogmatism, ecclesiasticism, hierarchicalism) which destroys the spirit of Christian charity. And a diversity without unity cuts the vital bond of the church's relation to Christ, its one and only Lord. But "diversity in unity, or a unity that comprehends diversity, is historically realistic, and makes it possible for our fragmentary, individual perspectives on the truth of the gospel to be complemented and corrected by cross-fertilization with the perspectives of other Christian individuals and groups. Such unity, which comprehends diversity, constitutes a dynamic fellowship that promotes growth "in the grace and knowledge of our Lord and Savior Jesus Christ" (2 Peter 3:18).

There seems to be fairly wide agreement in ecumenical circles regarding the validity of this general principle of diversity in unity. But we have not yet clearly seen precisely what this means when applied, in a corrective way, to the denominational situation that presently obtains. The principle of diversity in unity is gaining increasing acceptance, however, for it is recognized that only by this principle can we safeguard Christianity against the threat of a superdenomination or world-church, with a too powerful ecclesiastical organization, and clerical domination and control.

This evidently means that, although the church-merger approach to unity is good and in most instances represents real advance,[20] the church-merger pattern is not the clue to the final answer to our problem. We dare not forget that many centuries ago Rome succumbed to the lures of this easy substitute for Christian unity. If *this* is what is meant by the contemporary plea that ideal unity must be a "churchly" unity, we should be obliged to dissent, for such uniformity tends inevitably to become oppressive.

It would, however, be unwarranted theological arbitrariness to restrict the meaning of "churchly unity" to such a concept of monomorphic church structure. The type of unity for which we are pleading in the latter part of this paper, a unity that comprehends diversity, is quite definitely a "churchly" unity.

Saying that ideal unity comprehends diversity must not, however, be construed to mean that just any kind of diversification is compatible with true unity. The *kind* of denominational differentiation which now obtains obviously leaves much to be desired in the matter of unity. Various theological fixations, which are woven into the substance of the life of many denominations, throw difficult road blocks in the path of unity. One thinks of the Anglican fixation on apostolic succession, the Disciple fixation on immersion-baptism, the Lutheran fixation on the doctrine of the "real presence," Rome's fixation on the hierarchy, and the Orthodox fixation on the historic creeds. We must transcend these fixations. We must modify and correct this kind of denominational fixation.

This does not mean that it is incompatible with ideal unity for a denomination to retain a belief in the historic episcopate, or in the immersion mode of baptism, or in the "real presence," or in a Roman bishop, or in the need for confessional statements of the faith. But it does mean that the element of liberty in ideal unity demands of these denominational branches of the church that they cease holding these beliefs in an exclusive way. They must hold these and all other doctrinal formulations in a way that includes those who differ with them, thereby sharing their own witness in the larger fellowship of Christ's total body, in freedom. The unity we seek provides for a principle of comprehension. It is a unity in which we recognize that we are one by virtue of our common experience of the One Lord, even though our limited attempts to understand and express this experience involve us in doctrinal differences.

As to the precise form of the unity we seek, the live options now being debated in ecumenical circles are either full, visible, corporeal unity, or a unity of inclusive association or fellowship augmented by conciliar methods and procedures. The former, "catholic" pattern of unity seems to be decreasing in popularity; and the conciliar approach seems to be gaining in favor. Advocates of the latter concept urge greater association, both in cooperative action and in a fellowship which involves complete mutual recognition of one another's ministries and members. The author of this paper confesses his present leanings toward this latter alternative.

Advocates of this conciliar concept press their argument along five main lines:[21]

This concept is closer to the New Testament conception of unity, in which there was considerable flexibility and variety in forms of church expression within the "unity of the Spirit in the bond of pcace."

This pattern of conciliar connectionalism was also predominant throughout the early centuries of church life. In the early centuries, Christian unity was a matter of complete mutual recognition of ministers (bishops) and members; so that when a Christian moved from one city to another, he was immediately able to feel religiously at home in the new situation, despite the differences in forms of church life and worship. And this sense of unity found an instrument, for common voice and joint action, through church councils. This "autocephalic" structuring of church life (which lives on in Eastern Christianity to this day) was a happy state of affairs until Rome decided to inject the papal fly in the unity ointment and absolutize its own peculiar structural development, and accordingly set out to hierarchicalize the rest of Christendom.

The association pattern alone can make room within unity for the rich varieties of Christian experience and worship, which are part of the glory and fullness of the church's historical life, under God.

The association concept safeguards our individual liberty in Christ (as a full visible corporeal unity evidently would not) against the ever-present menace of overlarge and overpowerful ecclesiastical structures. Yet it safeguards this liberty in a way which prevents the emphasis on liberty from being distorted into an irresponsible individualism that disrupts the spirit of creative community.

The association pattern is truer to the Protestant principle, for it keeps alive the awareness that no one church form is sacrosanct. It thereby helps to rid our hearts of the denominational attitude which ceases any longer to examine and reform itself under the transcendent light of God's continuous revelation in Christ.

It remains to be seen however whether, and to what extent, the conciliar development of a unity of association will be able to remove the blocks that remain in the road to greater unity. Will the councils be able to sponsor the growth of some new structures which will make possible a more forthright mutual recognition of one another's ministries, leading to greater fellowship in the matter of pulpit exchanges, both temporary and permanent? Will they be able to instigate and augment the kind of theological development needed so that a mutual recognition of one another's baptisms and members can be frankly secured and established, and so that intercommunion can become more frequent and more meaningful?

What is needed is a closer and more inclusive kind of association than that which obtains at the present time—not a loose association in the sense that we occasionally swallow our denominational pride and agree to share in an interdenominational service, but the association of vigorous and sustained fellowship, of being bound together in the one family of God.

A refreshing and inspiring unity of fellowship is an actual reality, at the present time, at the higher levels of conciliar gatherings. Perhaps the greatest scandal, at the present time, is the wide contrast between this robust conciliar fellowship and the pitifully weak and meager ecumenical fellowship at the grass-roots level, in the local community, the place where most Christian people live out the meaning of their faith. This scandal must be removed. Ways must be found whereby all Christian people in a given community can come to experience a vastly greater and vastly more meaningful togetherness in the body of Christ than their present portion of ecumenical life. This can be achieved, perhaps, if parallel developments in the matter of worship and study can match those of cooperative social action. Ecumenical leaders with creative imagination are desperately needed to do this job at the level of local church life. Despite the fact that not nearly so much social glory awaits them as that shared by ecumenical leaders of the higher echelons, "great will be their reward in heaven."

Theological But Not Dogmatic

(6) A Christologically grounded unity will also be vigorously theological in nature. Only if it is such, can it avoid the pitfalls of pietistic spiritualism and reductionist rationalism. I would agree with John E. Skoglund when he argues that ideal unity "must mean more than the dulled denominationalism or 'getting together on good works' characteristic of so much of contemporary American popular Christianity.[22]

Theology qualifies the church's life when it seeks to understand God's gift in Christ, through faith. A religious unity lacking in the intellectual impulse tends to thwart the fulfillment of the truth of Christ.

Here again we would distinguish between two levels in unity. The primary level concerns the basic reality which is the absolute bond, the *sine qua non* of unity. This reality is the vital center of all valid Christian unity. It is the lordship of God in Christ, sharing in whose life we are made one. This is the vital bond which unites all men of faith in the one body of Christ, despite the diversity, and even contradictions, in their respective theologies.

Yet there is also a secondary level of unity. This concerns our growing together in an understanding of the meaning and truth of Christ's lordship. This theological element in ideal unity is the one thing that can secure the church against sheer arbitrariness and slipshod relativism in the interpretation of the Christ-reality. Christian unity can hardly be perfected apart from attaining "to the unity of the faith and of the knowledge of the Son of God" (Ephesians 4:13). Although *ultimately* it is the common spirit of loyalty to Jesus Christ as Lord which binds us together in the one body, this theological aspect is vitally important for vigorous growth in unity, and in some sense also indispensable.

If the distinction between these two levels in unity, between the vital bond of faith and the intellectual effort of faith to understand itself, be kept clear, it should be possible for the church to express and realize the confessional aspect of its life without lapsing into the error of confessional*ism*.

In regard to the theological aspect of the church's unity, it is hardly saying too much to affirm that we are already miles beyond a vague sense of oneness by virtue of the fact that we all share in common the name "Christianity," or all agree that "Jesus is Lord." Something of the extent of our theological growth in unity is evident in the words of the pre-Lund Commission on the nature of the church.

Every communion holds that the Church is not a human contrivance, but God's gift for the salvation of the world; that the sav-

> ing acts of God in Christ brought it into being, that it persists in continuity in history by the presence and power of the Holy Spirit. Every communion likewise believes that the Church has a vocation to worship God in His holiness and to proclaim the Gospel to every creature, and that she is equipped by God with the various gifts of the Spirit for the building up of the Body of Christ. And every communion believes that the Church is composed of forgiven sinners, yet through faith already partakes in the eternal life of the Kingdom of God. These agreements cover the Church's origin, the mystery of the Church's present being, and the Church's goal. They ascribe to the Church both a divine and a human element, both a possession and an anticipation of the age to come. They imply an insistence upon the holiness of the Church without any identification of this with a mere human moralism; and insistence upon the visibility of the Church without obscuring the tension between the Church as it now is, and the Church as it is destined to become.[23]

We submit that here is a quite substantial theological bond of unity, to which all bear witness, which is happily free from the evils of dogmatism, and yet is considerably beyond a pietistically vague Jesus-faith or a reductionist, rational creed.

In regard to the theological aspect of ideal unity, there are two basic distortions to be avoided. One is the frozen wastes of doctrinaire dogmatism. The theological aspect of unity is twisted into this distortion when it is interpreted as a demand for doctrinal congruity, The error here is to forget that ideal unity comprehends diversity in forms of expression. The second distortion is the fuzziness of sentimental pietism or theological indecisiveness. The errors here arc those of the spiritualistic and rationalistic views of unity, pointed out in the beginning of this paper. Such theological fuzziness leads to a situation in which Christians feel that it is wonderful to be united in fellowship, but nobody quite knows why.

The pitfalls of both dogmatism and sentimentalism can be avoided if we maintain an awareness that it requires the variegated witness of the whole church of God for the full truth of the gospel to find adequate expression. How else can the finite even begin to grasp the infinite adequately? Due to our human limitations, no one individual or one confessional group possesses the wisdom or ability to present a full and complete expression of the truth of the gospel. It takes the compounding of the perspectives of all to approach the ideal of adequacy, in the matter of ideal unity. Growth of awareness of the need for this compounding of perspectives will greatly strengthen the bond of unity; for it will deepen our sense of need for one another, adequately to be the church.

Openness to God's Leading and Willingness to Be Transformed

(7) Perhaps the most important word to be said concerns the matter of religious attitude, the attitude of humility and readiness for reform. The degree of success of the ecumenical enterprise will be directly dependent on the degree to which those involved are willing to be remade, reformed, and re-created by the larger vision of truth that may emerge.

It may well be that we have reached a point of growth in the cause of unity where not much further development is possible until we come to see that God is seeking to lead all of us to something higher, better, and somewhat different than what we have been and now are; and until, coupled with this saving vision, we are characterized by a humble willingness to "let go" and "let God" lead to a restructuring of the forms of expression of the Christian faith to which we yet cling.

It is true, of course, that Christians are united by a common purpose, namely, God's intention for man disclosed in Jesus Christ. This ethicoteleological aspect of Christian unity is eloquently expressed in Jesus' analogy of the kingdom of God. Luminous, empowering, and life-transforming as this light of Christ's disclosure of God's purpose for human existence is, the church's grasp of it, at any given time, always leaves much to be desired, both in terms of strength of commitment and clarity of vision.

The church, however, always tends to lose this awareness of the insufficiency of its own faith and forms. It succumbs to the false security of traditionalism. History shows that new visions of truth and holiness are established only through severe struggle with the forces of traditionalism. Religious people become very strongly wedded to the forms of the tradition in which they have been reared, often to the point of idolatrizing them.

We wonder, therefore, to what extent it is recognized by all that God is seeking to lead us to a goal which reaches vastly beyond anything that our limited ideals of the kingdom are able to envisage, at any given time? Our fallible vision doubtless leaves out many things which God, in his infinite wisdom, includes. And history teaches us that we often include things which we later learn are really not included in God's purpose. We are thus continually growing in spiritual wisdom, and must continually revise our ideals accordingly. This is as it should be.

Our ultimate commitment, then, should be solely to the creative and redemptive working of God, to the Lord Christ, whose power works at levels vastly deeper than human intelligence and purpose. Hence, the urgent need for a willingness of heart and mind to be continually reformed and transformed, lest we be found blocking the very purpose of God, as he seeks to bring about a fuller realization of the unity of Christ's body, the church.

NOTES

1. The Evanston Report (New York: Harper and Brothers, 1954), pp. 2-3.
2. *The Ecumenical Review,* April, 1960, p. 297.
3. *Ibid.,* p. 298.
4. Karl Adam, *The Spirit of Catholicism* (London: Sheed & Ward, 1939), pp. 235-237.
5. Cf. Emil Brunner, *The Misunderstanding of the Church* (London: Lutterworth Press, 1952), p. 117.
6. Thomas Campbell, *Declaration and Address* (Indianapolis: International Convention of Disciples of Christ, 1949), pp. 14-15.
7. Friedrich Schleiermacher, *The Christian Faith* (Edinburgh: T & T Clark, 1928), p. 690.

8. *The Christian Century,* July 10, 1957.
9. Adolf von Harnack, *What Is Christianity?* (New York: Harper & Brothers, 1957), pp. 143-144.
10. If now the road to a fuller and more perfect manifestation of the unity we have in Christ is not by theological reduction to a skeleton creed, but rather by direction toward the center, God's redemptive act in Christ, perhaps confessions, in this sense, are of vital importance. If so, Disciples must ask themselves anew: what does this mean in reference to the traditional slogan, "No creed but Christ"?
11. As quoted by W. A. Visser t' Hooft, *Our Ecumenical Task in the Light of History* (Geneva: John Knox House Association, 1955), p. 11.
12. *The Ecumenical Review, op. cit.,* pp. 281-282.
13. Gustav Thils, *Histoire doctrinale du mouvement oecumenique* (Louvain: Em. Warny, Editeur, 1955), p. 173.
14. *The Ecumenical Review, op. cit.,* p. 284.
15. Brunner, *op. cit.,* p. 10.
16. Daniel Day Williams, *What Present-day Theologians Are Thinking* (New York: Harper & Brothers, 1952), p. 132.
17. See John 16:14.
18. See 1 Corinthians 1:9.
19. See 2 Corinthians 13:13; Philippians 2:1.
20. At this point a word should perhaps be said relative to the proposal of a church merger between the Disciples of Christ and the United Church of Christ in America, a proposal now under serious consideration. I would argue that this is a worthy proposal, and that it can be carried through in theological integrity. Such a merger would represent real advance, for several reasons:

(a) It would furnish a more realistic basis for broader Christian fellowship.

(b) It would help to overcome the residue of sectarian feeling generated by the restoration phase of the Disciple movement.

(c) Because of the Evangelical and Reformed elements in the United Church, an organic oneness with this group would enable Disciples to transcend the limits of their single American tradition and appropriate, more adequately, the total Protestant tradition. To be sure, this might eventually mean a loss of Disciple identity, but it would represent the gain of a larger identity. I would agree with Virgil Sly, when he concluded his address at the Consultation on Christian Unity at The College of the Bible in April, 1959, by saying, "I am convinced that the continuing identity of Disciples of Christ is not of major importance. The important thing is whether Disciples of Christ have completely identified themselves with the purposes of Christ for his world."

(d) Joining the new Union would provide a framework within which Disciples could more effectively make their contribution to the whole church. The day is past for Disciples to make a separatist denominational witness. From here on out, they must seek to bear their witness within the larger framework. Each group possesses values and insights which need to be shared for the enrichment of the larger fellowship.

21. Cf. H. P. Van Dusen, *Ecumenical Review, op. cit.,* p. 315.
22. *The Ecumenical Review, op. cit.,* p. 320.
23. *Faith and Order Commission Papers,* No. 7, "The Church," p. 13.

INDEX

INDEX